The Game Changer

"It is no secret that I have and will always devour anything Lana Ferguson writes. *The Game Changer* is her first dab at sports romance, and boy, I was immediately obsessed. This book has Ferguson's addictive brand of delicious spice and storytelling, plus one of the tropes I'll never get tired of reading: brother's best friend. Besides, we get to follow a giant ginger on skates around the ice and a baker who calls him Cupcake. It doesn't get better than this."

—Elena Armas, *New York Times* bestselling author of
The Fiancé Dilemma

"*The Game Changer* is a fun tale to read that revolves around the world[s] of hockey and baking. Ian and Delilah are two likable characters trying to do the right thing even as those around them try to tell them what to do. Readers will enjoy their banter and watching them fall in love. Don't miss this enjoyable tale."

—Romance Reviews Today

"A great addition to steamy romance readers' summer TBR lists!"
—The Nerd Daily

"A real banger. . . . *The Game Changer* has sensuality, banter, wit, and romance in spades, and I promise you will not be able to put it down once you start reading it."   —Romance by the Book

"I just gobbled this book up. It was very spicy, very fun, very swoony, and so much fun to read. It has a lot of depth to it while still remaining utterly entertaining." —Read & Wright

The Fake Mate

"An overall delightful experience. . . . Funny, sweet, and very hot, *The Fake Mate* is the ideal venture into mystic romance."

—Shondaland

"A steamy, worthwhile romance with plenty of banter, tapping into the popular grumpy-meets-sunshine trope."

—*Kirkus Reviews*

"Charming. Funny. Primal. Ferguson's paranormal romance manages to be sweet and spicy at the same time, with two likable leads who can't ignore their wolfish urges. . . . Readers will tear through this omegaverse novel." —*Booklist*

"This mash-up of *Grey's Anatomy*, Ali Hazelwood, and high-heat Reylo fan fiction will make even the most seasoned romance readers' hearts beat a little faster." —Shelf Awareness

PRAISE FOR

The Nanny

"I need more books like *The Nanny*, stat. A smart, educated heroine (Yes, please!) meets a driven, career-focused single dad. Sparks fly . . . and fly, and fly. Seriously, this book is like if Ali Hazelwood and Tessa Bailey had a smutty baby. I devoured every page and was sad to see it end. This is the spice BookTok wants! Now I need Lana Ferguson to work faster, because I want to see everything she writes."

—Ruby Dixon, *New York Times* bestselling author of *Bull Moon Rising*

"Ferguson makes the will-they-won't-they sing with complex emotional shading and a strong sense of inevitability to her protagonists' connection. . . . Rosie Danan fans should snap this up."

—*Publishers Weekly* (starred review)

"This steamy romantic comedy puts a modern spin on traditional tropes, bringing the falling-for-the-nanny and secret-past storylines into the twenty-first century. . . . Readers who enjoyed Julie Murphy and Sierra Simone's *A Merry Little Meet Cute* will adore this positive, upbeat, sex-filled romp." —*Library Journal*

"Everything about *The Nanny* is enjoyable: the plot, the pacing, the compelling characters, and especially Ferguson's wise and funny voice. It's also extremely refreshing to see sex-positive characters who approach intimacy with maturity. . . . If you're a fan of dirty talk and slow-burning chemistry, you'll love *The Nanny*."

—*BookPage* (starred review)

BERKLEY TITLES BY LANA FERGUSON

Overruled

LANA FERGUSON

BERKLEY ROMANCE

NEW YORK

BERKLEY ROMANCE
Published by Berkley
An imprint of Penguin Random House LLC
1745 Broadway, New York, NY 10019
penguinrandomhouse.com

Copyright © 2025 by Lana Ferguson
Excerpt from *The Mating Game* copyright © 2025 by Lana Ferguson
Penguin Random House values and supports copyright. Copyright fuels creativity,
encourages diverse voices, promotes free speech, and creates a vibrant culture.
Thank you for buying an authorized edition of this book and for complying with
copyright laws by not reproducing, scanning, or distributing any part of it in any form
without permission. You are supporting writers and allowing Penguin Random House
to continue to publish books for every reader. Please note that no part of this book
may be used or reproduced in any manner for the purpose of training artificial
intelligence technologies or systems.

BERKLEY and the BERKLEY & B colophon are registered trademarks of
Penguin Random House LLC.

Book design by George Towne

Library of Congress Cataloging-in-Publication Data

Names: Ferguson, Lana, author.
Title: Overruled / Lana Ferguson.
Description: First edition. | New York : Berkley Romance, 2025.
Identifiers: LCCN 2024050606 (print) | LCCN 2024050607 (ebook) |
ISBN 9780593549391 (trade paperback) | ISBN 9780593549407 (ebook)
Subjects: LCGFT: Romance fiction. | Novels.
Classification: LCC PS3606.E72555 O94 2025 (print) | LCC PS3606.E72555 (ebook) |
DDC 813/.6--dc23/eng/20241223
LC record available at https://lccn.loc.gov/2024050606
LC ebook record available at https://lccn.loc.gov/2024050607

First Edition: July 2025

Printed in the United States of America
1st Printing

The authorized representative in the EU for product safety and compliance is
Penguin Random House Ireland, Morrison Chambers, 32 Nassau Street,
Dublin D02 YH68, Ireland, https://eu-contact.penguin.ie.

To Kristen, for always being the daddy I deserve.

Overruled

Prologue

DANI

"THIS IS THE last time."

I can feel his chuckle against my throat, the scrape of his teeth following after just before he soothes the mark with his tongue. "You said that last time."

The warm press of his chest covers the length of my spine as he curls over me, and I grit my teeth when I feel his hands sliding around my hips, his fingers digging into my skin as I arch beneath him.

I don't give him the satisfaction of a response—it only makes him more intolerable—instead giving him a silent urge to keep going as I push back against the hot length of his cock, which slots between my legs. I should make it less easy, I know that; there is nothing I hate more than knowing it's so *easy* for him to make me fall apart—but that's a conundrum I haven't been able to figure out in the months we've been doing this. Hell, Ezra Hart might as well be a fucking glitch in the Matrix for how much I don't understand about his infuriating appeal. My lips part when

I feel him nudge against me, the thick head easing against my core in a slow, frustrating tease.

And Ezra, being the absolute dick that he is, immediately catches on to my impatience.

"You in a hurry, Dani?"

"You're a fucking asshole."

Another soft laugh caught in the bend of my neck as his nose traces back and forth there. "Tell me something I don't know."

"Stop fucking teasing me," I huff.

He feathers a barely there kiss against my shoulder, and I can practically feel him grinning, the bastard. "Just savoring. Might be the last time, right?"

"*Will* be the last time," I grind out.

"Mm. Sure."

I open my mouth to tell him where he can shove his perfect dick—other than in me, of course—but then I feel the slow, maddening stretch of him as he eases inside. My angry words come out as more of a whimper, and I hate that too. Hate that I'm here, giving in to this for the umpteenth time, that I'm giving him one more encounter to gloat about when I see him in the light of day.

"I think we both know it won't be the last time," he breathes, tightening his grip on my hips.

I hate that he's probably right.

One

DANI

"OBJECTION. LEADING THE witness."

I bite my tongue, quietly seething as I resist the urge to look back at the owner of the deep, honeyed voice calling out in a bored tone.

"Let me rephrase," I say as evenly as I can manage, keeping my attention on the man in front of me. "You said in your statement that you would often see a visitor coming to the house while Mrs. Johanson was home alone. Is that correct, Mr. Crane?"

The man nods, peeking warily at the woman in question. "That's correct."

"And during those visits, where was Mr. Johanson?"

"He was usually at work, ma'am."

"And this visitor, was it a man or a woman?"

"It was a man."

I bite back a grin. "I see. How long would this man stay?"

Mr. Crane reaches to scratch at his thinning hair, shifting in his seat. It had taken me a hell of a lot to get him on the stand; in the end it was only because of Mr. Johanson's promise that he would keep his gardening job regardless of the outcome of this trial that he finally agreed.

"It varied," Mr. Crane said. "Sometimes an hour. Sometimes more."

"So it's safe to assume that Mrs. Johanson knew this man . . . well, correct?"

"Objection." I hear a sigh behind me. "Speculation."

"Rephrase," I say tightly, still refusing to look at him. It's clear he's only objecting to trip me up at this point, since the basis is ridiculous. "Did you ever see Mrs. Johanson and the man interacting when he would visit, Mr. Crane?"

Mr. Crane shakes his head. "No, ma'am. He always went straight inside the house."

"But it was always the same man?"

"Yes, ma'am. As far as I could tell."

I know any other attempts to steer this conversation to the *obvious* truth of Mrs. Johanson's infidelity will only result in more bullshit objections from my opposing counsel.

"Thank you, Mr. Crane." I give my attention to Judge Hoffstein. "No further questions, Your Honor."

I try not to look at him when I return to my table, I really do— but that pull is there, the one I so desperately wish didn't plague me anytime we're in the same room together. I can feel his eyes linger on me when I'm finally able to avert my gaze, feel them like the weight of his fingers along my skin as I retake my seat.

He stands slowly, one hand reaching to fasten the button of his suit—a deft, practiced motion that makes the tendons in his too-large hands flex—and I can't help the way my eyes are drawn there, remembering the warmth of them on my body hardly even a week ago. I catch a hint of a smirk when I turn my face to meet his eyes, feeling warmth creep up my neck as I clench my teeth.

Fucking Ezra Hart.

I train my eyes forward, keeping them on the nervous older man on the stand, in quiet support.

"Mr. Crane," Ezra starts. "Did you know Mrs. Johanson's visitor?"

"No, sir," Mr. Crane answers. "I was told that—"

"That's hearsay," Ezra cuts him off. "What you *heard* is irrelevant." He shoves his hands in his pockets, strolling casually to the side and flicking his gaze to mine for the briefest of moments. "I'm asking if you ever actually *met* Mrs. Johanson's visitor."

Mr. Crane's eyes dart to mine, looking unsure. "Well, no, I didn't."

"So there's no possible way for you to know the purpose of that man's visits. Correct?"

Mr. Crane is quiet for a moment, and my heart thuds in my ribs. There's no way that Ezra can possibly suggest—

"No, sir," Mr. Crane answers. "I could not."

"I see." Ezra's mouth turns up in the ghost of a smile. "Just as you couldn't know of Mrs. Johanson's recent interests in spiritual direction?"

"I . . ." Mr. Crane blinks with confusion, and I can feel the same emotion playing on Mr. Johanson's and my faces. "No? I didn't know that."

"Of course you didn't," Ezra practically coos. "It's not something she advertised. The only people who knew this were her close friends. Well, and her husband, of course." Ezra looks back at our table. "Although I very much doubt Mr. Johanson would recall this, given that he rarely took note of Mrs. Johanson's interests."

"Objection," I call. "Speculation."

"Withdrawn," Ezra says with a grin. "Mr. Crane, did you know that the man you saw coming in and out of Mrs. Johanson's house was her spiritual advisor?"

Oh, what a load of horseshit.

"Objection, Your Honor." I almost laugh. "This is irrelevant."

Ezra directs his attention to the judge. "This is completely relevant, Your Honor, I assure you."

Judge Hoffstein nods minutely. "Overruled."

"Thank you." Ezra inclines his head. "You see, Mrs. Johanson's visitor, a Mr. Jacobs, had been contacted several weeks prior by Mrs. Johanson to oversee her spiritual direction. There was nothing nefarious about their encounters. If you'll be so kind as to take a look at Exhibit 13, which was already admitted into evidence—you'll note the credentials I've provided to prove Mr. Jacobs's involvement with the local church."

Son of a bitch. How did we miss that?

Ezra looks smug as the judge peruses the bit of evidence in question; to an outsider, Ezra would simply look contemplative, but I've seen that look on his face too many times. In *and* out of the courtroom.

"Mrs. Johanson was simply exploring her new faith," Ezra continues. "There is no evidence to suggest that she and Mr. Jacobs were meeting under false pretenses, and she paid him for his time. Therefore this line of questioning isn't relevant to this alimony hearing."

Ezra waits until the exhibit has been passed to the bailiff before he turns back to the witness. "Thank you for your time, Mr. Crane." He looks to the judge. "No further questions, Your Honor."

Ezra takes his seat on his side of the courtroom, a small smile on his lips, practically laughing at the way I'm nearly incandescent with rage right now. I feel Mr. Johanson lean into me, whispering, "She can't seriously pull this shit, can she?"

I want to tell him no, that cheating spouses get what they deserve—that *doesn't* include an overly fat alimony check—but I know that without any concrete evidence of infidelity, which we haven't been able to unearth no matter how hard we've looked, it's likely Mrs. Johanson will be milking her soon-to-be-ex-husband dry for years to come.

Fucking Ezra Hart.

I PINCH THE bridge of my nose as I wait for the elevator to open, trying to stave off the headache forming behind my eyes. It had taken weeks to find out about Mrs. Johanson's little *spiritual advisor* who came twice a week like clockwork, unbeknownst to her husband while he was at work, and it had felt like an ace in the hole. Until Ezra swooped in and plugged it right up, that is.

I've heard him called "the Heartbreak Prince" at several legal mixers I've attended, and even in a city as weird as Austin, I find it a stupid fucking moniker. One that he absolutely eats up, I'm sure. His win record is astounding, and every time I have to be in the same courtroom with him, I know I'm in for a world of bullshit. Not to say I haven't won against him, because I have—but not nearly as much as I'd like, today included.

The elevator dings, and I climb inside, grateful to find it empty as I settle against the back wall to let my head thunk against the cool metal. I close my eyes as I wait for the doors to close, only snapping them back open when I hear something nudging between them to force them apart.

"Room for one more?"

I narrow my eyes at him. "You could always take the stairs. Get a workout in."

Ezra laughs as he strolls into the elevator, leaning against the bar at the back wall as I scoot away from him. "You've never had any complaints about my body."

I glare up at him as the elevator doors slide closed, trapping us inside. He always knows exactly what to say to push my buttons, just like he knows that his stupid face and body are lethal distractions when it comes to remembering how much I dislike him. It's not the dark blond hair that always looks like someone just ran their fingers through it, not the full mouth or the piercing green eyes or the amazing bone structure that makes his face look carved—it's all of it, really. The broad shoulders that fill out his tailored suits a little too well, his long fingers that stir up wicked memories, even his stupid cologne makes you want to lean in closer to get a better whiff.

At least he only has four to five inches on me—I've always been on the taller side, and not having to crane my neck up to his six foot three from my five foot nine gives me an ounce of satisfaction. Especially in my heels.

"Yeah, well, that's just about the only good thing you have going for you," I mumble back, facing forward to watch the numbers tick by and mentally urging them to go faster.

There's a contrast between us in the reflection of the shiny metal doors—my inky black hair to his golden brown, my pale skin to his bronzed, his brawn to my lithe figure—looking at us side by side, one would never think to put us together.

Which we aren't, I mentally correct. Together. Because we aren't.

Except . . .

"Really?" He inches a little closer. "I'm told I'm pretty charming."

"Are those people on your payroll?"

"I can think of a few times when *you've* found me charming, Dani."

I roll my eyes. I'm used to people calling me Dani; when you have a name like Danica, I guess it's easy to jump to the nickname—but something about the way Ezra says it always makes my stomach do something funny. I'm sure I'm not the only one Ezra amuses himself with. There's no doubt in my mind that Ezra's easy playboy act comes from vast amounts of real-life experience—but I can't help but wonder if anyone else in what is surely a very wide net of his sexual conquests succumbs to his annoyingly effective charms quite as often (albeit begrudgingly) as I do.

"I can assure you I have never found you charming," I toss back dryly. "Maybe mildly amusing. Your dick, at least."

He clutches his hand to his chest, and I try not to notice how large it looks against his tie. "Only mildly? That isn't what you said when you were screaming my—"

The elevator doors slide open as we come to a halt, and I immediately bolt out of it, trying to put distance between Ezra and me before he notices how flushed my neck most likely is. Not that he lets me escape that easily, since I hear his footsteps, heavy and quick as he catches up to me.

"I'm free tonight, you know," he says casually.

I keep my expression blank, hoping the people milling around in the lobby don't notice how close he's walking beside me. "Good for you. Sounds like an excellent time to take up a hobby."

"Oh, but I would much rather enjoy the one I've already got."

I glance at him from the side, frowning. "What's that?"

"See, there's this certain opposing counsel that makes the most delicious noises when my fingers are—"

I spin on my heel, hissing under my breath as we come to a stop in front of the large glass doors that lead outside the courthouse. "I told you," I grit out. "Last time was the last time."

"Right." He flashes me his perfect white teeth—stark against the deep pink of his lips—and I have to force myself to keep my eyes on his. "But you said that the time before that." He leans in a little closer, practically looming over me as he lowers his voice. "And the time before that . . . and the time before that . . ."

"I mean it this time," I argue, trying to convince him or me, I'm not sure. "It was stupid to begin with. You're an asshole, and I was . . ." *Hard up? Horny? Out of my mind?* "It was a lapse of judgment on my part."

"Eight lapses of judgment," Ezra says with a low whistle. "I think they call that a bad habit, Dani. Maybe *you* need a hobby. You know, besides me."

I clench my fists at my sides; I know he's teasing me, but it hits a little too close to home. Especially because I *know* that constantly sleeping with Ezra—someone I barely tolerate outside of what we do behind closed doors—is the stupidest thing I've ever done. After everything with Grant . . . you'd think I would make smarter decisions when it comes to the opposite sex.

It's just sex, I soothe myself. *Just scratching an itch.*

Even if I've scratched this particular itch more times than I'd like.

I make a frustrated sound, shoving him away and pushing

through the doors as I stalk off quickly. He doesn't follow me this time, but I can hear his stupid laugh even from halfway down the steps.

Fucking. Ezra. Hart.

I FEEL A little less out of sorts when I'm back at the firm; I'm not thrilled to tell my boss how miserably today went with the Johansons, but at least here I can put the headache of Ezra's and my antagonistic . . . whatever we have . . . at the back of my mind for a little bit. I drop my case files in my office, noticing on my way out that Nate's and Vera's are empty; I guess they've already headed home for the day.

The door to Manuel's office is cracked at the other end of the hall, however, and I step toward it to update him on everything before I finish up for the day myself. I find him sitting behind his desk poring over a stack of papers, his neat, salt-and-pepper hair swept into his usual perfect style. I don't think I've ever seen Manuel Moreno with a single hair out of place.

"Danica," he greets as I knock lightly against the open door. "Come in, come in. How did it go today?"

I purse my lips. "Not as well as I would have liked. The guy she was seeing was apparently her 'spiritual advisor.'"

The deep wrinkle that lives permanently between Manuel's brow worsens. "That's the horseshit they're spinning?"

"Well, horseshit does happen to be a specialty of Ezra's."

"I want to hate the bastard," Manuel snorts. "But he's damn good."

I refuse to even acknowledge how "good" Ezra is.

"I've got a lead on a housekeeper that quit a couple of months ago," I tell him. "I'm trying to get in touch with her. Maybe she saw something between them of a more *physical* nature. Thankfully I mentioned her as a potential witness in the pretrial order."

"Great. Let me know."

I'm about to return to my desk when he stops me.

"I actually wanted to talk to you," he calls.

I turn back. "Yes?"

"We had a potential client call today. A Mrs. Casiraghi."

I frown. "Why does that sound familiar?"

"Her husband owns Casiraghi Development."

"Shit." My mouth parts in surprise. "The real estate mogul?"

"He owns half the city, practically. God knows how many others."

"They're divorcing?"

"It appears so. A friend of mine recommended us."

"That's great." I wince. "Well, not for *her*, but . . ."

"I was thinking that you should take it."

I blink back at him. "What?"

"You've been here for six years now. You mentioned last year that you were interested in a junior partner position, and with Hinata retiring . . ."

"Wait, are you saying . . . ?"

"I'm saying that Mrs. Casiraghi stands to make this firm an enormous amount of money if she comes out on top of her divorce. She claims to have all sorts of evidence of his infidelity."

"Holy shit."

"But there's a catch."

"There always is."

"She signed a prenup."

I groan. "Of course she did. How solid is her evidence?"

"I guess that's for you to find out."

"Not making this easy for me, huh?"

"High risk, high reward," he chuckles before his expression turns serious. "I think winning this case would be the perfect thing to bring to the other partners and prove you're ready to step up."

"You'd be willing to go to bat for me?"

Manuel rolls his eyes. "I've known you since you were seven. As many T-ball games as I went to with you and your parents, I have 'gone to bat' for you plenty of times in your life."

"That's corny, but I'll take it," I laugh. "I just . . . You already stuck your neck out giving me this job, and I don't want anyone to think I'm getting special treatment just because you and Dad are old friends."

"You graduated top of your class. It was hardly a burden to offer you a position here. Just like it won't be when you win this case, and I show the other partners what an asset you are."

"I . . . Wow. Yes. Of course. This is . . . Wow."

"You have a meeting with Mrs. Casiraghi at the end of the week," he informs me. "She's a character, but I think you can handle her."

I nod aimlessly. "Yes. I . . . Thank you, Manny."

"Don't mention it." He waves me off. "Feel free to loop Nate and Vera in. I'm sure they'll be foaming at the mouth to be a part of it regardless."

I grin. He isn't wrong about that. This is one of the biggest cases we've had since I started. I can already hear Nate squealing. "I will."

"Don't stay up at your desk all night," he chides. "You have to sleep sometime."

I roll my eyes. "Yeah, yeah."

He gives me a dismissive gesture as he returns his attention to his paperwork, and I leave his office with a wide smile on my face and a fluttering in my stomach. I've been waiting for this opportunity for the last year or more, and now, with it so close, I can feel a bubbling excitement humming under my skin.

A buzzing in the pocket of my slacks distracts me as I walk back to my desk, and all the elated feelings simmer out into annoyance as I take note of the message from "Asshole."

Asshole: I'll be home all night if you change your mind about . . . coming.

I grimace. That was terrible, even for him. Which makes the little flicker of warmth in my gut all the more infuriating. Sleeping with Ezra Hart had been a bad idea the *first* time it happened, something I blame on temporary insanity and thinking with my vagina—and the next seven times definitely didn't help things.

If only he wasn't so *good* at it. Bastard.

I tap out a quick response, shoving down the urges that pop up in spite of his stupid fucking text.

Me: Sorry. Better things to do.

I feel smug for about three seconds before my phone pings again.

Asshole: I highly doubt there's better than me, but keep telling yourself that. 😉

I scowl, shoving my phone in my pocket.
Fucking Ezra Hart.

Two

DANI

"DO YOU HAVE those files on the Preston case?"

I glance up from my desk to where Nate is lingering in the doorway. He's older than me at thirty-five, but his cornsilk-blond hair and bright blue eyes give him a boyish sort of look that makes you want to baby him. It's something he capitalizes on frequently. The man has dimples, for Christ's sake.

I jerk my head toward the top of the filing cabinet. "There are copies there."

"Cramming for your Italian madame?"

"Basically." I shake my head as I continue reading through the article I found online. "Did you know she comes from her own money? Her family are the Loredans." When Nate gives me a blank look, I add, "As in Loredan Jewelry."

"Yeah, I don't follow."

"This is why you don't have a girlfriend," Vera snorts as she pops up in my doorway. "They're like the Italian Cartier."

Vera regards Nate with the same level of barely checked impatience that stems from his constantly badgering her, and like clockwork, I watch his gaze flicker over her face, lingering on her dark eyes and her warm brown skin with an interest I'm fairly certain she's oblivious to. Or maybe she's aware and just isn't interested. Vera's an absolute vault unless she feels like sharing; she has been since we graduated from law school together.

Nate's mouth quirks. "Is that supposed to mean something to me?"

"Wow, seriously," Vera tuts. "It's truly a wonder that you're single."

Nate makes a kissy face. "Just saving myself for you."

"Guys." I rub my temples. "Can we all pretend that this is the biggest case of my career for five seconds?"

"So if she's rich . . ." Nate leans against the filing cabinet, crossing his arms. "Why is she pushing to fight the prenup? Why not just ditch the bastard and snag herself a pretty boy toy?"

"Really?" Vera cuts him a look. "If the prick really did cheat on her, he's lucky she isn't taking his balls."

Nate's eyebrows shoot up. "Tell me again how *you're* single?"

"Saving myself for you," Vera echoes blandly. She looks at me then. "I came to tell you that she's here, by the way."

I shoot up from my desk so fast that my knee knocks against the underside. "Fuck," I mutter, rubbing the sore spot. "Why didn't you lead with that?"

"I got her some coffee and set her up in the conference room. I figured you'd need a second to do some Lamaze or something before you go in there. You've been running around like a wild ferret all week."

"That's sweet of you," I deadpan.

Vera shrugs. "That is what people say about me."

"Lamaze is for pregnant women," Nate points out.

Vera arches a brow in his direction. "How do you know *that* but not about Cartier?"

"I don't have those answers for you," Nate tosses back.

I blow out a steady breath, ignoring my coworkers and their back-and-forth. Usually, I'm more than happy to sit back and watch their weird mating ritual, but today I'm all nerves, which isn't me.

"Okay," I say, interrupting some argument about meditative breathing. "I'm going in."

Nate shoots me a thumbs-up. "Good luck. Tell her I'm available if she comes around to the boy toy idea."

"I doubt she has enough room to house your big head," Vera scoffs.

Nate grins. "How many square feet is your place again?"

I grab my portfolio and my notes before I leave them behind in my office to make quick steps down the hallway, my heart thudding in perfect time with each click of my heels against the sleek black tile. The conference room door is closed as I approach, and I linger outside of it for a moment, smoothing my hands over my gray pencil skirt and straightening my red silk blouse as I take another fortifying breath.

"You've got this, Dani," I mutter, reaching for the brass handle.

Mrs. Casiraghi sits on the opposite side of the long conference table in the center of the room, her back straight in the leather chair as she gingerly sips her coffee. Her graying hair is pulled back in a sleek bun, her clothes neat and pressed and screaming subtle wealth. She turns to look at me when I enter, her lips pressing into a faint line and her brow arching.

"Mrs. Casiraghi," I greet her as I close the door behind me. "Sorry to keep you waiting." I move to settle in a chair opposite her. "I'm Dani." I reach across the table to offer her my hand. "Dani Pierce."

Her steely blue eyes assess me, traveling down the front of me before climbing back to my face. "You don't look like a Dani."

"I'm sorry?"

"Dani is a child's name," she goes on, her accent giving her voice a slight edge. "Are you a child?"

"I . . ." Part of me is bristling, but another part notices that she doesn't look as if she's mocking me when she says this. It's more like she's sizing me up. "My full name is Danica."

Her red lips part in a smile, her eyes crinkling at the corners. "Ah, yes. Much better. Danica sounds like a powerful woman." She takes another sip of her coffee. "I like powerful women."

This entire exchange is bizarre, but my mouth is still turning up at the corners. I decide, for whatever reason, I like Mrs. Casiraghi. "You strike me as someone who knows how to spot one from experience."

"I *used* to think I was a powerful woman," she muses quietly. "These days . . . I'm not so sure."

"That's where I come in," I tell her with confidence. "Manuel told me a little about your situation, and of course I've had time this week to research you, but I was hoping to hear things straight from you, if I can."

"Well, that is why I'm here," she says. She eyes me again. "Are you married, Danica?"

I shake my head. "No, ma'am. Never took the plunge."

"Pity." She nods idly. "You are a pretty young woman."

"And powerful," I say with a grin.

Her lips twitch. "Yes, and that."

I doubt that Mrs. Casiraghi has any interest in hearing all the things that ensure I will most likely *never* take the plunge—my parents' farce of a marriage, Grant walking out of my life, my cynicism of the construct in general—so I keep the conversation focused on her.

"I'm surprised you would think it is a pity, given your situation," I offer. "No offense intended."

She waves me off. "No offense. It is not marriage I am angry at. Marriage is beautiful. It is my husband that betrayed me."

"Of course." I flip open my portfolio to the legal pad inside, grabbing a pen and unclicking it. "Can you tell me more about it?"

"There is another woman," she tells me.

"I'm very sorry to hear that."

"It is Lorenzo who will be sorry."

My lips twitch. I might *really* like Mrs. Casiraghi.

"That's the idea," I tell her. "Manuel says you have proof of his infidelity?"

"He has been calling her," she answers coldly. "I have records that I pulled. There are emails also. My husband is surprisingly crass with his mistress. I can't imagine why woman would want to be wooed with talk of his cock." She clicks her tongue. "It hardly works anymore."

I have to bite my lower lip to hold back a laugh as I make notes. "You have copies of these exchanges?"

"Of course. His assistant is as spineless as he is." She reaches down to a clasped leather bag and starts pulling out manila folders. "The little man was shaking when I made him let me into Lorenzo's office."

I take the folders from her, flipping through them. "I have to warn you that even with evidence like this, the defense is going to say that it's circumstantial. They'll claim he was hacked, or that someone else was using his computer, or any number of things."

"I am aware that Lorenzo will try to slither his way out of his own mess," she says. "But as you say. This is where you come in, yes?"

A slow smile creeps onto my face. "Right. That's where I come in."

"Good. Then we understand each other."

"I'm going to do everything in my power to make sure your husband pays for his indiscretions, Mrs. Casiraghi."

She tilts her chin, looking me in the eye. "Call me Bianca."

"Bianca." I nod back at her. "Another name for a powerful woman."

Her answering smile is cool, almost predatory. "Let us hope so, Danica."

"HOW DID IT go?"

I run my fingers through my hair, noticing Manuel in my doorway. "I think it went well. I gave her a list of all the information I need on her finances, and we went over what she can expect going forward."

"And? What are your thoughts about her chances?"

"The evidence she mentioned is mostly just phone records and email printouts. Nothing concrete, unfortunately, but she seems to think that some digging will reveal more." I smile, remembering. "Her exact words were 'my husband is not as brilliant as he thinks himself to be.'"

"I got the impression that Mrs. Casiraghi is not a woman to be fucked with," Manuel chuckles.

"So did I. Nate and Vera both agreed to help with discovery. I imagine there will be a lot of records to dig through."

"Good," he tells me. "We need all hands on deck with this one."

"I think our chances are good, considering. I'm optimistic."

"Well, one of us has to be."

I snort. "And we both know that isn't going to be you."

"It isn't one of my strong suits. Have you told your parents yet?"

I frown. "Not yet. I wanted to wait until after I'd actually spoken to Bianca."

"I'm sure they'll want to celebrate."

"That's what I'm afraid of."

"It's not the most terrible thing in the world that your parents are such good friends, Dani."

I scowl at him, hating that he can read me so well. "It might be when they've been divorced for fourteen years."

"In our line of work, we call that the perfect divorce."

I don't respond to that, just shake my head. Manny and I have a different opinion on my parents' "perfect divorce." He knows I don't think such a thing really exists. If there aren't any perfect marriages—and I've long decided there aren't, since the one I held to the highest standard was never real—then it stands to reason that there can't be a perfect version on the opposite end of the spectrum. Once you find out the life you knew was a lie, you stop believing in a lot of things.

"I'll call them tonight," I tell him instead.

"Good. Your dad and I are golfing Sunday, and you know I hate lying to him."

"I'm aware. It's annoying, really."

He gives me a small smile. "Make sure to keep me updated on things with the Casiraghi case."

"Your office is thirty feet from mine. I can just shout when I have news."

He rolls his eyes. "Whatever works."

He pushes away from the doorframe as if he's moving to leave, and I stop him.

"Do we know who the husband has hired yet?" I notice Manuel wince, and a foreboding feeling creeps through my limbs when he turns back to give me a withered look. "No."

"I'm told Mr. Casiraghi called Hart and Associates last Wednesday."

"Goddamn it," I huff. "Why didn't you tell me?"

"I didn't want you to get any more stressed out about your meeting with Bianca. I know how weird you get where Ezra Hart is concerned."

A flush creeps up my neck, and with my pale complexion, I know it will be noticeable. "I do not get *weird*," I bite out. "I just hate the guy."

When I'm not fucking him, that is.

"He's not my favorite person," Manuel offers, "and it's going to make winning that much harder, but you've beaten him before."

Not as many times as I'd like, I think bitterly.

"I'm sure he's already crafting some bullshit defense about how the woman Lorenzo has been emailing is his personal trainer, and that's why she's so interested in his body."

Manuel laughs. "Most likely. You'll just have to find something Ezra can't twist. You can't skirt around solid evidence."

"Right." I nod, mostly to myself. "*Right.* I'm going to kick his ass."

Manuel winks as he turns to go. "I have no doubt, kid."

I sit at my desk and fume for a few more minutes, thinking about the stupid texts Ezra has sent this week where he conveniently left out that he'd be my opposing counsel. I sure as hell hadn't waited more than a day before bragging about possibly representing Bianca. Did he know then? My earlier smugness now makes me feel a little embarrassed. God, he was probably laughing at me the entire time.

I snatch my phone from the corner of my desk, opening our text thread and furiously shooting one off.

> **Me: How long have you known you were representing Lorenzo Casiraghi?**

I watch the dots appear with narrowed eyes, waiting for his response.

> **Asshole: At least a few days before your charming text. Did you end up landing the missus?**

> **Me: You're the literal worst person I know.**

> **Asshole: Aw. I miss you too.**

He sends me a GIF of Paul Rudd on the *Hot Ones* show saying "Look at us. Who would have thought?" and I roll my eyes.

> **Me: You know you won't be able to bullshit your way through this one.**

Mr. Casiraghi doesn't seem the
type to have "spiritual advisors."

Asshole: Are you implying
something about my
methods, Dani?

Me: That they're bullshit. Yes.

Asshole: I'm wounded. Are we
fighting? I hate it when we fight.
Maybe you should come over so
we can talk about it.

Me: You'd like that wouldn't you?

His reply takes a bit longer than his previous ones, and I don't
notice my teeth pressing against my bottom lip until it pops up on
the screen.

Asshole: I promise you, Dani. We'd
both like it if you came.

I shift in my desk chair, remembering the last time I'd been to
his place. Heat courses through me, the memory of his tongue on
me and his body against mine leaving me disgusted with myself
but still entirely horny. I hate that he always seems to catch me
when I'm at my most stressed, that he knows orgasms are my
weakness when I'm wound this tightly.

I can't go to his place again. I know I will regret it tomorrow. I *know*.

I hear a *ping* as another text comes through.

Asshole: I've been thinking about
touching you all week.

I grit my teeth, closing my eyes as a shudder passes through me.
I am *not* going to his place.
I'm not.

Three

EZRA

I SMILE AGAIN at Dani's short response of "Fine." Then I check the time, thinking she should be here soon. I've been waiting patiently to see if Dani would end up as my opposing counsel on the Casiraghi case, hoping for it, actually, knowing she'd be prickly and sour about it. It shouldn't be so appealing when she puffs up like my cat's tail, but something about it really inspires the need to rile her up even more when it happens. Touching her is always that much sweeter when I have to work for it.

The aforementioned feline rubs against my ankle then, and I reach to scratch behind Purrgood Marshall's ears.

"She likes you, at least," I tell him.

Purrgood arches his fluffy gray body, flicking his tail as he stares up at me, looking bored. He scampers away after another quick rake of my nails against his spine, and I move across the apartment to the wet bar to make myself a drink. Two fingers of scotch usually helps prepare me to handle Dani's verbal assault, which she insists on before she defrosts. A good therapist might suggest there is something seriously wrong with me if they knew how much I enjoy our strange dynamic.

Dani has no qualms with making it immensely clear what she thinks of me as a person, and for the life of me, I can't even begin to explain why that makes her inability to stop coming to me to fuck her stress away all the more appealing. Touching Dani is like scooping the honey out of the hive after the beesting. Totally worth the pain.

I'm sipping my drink and looking out the wide wall of windows on the other side of the large leather sectional in the living room when I hear three sharp knocks from the front door across the room, and my skin hums with anticipation as I set my scotch glass on an end table and practically jog to answer the door.

Her perfectly arched dark brows are pulled together over her stormy gray eyes when I open the door, her pink mouth pursed as she taps one heeled foot. I smile at her arms crossed tightly over her chest; she always looks like someone forced to solicit for community service when she comes over.

"Hi, honey," I say sweetly. "How was your day?"

She rolls her eyes as she pushes past me. "I can't believe you let me brag about the Casiraghi account knowing you were opposing counsel."

"Don't be cross, dear," I coo. "You're just so cute when you're excited."

She narrows her eyes at me. "You're such an asshole."

"So I've been told."

Purrgood trots out from wherever he's been hiding to rub against Dani's leg, and for a moment, I'm almost jealous of the way her expression changes, the way her mouth twists in a small smile as she crouches to pet him.

"You're making me envious of the cat," I tell her.

Her smile dissipates as she shoots me a look. "He's the only non-asshole in this apartment, so."

"Ah. So I'm sure it's just Purrgood you came over to see, right?" I step around her to lean against the back of the couch. "Should I leave you two alone?"

"I don't even know what I'm doing here," she grumbles as she straightens.

My eyes move over her rounded hips, which look soft even in her tight pencil skirt, my fingers twitching at the memory of how they feel underneath. "You know exactly what you're doing here."

"I don't," she huffs, crossing her arms again. "It's such a bad idea."

She doesn't even realize, I think, the way she's gravitating closer—like her brain and her body aren't on the same wavelength when it comes to me. She's near enough now that it makes it easy to reach out and graze my fingertips against the material stretched over the outside of her thigh, feeling her shiver under my touch.

"Sometimes the worst ideas feel best," I murmur.

It's almost imperceptible, the shift in her attitude—but I notice her shoulders relaxing, and the tight lines on her brow begin to smooth as her lips part. Her throat moves with a swallow as I let my palm rest against her hip, coaxing her closer. This is the part that makes all her barbs worth it. When she forgets she hates me and gives in to the electric pull that lingers between us.

"I said I wouldn't do this again," she says.

I can feel the tops of her thighs brush against mine; she's so close now that I could lean forward just a little and press my mouth to hers. "And yet here you are."

"I really fucking hate you, Ezra."

It really does have to be some sort of psychosis, the way that makes me smile. "I know, Dani."

My lips ghost against hers, and the spark between us lights up like a match—her hands shoving into my hair and her body pressing into mine as she tugs me impossibly closer. Everything between us is always rough and rushed, but I like that too. I like knowing I can ruffle Danica Pierce's feathers, this prickly woman who takes no shit.

But she's far from prickly when she's with me like this.

I let my hand slide up her spine until I can cup the back of her neck, tilting my head to sweep my tongue into her mouth as she lets out a soft sound that makes my cock ache. Her long black hair is silky as I plunge my fingers into it, and I close my fist to muss it, the need to mess up her perfect poise like a drug in my veins.

"Couch," she breathes into my mouth.

I duck my head to swirl my tongue over the pulse at her throat. "I could do so much more to you in my bed."

"That's not what we do," she huffs.

Which is true, since she refuses to let me have her anywhere that might suggest this is anything more than it is, but you can't blame a guy for trying. The thought of her naked in my sheets is a tempting one.

She's unbuttoning her blouse as I lead her around the couch, her mouth never leaving mine as I fumble with the zipper of her skirt to shove it over her hips. She drops to the couch cushions when I give her a gentle shove, roughly popping open the button of my jeans as she watches. She won't look me in the eye; she never does when we're together like this. Almost like she can convince herself she's here with someone else and not the person she decided was a pretentious asshole within five seconds of meeting him. Not that I can blame her, since it's true, but still.

My cock is already hard and straining against my black boxer briefs as I shove at my jeans, watching her fingers slide over the thin material of her white lace bra, which is sheer enough to give me a peek at her nipples. My mouth waters as I kick my jeans off, because I know exactly what they taste like.

"Take your bra off," I grate out, palming my cock through my underwear to give myself a second of relief before reaching for the hem of my shirt to pull it up and over my head.

Dani's eyes are still trained between my legs, scowling now. "Don't tell me what to do."

"Should I ask nicely?" I drop to my knees, running my hands up the insides of her thighs. She watches the path they take, her chest rising and falling more roughly now. "Or do you just like it better when I do it for you?"

"Fuck you," she mumbles.

So prickly. I grin anyway. "I plan to."

Her head falls back when my hand splays wide over her hip, my thumb dipping between her legs to tease her through the thin fabric of her underwear. Part of me wants to gloat when I find it already wet; she can pretend she hates me all she wants, but she *loves* this.

"Maybe I should start here instead," I drawl. "You're always more agreeable after you've come on my tongue."

I see her teeth sink into the soft flesh of her lower lip, and I keep my eyes on what I can still see of her face as I lean in to press my tongue where my thumb just was, tasting her through the material.

"*Ah.*"

My fingers curl under the waistband of her underwear, slowly tugging them down. Her legs part wider, and I think to myself that she and I would be much better friends if she would just let me fuck her with my tongue every day.

"Be honest," I murmur as I lean in. "You've been thinking about my mouth all week."

"Of course I have," she gasps as I slide my tongue up the crease of her. That's new. It gives me pause. But then her lips curl as she adds: "Hard not to, with the bullshit always spewing out of it."

I snort. That's more like it. "Is that all?" She squirms as I slide my tongue through her folds again, teasing the little bud hiding at the top. "Surely this is a better use of your thoughts."

"It's the only time your mouth ever does anything good," she practically hums.

I give her clit one long suck that makes her cry out, releasing her with a wet *pop* as I laugh quietly. "I can live with that."

I wrap my hands around her thighs and pull them over my shoulders, diving between her legs so I can rob her of any more coherent thought. She can't berate me if she's dizzy with pleasure—it's something I learned early on. I only linger briefly near her entrance, licking a hot stripe between her legs before focusing my attention solely on her clit. Dani doesn't like teasing, doesn't want me to be gentle and sweet with her. No, Dani comes to me for release, and if that's all she wants from me, I am more than happy to give it.

"Oh. *Oh.*"

I would smile if I could, relishing the sensation of her fingers winding in my hair as she tugs the strands so hard it stings. I keep my lips firmly attached to her clit, sucking her as hard as I possibly can as I press two fingers at her entrance to slip them inside.

"*Fuck*," she rasps.

I'm still watching her as I work her over, enjoying the pink flush that spreads all over her pale skin as she holds my face exactly where she wants it. I pump my fingers in and out of her, dragging them along the front of her inner walls to drive her wild. I flick my tongue against her clit even as I continue to pull at it with my lips, feeling her thighs quivering on my shoulders and her pussy growing more and more slick as I push my fingers deep to keep her full like I know she likes when she comes.

"Damn it, Ezra. *Fuck*."

It's not exactly shouting my name in bliss, but I'll take what I can get.

I keep my fingers inside even as I pull my mouth away, watching her tremble as her pussy flutters and clenches with her orgasm. There is a small part of me that wishes she'd just fucking *look* at me when she comes, so that she can see exactly who's doing this to her, but I don't know why. Maybe it's because I know it would be even more fun to tease her later if I knew she couldn't deny that I make her come harder than she ever has.

She's never said that, but I am happy to assume. Since I *am* pretty pretentious, after all.

She's panting on the couch when I let my fingers slip away, her eyes glassy and wide as she stares up at the ceiling. I can't help the urge to try to get a better look at her, climbing up onto the couch and curling my body so I can press a kiss to the corner of her mouth.

"See? Much more agreeable."

"Fuck you," she says again, but it sounds less threatening in the breathy way she says it.

"Happy to," I mutter, letting my lips slide against the skin under her jaw. "On your knees. Grab the couch."

"Stop fucking telling me what to do."

Again, much less threatening since she's already complying.

Her body is lithe and lean, her spine a pretty curve as she arches back toward me, most likely without realizing she's doing it. I shove my underwear down and off before grabbing the condom I stashed on the end table earlier and rolling it on. I grip her hips, the softness there a stark contrast to the hardness of her demeanor. For a moment I'm content to just look at her as I let my cock graze between the curves of her ass, her fair complexion glowing and bright against mine.

I curl my body until my tongue can trace the lone freckle at her shoulder blade, the one I noticed the first time we were together and that I have been obsessed with ever since, hearing her suck in a breath as I pull back to let my cock press against her. I don't move for a bit, just holding still against the heat of her, smiling into her skin when she starts to squirm.

"I don't have all night," she huffs.

So fucking *prickly*.

I push inside slowly, wanting to draw this out a bit since I know she'll be out the door seconds after it's over—and that feels as foreign as the desire to have her look at me when we do this. Maybe it's my ego that feels bruised. Maybe it's that I don't like not having the upper hand. I try not to examine it too closely.

"Fuck, you feel good," I sigh against her neck. "So damned hot inside you."

"Move," she demands, pushing back against me.

My teeth graze her throat. "Say please."

"*Please* move, asshole," she says through gritted teeth.

"Well, since you asked nicely . . ."

I rear back just to roll back inside, my mouth going slack against her skin as that familiar rush courses down my spine. Dani isn't my first hookup, but she's by far the best. Everything about her has me constantly seconds away from losing it—from the slick heat of her cunt to the rough spew of her words. Maybe I really *am* losing it.

Her head lolls forward as I do it again, and I let my hand slide up her back to curl over her shoulder, holding her steady as I start to pound a steady rhythm. There's a sharp slap of skin that rings out in my apartment with every thrust, a staccato beat that plays in time to her gasps and her low moans. I let the palm of my free hand rub over the swell of her ass, biting my lip as I give it one sharp smack that makes her tense up around me. Not enough to bruise, just enough to make her shudder.

"*Bastard*," she hisses.

I do it again, my eyes nearly rolling back with the way she clenches around me. "Stop pretending you don't like it. We both know you do."

Not that she'll ever admit it. The first time had been an instinctual accident, one I had expected to have her pulling off me and storming out of my apartment—so it had been a surprise when a heavy moan had fallen out of her mouth instead, her entire body shivering. I haven't forgotten. Doubt I ever will.

"That's it," I rasp as I slam back inside, letting another light *crack* of my palm fall against her ass. Her pale skin turns pink quickly, and I like knowing she might wear my handprint around for a few hours after this. "You can be a good girl when you want to be, Dani."

"Hate you so much," she slurs as both of my hands move to her hips to grip her tight.

"Maybe." I can feel that familiar pressure building, feel the allover rush that tells me this won't last much longer. "But you're still going to come on my cock."

I let one hand slide over her hip to press between her legs, finding that swollen bundle of nerves and circling it with a steady pressure from my fingers as I move in and out of her again and again. My head falls forward and my eyes drift closed, focusing on the way she feels, on the sounds she's making, letting them pull me closer to the edge.

"I'm—*shit*, I'm—"

I let out a string of curses as I feel her trembling around me, her entire body quaking as she pushes back against my still-thrusting cock as I move faster than before to chase my own release. It hits me just as hard as it always does with her, drawing a shout from my lips as I stay flush against her ass while I pulse inside the condom. Not for the first time, my hazy thoughts wonder what she would feel like without one, not that it would ever happen.

She's boneless beneath me as I catch my breath, but even in her languid state, I can sense her closing herself back off. I let my head drop to her shoulder just for a moment so I can savor the orgasm for a second more before she runs off, breathing out a sigh before I pull out of her with a wince.

Dani is all business as I fall back naked against my couch, and I watch her lazily as she quickly grabs for her clothing and starts to button herself back up as if she didn't just take me on my couch while moaning my name.

Okay, so she didn't do all of that exactly, but it's nice to pretend.

"What," I call as she pulls her skirt back over her thighs. "No dinner?"

She rolls her eyes. "Hardly."

"Fine." I make a show of letting my fingers rub across my mouth when her eyes slide over to meet mine. "I already ate anyway."

She wrinkles her nose, and for a second I think she might laugh, but she schools her expression quickly to the more usual annoyed look she reserves for me. "We have to stop doing this."

"Sure," I laugh, since arguing will do no good. We both know she'll be back.

I haven't really let myself consider the possibility that she won't.

"I mean it," she stresses. "No more."

"Of course," I answer with a lazy grin. "Whatever you say, Dani."

She blows out a breath as she buttons the last button of her blouse. "Asshole."

She bends to pet Purrgood once more near the door, but I don't get so much as a goodbye—just the soft clicking of her heels across my wood flooring before my apartment door slams shut behind her. I let my head fall back against the couch, sighing and wondering not for the first time what it is I'm doing with Danica Pierce.

AFTER A QUICK dinner (sans Dani, unfortunately) followed by a shower and feeding my cat, I'm more than ready to crash into bed; I always sleep better after Dani leaves, if for no other reason than she always seems to wear me out in the best way. So I'm annoyed when my cell phone starts to vibrate on the side table just after I've plugged it in to charge for the night, frowning as I reach to click on the lamp and feeling it turn into a scowl when I notice the name.

"Hello?"

"Took you long enough to answer."

I purse my lips. "Hello, Alexander. Good to talk to you too."

"Cut the shit, Ezra," he huffs. "Did you go over Lorenzo's financial records yet?"

"I've been going over them all week. You already know this."

"I heard Bianca hired Danica Pierce."

"Yes, I've heard."

Then I heard Dani moaning on my couch, I don't say.

"Best news we've got this week," my father chortles. "She'll make it an easy win."

I bristle at that. "Don't be too sure. She's won against me before."

"Only because you got sloppy."

I feel hot anger bloom in my chest, but I tamp it down. I learned early in life that you don't talk back to Alexander Hart.

"Is there any other reason you called so late?"

"We're holding mediation next week," he tells me.

"Does Dani—" I hesitate, correcting myself from calling her so casually. "Has Danica's firm cleared this?"

"No, but you're going to make sure they do. Lorenzo wants this taken care of quickly. He's already got a settlement plan laid out that you can offer Bianca. She's got her own money. She shouldn't put up much of a fight."

She might since her husband is a cheating bastard, I don't say.

"I'll reach out to their office and set a meeting on Monday."

"Good." I can hear my father settling into the large leather wingback in his study, hear the strike of a match as he most likely lights up a cigar. "You know how important it is that we take care of this for Lorenzo. He's an old friend of mine."

Like I care.

"I don't need the reminder," I scoff. "I can handle it."

"Don't get smart. I can still give the case to your brother. At least I know he won't fuck anything up."

My teeth grind together at the thought of Eli, my older brother and Alexander's perfect, asshole firstborn, in the courtroom with Dani.

"I said I'll handle it," I answer tightly.

"See that you do. Don't get sloppy." There's a brief pause before he continues. "Your mother wants you to come to dinner this week."

I grip the phone a little tighter, the mention of my mother always setting off waves of sadness that I can barely swallow. "I'll try to come by."

He hangs up without so much as a goodbye, and I angrily toss my phone back on the side table as I fall back against the pillows. I tell myself that at least I'll get to annoy Dani first thing Monday morning.

It's that thought that has me smiling as I drift off to sleep.

Four

DANI

"BILL ISN'T COMING?"

My mother makes a disgruntled sound, rolling her eyes in my father's direction. Her black hair, which looks so much like mine save for the slight streaks of gray, is pulled into a high ponytail, her perfectly tailored brow tilted high. "He's playing golf with a client."

"Oh?" Dad gives her a look over the brunch menu. "Did he ever snag the Feinstein account?"

"He's still 'reeling that one in,' he says," Mom laughs. "Patty have a class today?"

"Pottery," Dad tells her. "She started up a daddy and daughter art hour or something."

Mom practically coos, "Oh, that's lovely."

I watch all of this unfold with the morbid fascination one might reserve for two different species interacting with each other in the wild. In my professional experience, separated couples usually tend to, well, *stay* separated when they divorce. It's the natural order of things. They aren't supposed to remain *best friends*. They aren't supposed to meld into this weird foursome of solidarity with themselves and their new spouses.

But that's exactly what my parents did.

Until I was seventeen, I thought that Perry and Katherine Pierce had the perfect marriage. They did everything together; we were a unit. I thought the sun rose and set on their love for each other. That is . . . until they sat me down and told me they were getting a divorce. That they would still be *friends*—but they just weren't in love. Just like that. Like they were telling me what we were going to have for dinner that night. One minute they're the perfect couple, and the next, they're telling me they never actually loved each other at all. At least, not like I thought they did. Regardless, I learned a long time ago that good marriages don't really exist. They're all destined to end.

I take a sip of my water, listening to my mom and dad continue to chat about varying news regarding their respective spouses. Don't get me wrong, my stepparents are great, but it's still weird that we all spend every holiday together like some warped version of *The Brady Bunch*.

"So have you met your client yet?"

I blink, realizing my dad is talking to me now. "Oh, have you remembered I'm here? I wouldn't want to interrupt family time."

"Oh, stop your pouting, Danica," Mom tuts. "We were just catching up."

"You talk on the phone almost every day," I grumble.

Dad laughs. "You don't talk to your best friends on the phone every day?"

I don't even want to begin to try to get into the weirdness of my mother being my father's best friend while they're both married to someone else.

"Yes, I've met the client," I say instead, changing the subject. "She's . . . a character."

"That's what Manuel said too," Dad says. "'A real ice queen' were the words he used, I believe."

I frown, not liking that assessment of Bianca. It doesn't feel right.

"I would say she's more of a . . . powerful woman," I tell him, a slight smile on my lips. "I like her."

"Well, you'd better," Dad snorts. "If you can't prove her husband was a cheating son of a bitch, she'll be out millions."

"I heard she doesn't even need the money," Mom points out. "Why is she fighting the prenup so hard?"

It's a question I've heard numerous times since Bianca signed on with us. It's even one I've wondered about myself—despite having talked to the woman in question. But it's also one I'm still not sure I have the full answer to, so I just shrug.

"Who cares? If he cheated, he deserves to be hung out to dry."

"Hear, hear," Dad says, raising his mimosa.

I cock an eyebrow at him. "Maybe you should make that your last one."

"Oh, don't be a square, Danibaby," he chides. "We're celebrating, remember?"

I snort into my water glass. "Seems you two are celebrating a lot more than I am."

"Well, we can fix that," Mom says with a snap of her fingers. "Let's get something covered in syrup and more mimosas!"

"We really don't need any more—"

My lips press closed as I realize everything I'm saying is going in one ear and out the other, since Mom is already waving down a waitress and Dad is tipping back his glass to finish off the rest of his second drink. I swear, sometimes it feels like *I'm* the parent in this group and Mom and Dad are the unruly children I have to keep a firm hand on. You'd never know that Dad is a retired judge and Mom a tenured professor, watching them act out like they are.

I order a fruit salad with some turkey bacon, which causes all sorts of ruckus from my dad about living a little, and they both make good on ordering something covered in syrup and—much to my dismay—more mimosas.

"So." Dad leans back in his chair, scratching at his thick, graying mustache. "What are you bringing to the party?"

I frown. "Party?"

"The Fourth of July party!" My mother waves a hand, clucking her tongue. "I told you that you were in charge of the apple pie."

"I don't have time to make a pie," I argue.

"But your apple pie is famous! You know everyone will be asking about it."

"Did we forget that I just took on the biggest case of my career?"

Dad shoots me a look. "If you think that's getting you out of coming to the party, you can think again."

"We all know your Fourth of July thing—"

"The ninth annual Pierce Fourth of July Bash," Dad corrects.

I roll my eyes. "Your *party* is just an excuse for all of your old work friends to get tipsy and for you to almost burn your hand off shooting fireworks."

"Haven't lost anything yet." Dad grins, wiggling his fingers at me. "You're coming."

"I'll check my schedule," I mumble.

Mom laughs. "You know our Danica can't do anything without making sure we completely understand how begrudged she is about it."

"It is one of her more adorable personality traits," Dad chuckles. "No idea where she gets it from though."

Mom taps her chin with one manicured nail. "Maybe from your dad? You know he was an old grouch."

"He was also a raging alcoholic," Dad says. "Which I hope our Dani isn't."

"That's fine," I huff. "Please continue to talk about me as if I'm not here."

"We're just teasing," Mom tells me, reaching to pat my hand. "You're just always so serious, honey. Makes me worry you're going to keel over before us."

"Lovely," I deadpan.

"Feel free to bring a date to the party," my mom adds, practically winking at me like a cartoon character.

I bristle. "I'm not bringing a date."

"Honey . . ." My mom's eyes turn sympathetic. "It's been years. You can't keep letting Grant hang over your head like some sort of—"

"Can we please not talk about this right now?" I say through gritted teeth.

Or never, I don't say. Grant is a nonstarter for me. He always will be.

Dad shoots Mom a worried look, clearing his throat and blessedly changing the subject. "So, do you know who the opposing counsel is yet?"

"I do," I grind out with a scowl. I definitely don't want to remember Ezra fucking me silly over the back of his couch a few nights ago while I'm sitting with my parents and skirting conversation about my ex. "Unfortunately."

Dad looks at me expectantly. "Well? Who is it?"

"I—"

My mouth continues to hang open, whatever I'd been about to say trailing off into open air and wafting away as my eyes catch sight of a familiar figure entering the dining room from the bar seating area in the room beyond. I don't think my brain fully realizes that I'm just staring at him as he winds through the linen-covered tables effortlessly, his hands in his pockets and a sly smile on his mouth as if he's taking a leisurely stroll through the park.

And that's when I realize he's headed right for our table.

My eyes dart around as I try to look for an escape; being within a ten-foot radius of Ezra Hart while my fucking parents are around is on the very bottom of my to-do list—right under Pap smears and custody hearings. I'm seconds away from shooting up from the table and breaking out into a run without any explanation, but when Ezra raises a hand in greeting, I realize there's no getting out of this.

"Dani," Ezra practically purrs. "What a nice coincidence seeing you here."

My eye twitches. "It's . . . a coincidence. That's for sure."

"Are these your parents?" Ezra looks between my mom and dad, completely disregarding the silent "go the fuck away" I'm signaling with my eyes as he offers his hand to my mother. "Or maybe this is your sister?"

"Oh, he's a charmer," Mom says with a flush, taking his hand to shake it.

Dad wags a finger in Ezra's direction. "I know you. How do I know you?"

"Can't say," Ezra answers casually, still ignoring the silent waves of irritation rolling off me. "Dani and I are more 'closed door' sort of friends." My mouth falls open, and my mother gives Ezra a strange look, but then he adds, "I work for another firm."

Dad snaps his fingers. "Hart! You're the Hart boy. I've followed your career. Hell of a win rate."

"I appreciate that, sir," Ezra preens.

"Never had you in my courtroom, unfortunately," Dad goes on. "Been retired for a while now, but I still keep up with things in the court reports."

Mom pats Dad's arm. "Perry was a judge for thirty years."

"Oh?" Ezra chances a glance at me, his jaw twitching with his tempered smile when he notices my narrowed eyes. "Dani never mentioned."

"The Heartbreak Prince!" Mom makes a delighted sound before she slaps Dad's shoulder. "That's what they call Ezra. So clever."

About as fucking clever as a Saturday-morning cartoon.

I clear my throat. "What are you doing here, Ezra?"

"Same as you, I imagine," he drawls, shooting me a megawatt smile that makes me scowl even as my stomach swoops. "Having brunch." He winks at my parents. "With lesser company, surely."

"Well, we're kind of busy," I say tersely. "So . . ."

Ezra completely ignores me. "Did Dani tell you we'll be going against each other on the Casiraghi case?"

"She hadn't gotten around to it," Dad says. "You've given her a run for her money in the past."

"It's because he's fluent in bullshit," I mutter.

Ezra remains unfazed. "I've definitely never come up against anyone like your daughter. She's . . . very good." He pauses, his mouth hitching in a slow smile. "When she wants to be."

I feel my neck flush with heat, my nostrils flaring in what has to be a comical expression as I remember the other night.

You can be a good girl when you want to be, Dani.

"Nothing like a little friendly rivalry to make things interesting," Dad pipes up, oblivious to the fact that Ezra is trying to engage me in some kind of odd mating dance that I refuse to be a part of. "I can't wait to see how things play out."

Ezra's eyes are still fixed on me, giving a surreptitious glance down the front of me before his head snaps back to my parents to flash another practiced smile. "I'm always in for a surprise when it comes to Dani, but it's never boring." Ezra checks his watch. "I'd better go back to waiting on my client. It was really great to meet you both."

"It was nice to meet you," my mom offers.

Ezra's eyes catch mine, an annoying twinkle there that lets me know how amusing he finds all of this. "Always good to see you, Dani."

I can't manage more than a stiff nod, the familiar knot forming in my belly, one that always seems to work in tandem with the warming of my blood, leaving me aggravated. Especially since I can never really pin down if it comes more from irritation or arousal.

"He seemed nice," Dad notes as Ezra strides off.

I catch Mom nodding from the corner of my eye. "Handsome too. Dani, have you ever—?"

"I need to go to the bathroom," I spit out, pushing up from my chair. "I'll be right back."

I don't wait for them to reply as I make a beeline for the restrooms, turning sharply just before I reach the hallway to cut across the edge of the dining room toward the bar area. I find him there, slung casually in one of the oversized leather stools at the horseshoe-shaped bar, his fingers drumming lightly over the dark polished wood as he watches some sports game on the overhead television.

I shove his shoulder lightly. "What the hell was that?"

"Oh, hello, Dani. Miss me already? That has to be a new record."

"I miss you about as much as I miss teeth cleanings."

"Mm, sounds like you're thinking about me in your mouth."

"I actually cannot stand you."

Ezra's smile is slow, lazy even. It makes the knots in my stomach tighten even further. "I like you best off your feet anyway."

"You think you're cute," I huff.

He bats his eyelashes at me in an overexaggerated fashion. "I think I'm adorable."

"Why are you here? Really?"

"I told you, I'm meeting a client."

"Is it Mr. Casiraghi?"

"I have more than one client," he chuckles.

"Are you implying I don't?"

"Calm down, Sour Patch," he laughs. "I would never."

"Don't call me that."

He drums his fingers over the bar again, still looking annoyingly smug. "Your parents seem nice."

"What's that supposed to mean?"

"That your parents seem nice?" he repeats with a grin. "No hidden meaning."

"There's always a hidden meaning with you."

"I think you *think* there is, but I'm actually very simple. I say what I mean, Dani."

I narrow my eyes, still trying to figure out if there is some sort of angle here that I'm missing.

"Brunch with my parents is awkward enough without you mucking things up."

"Didn't seem very awkward to me."

"Right," I snort. "Only because my dad's wife and my mother's husband couldn't be here to parade their weird little four-way friendship that drives me up the fucking wall."

Ezra cocks his head. "They're divorced?"

"But still the *best* of friends," I say bitterly.

"That sounds like it would be tough to deal with as a kid."

"Didn't happen until I was seventeen. Fucking blew my world up, but I—" I close my mouth. What am I doing? Ezra and I don't do this. This sort of thing is for friends with benefits who are actually friends. "Whatever. I wanted to tell you that just because we . . ." I swallow, refusing to acknowledge it out loud. "It doesn't mean you can insert yourself into my personal life."

"I could make a joke about *inserting myself*, but I'm a gentleman."

"Sure you are," I scoff.

"Did you come all the way over here just to yell at me, or did you *actually* miss me?"

"Hardly."

"Too bad," he murmurs.

My nose wrinkles. "Why?"

"Because I've missed you."

I refuse to let surprise show on my face; I remind myself that things like that are all part of Ezra's game. That making me think he's actually being nice would be like a gold star to him.

"Sure you have," I reply blandly.

His fingers slide from the bar to tease against the tips of mine, his touch so slight that I might not even notice it if not for the sparks of electricity it causes to shoot along my skin. "I can show you just how much," he tells me, his voice lowering to a level that makes me want to press my legs together. "If you want to come over later to . . . go over things."

I tell myself that the shiver along my spine is one of distaste. The mistruth is like a lifeboat in an entire sea of lies that I've been treading these past few months.

I yank my hand away. "Not happening. I'm busy, and I already told you we aren't doing that anymore."

"Suit yourself." Ezra shrugs. "I guess I'll just see you at my office to discuss the settlement proposal in a few days then?"

"They tell me it's mandatory," I reply dryly.

"Can't wait to see you either," Ezra chuckles.

"Try to keep the bullshit to a minimum, if you can."

"But, Dani," he says with a wide grin, "you look so pretty when you're pissed at me."

I throw up my hands, spinning on my heel with a frustrated sound as his laughter chases after me. I don't know how many times I've told myself not to let Ezra rile me, but it seems like my brain still hasn't gotten the message, like he has intimate knowledge about all my buttons and exactly where to press them. I clench my fists as I stomp back to my parents' table.

I'm definitely *not* still thinking about the way my skin tingles where he touched me.

Five

DANI

I CAN THINK of a dozen things I would rather do than visit Ezra's firm.

That very real list includes, but is not exclusive to: having a colonoscopy, seeing people from my old high school at the grocery store, getting a flat on I-35 before a court date, listening to my mother talk about her and Bill's sex life . . . I could go on.

Yet, here I am, walking through the wide-open space of the entryway as I step off the elevator and onto the floor where the Hart & Associates offices are located. The foyer is carefully decorated in a way that only a group of rich men can manage—sleek, black furniture and obnoxious wall art that looks like something from Wayfair but probably costs five times as much—it even comes complete with a perfect blond receptionist who stands to greet me when I get close.

But her, I like.

"Hey, Maggie," I tell her, returning her smile. "Love your dress."

She smooths her hands over her hips, flashing me a brief coquettish pose. "You like? I got it from T.J.Maxx."

"Shut up," I gush. I give her another once-over. "Damn."

"I know. I look amazing." She winks as she settles back into her desk chair. "Which Mr. Hart are you here for?"

"You say that as if any of them are preferable choices for company."

Maggie holds up her hands. "No comment."

"I have an appointment with Ezra," I say flatly, the reminder tasting bad on my tongue.

"Ah." She checks something on her computer. "Right. They're set up in Room B."

"Perfect." I flash her a playful roll of my eyes. "Wish me luck."

"Go get 'em, killer."

I wait until I'm out of sight down the hallway before I reach behind me to run my fingers through my ponytail, not wanting a hair out of place before I face my nemesis.

Can we really say that if you're constantly having sex with him?

I shake the thought away as I straighten my blouse just outside the door to the conference room. I take a deep breath as I reach for the door handle, giving myself a silent pep talk to ensure that I *don't* let Ezra get to me, that I don't succumb to the verbal fishing lures he uses to try to reel me in to a fight. Especially since I'm almost certain he considers fucking with me foreplay to, well, *actually* fucking me.

Ezra is already slung in one of the large leather conference chairs like some sort of king—having turned it away from the table and leaned back into it so he can let his legs spread wide in front of him. I allow myself three seconds to take this in and then make a mindful decision to focus on the paralegal who's sitting across from him instead. I give the other man a polite nod, making sure to greet him *before* Ezra just because it gives me a tiny tremor of satisfaction to do so.

"Good morning, Dani."

I cut my eyes to the other side of the table, suppressing a small shiver at Ezra's mention of my name. Why do two syllables out of his mouth make my stomach erupt in butterflies? My name on his tongue always feels like more than an address. It feels like a promise to *undress*. It's irritating as hell.

"Morning," I answer curtly. "Is anyone else joining us?"

"Just us three. Unless you wanted it to just be the two of us? I'm sure I can send Kevin here on an errand if you'd rather—"

"Us three is perfectly fine." I settle into a chair three spaces away, opening my briefcase. "I've brought all the necessary financial paperwork for disclosure. We're excluding Mrs. Casiraghi's trust fund as previously agreed; we're only including assets gained between them during the course of their marriage." I glance up at Ezra then, finding him smiling at me infuriatingly. "You wanted to discuss the possibility of a settlement?"

"Ah. Right. Mr. Casiraghi hates the idea of dragging his wife—"

"Soon-to-be-ex-wife," I correct.

Ezra's grin widens, and my stomach does that *thing* again that I hate. "Right. Sorry, he hates the thought of putting her through such a public trial unnecessarily and is prepared to settle to avoid the whole thing if she's agreeable to it."

I have to force my eyes to remain steady, holding back a preemptive eye roll.

This should be good.

"And what is Mr. Casiraghi prepared to offer for this settlement?"

"He's prepared to let their home here in Austin go to Mrs. Casiraghi, ten percent of the business's current net worth, as well as a five percent share in the company for any future assets."

I read once that the human brain registers four seconds of silence as rejection, so I make sure to count to a full five before I give Ezra an answer. "I think I can safely say that my client will not be accepting that offer, since it's, to be frank, a bullshit offer. Seriously, Ezra. Didn't I tell you to keep the bullshit to a minimum?"

"I think it's more than fair," Ezra answers coolly. "Considering there's a prenup in place."

"One that would be rendered null and void per the infidelity clause."

"You haven't produced any evidence to prove that those claims aren't entirely circumstantial."

"Well, unless it's his *spiritual advisor* that's been sending him all of those emails . . ."

Another grin for my trouble. "You always seem to be beating around the bush, Dani."

"Like to beat *something*," I mutter under my breath. I look him in the eye when I speak to him again. "I will have to check with my client, but don't hold your breath on that offer." I let my lips curl. "Or do. It makes no difference to me."

"That's unfortunate," Ezra says, his voice still aggravatingly upbeat. He reaches a hand across the table without even looking at his paralegal, Kevin, waiting until the man in question deposits a thick binder. "In that case, all I can offer you today are Mr. Casiraghi's financial disclosure documents. My client was afraid you might react that way to his very generous—and unnecessary, I might add—offer, and in the case that you and your client might not want to accept, he regrets to inform you that he will have to disagree to Mrs. Casiraghi's proposed terms to leave her trust out of the combined assets."

I blink at him stupidly, caught off guard for a second. "Excuse me?"

"Mr. Casiraghi has helped manage her trust for the entirety of their marriage to the benefit of his wife. It has seen rapid growth because of his investments. My client feels that if *your* client insists on dragging him through a very lengthy and unnecessary bout in court, as well as attempting to besmirch his good name, then *all* assets between the two of them should be on the table."

"'Besmirch his good name'?" I sputter. "What is this, a Jane Austen novel?"

Ezra shrugs. "Don't shoot the messenger."

"Typical," I scoff, snatching the binder from him. "Is there anything else you need from me?"

"Are you offering something else?"

I feel warmth creep up my neck. "No." I tuck his binder into my briefcase, pushing away from the table to stand. "Honestly, this entire meeting could have been an email. I don't even see why I needed to come in."

Ezra stands with me, stuffing his hands in his pockets easily and giving me that slow, lazy smile that flips my stomach. Something that only adds fuel to the fire that is my anger at this entire debacle. "I'm always happy to see you in person, Dani."

"Well, that makes one of us," I toss back. "I'll be in touch with my client's official decision in regard to your client's settlement offer. Again, feel free to hold your breath until my call."

"Have a good day, Dani." He completely ignores my frosty attitude, acting as if we just had a casual brunch together. "I'm sure I'll see you soon."

I bristle at the implication, but say nothing as I turn to leave the room with my things in hand. My steps back toward the front foyer are much heavier than before, irritation evident in my stride. I think I might actually be muttering obscenities under my breath. Why do I let him get under my skin like that? Why is it that *everything* Ezra says seems to turn me into the human equivalent of a snapping turtle?

I blame my distracted thought process for not watching where I'm going properly, and when I bump into a large, hard body, I wince, immediately offering up an apology.

"Sorry, I didn't see—"

I recognize him immediately; he's had as much press as his brother, after all, but the elder Hart brother, Eli, looks entirely different than Ezra. Harder, somehow. His dark hair is neatly combed, and his piercing blue eyes, which he narrows in my direction as if I'm some sort of bug, give me a much different but no less irritating feeling than those of his brother.

"Ms. Pierce," Eli says stiffly. "Pardon me."

"No, it was my fault. I didn't see you."

"All right."

Damn. Usually there is least one more pretend back-and-forth of the blame game before we just settle on it, but okay.

"You met with my brother?"

I feel my spine go a little straighter. "Just left, actually."

"Mm." He gives me a once-over, but something about it makes me feel . . . cold. It's a stark contrast to the way I feel when Ezra does something similar. Weirdly, at this moment, I might prefer the frustrating warmth of Ezra's gaze over the unsettling coldness of his brother's. "Well. I suppose I should offer you good luck on the case."

I wait for him to actually *offer* said good luck, but since all he gives me after that is a tight nod and a brush-off as he moves around me like I'm a traffic cone—I guess that's as good as it's going to get. I turn my head to watch him go with a frown; he wasn't rude exactly, but he wasn't . . . *not* rude either. I puff out a breath as I continue on, putting the interaction behind me.

Damn Harts. Assholes, the whole bunch.

"AND THE SETTLEMENT they offered," I say heatedly, continuing what's turned into a twenty-minute rant about the most infuriating man I've ever met while my friends and I sit at the bar of our favorite hangout. "It was ridiculous. Actually insulting."

"I'm assuming Mrs. Casiraghi told them to fuck off?" Vera asks.

I make a face. "Not in so many words, but basically. I told Ezra to expect as much."

"I think he likes to piss you off," Nate inserts. "Does it make the sex better or something?"

I groan. "Can we not talk about that?"

"No one asked you to tell me," Nate says.

Vera frowns. "She didn't. You overheard us talking."

"And I was very hurt to have been kept out of the loop," Nate *hmphs*.

"So sorry," I answer, rolling my eyes. "Next time we can just call Manuel in too and loop him in."

"Ignore him," Vera says. "It's how I make it through the day. What happened after?"

I shrug. "Nothing much. I basically packed up and left in a hurry after that. Ran into Ezra's brother on the way out. That was fun."

"You met Eli Hart today?"

I curl my lip in distaste, taking a sip of my amaretto sour before answering. "Unfortunately. He might be a bigger asshole than Ezra. I can't tell."

"Please." Nate snorts loudly. "We both know you don't hate Ezra as much as you pretend."

Vera twirls the straw in her drink. "She's allowed to hate him and enjoy his dick. The two aren't mutually exclusive."

"*Exactly*," I stress, snapping my fingers. "If anything about him were half as enjoyable as his dick, I'd marry the man."

"No you wouldn't," Vera and Nate both say at the same time.

Nate and Vera are *very* aware of my thoughts on relationships. Nate, the romantic, thinks someone will sweep me off my feet one day. Vera, the realist, thinks Nate is an idiot.

"Fine," I agree, grumbling.

"Sounds like you're dangerously close to objectifying Ezra Hart," Nate accuses. "Not very feminist of you."

"You are not allowed to talk about objectification," Vera scoffs. "Or feminism. Actually, why did we invite you again?"

He reaches to pluck one of her neat braids in an attempt to twirl it around his finger, laughing when she smacks his hand away. "How can you continue secretly pining for me if I don't make myself available? I'd hate for you to have to stoop to gazing wistfully into my office."

"You know, I don't like you *or* your dick," Vera says flatly. "So I'm wondering what I gain from these interactions."

Nate blows her a kiss. "Don't knock it until you try it, darling."

"Can you guys do your weird verbal foreplay somewhere else?" I rub my temples. "I have a headache."

"You invited us out for a drink," they both say at the same time again.

"Stop that," Vera huffs.

Nate laughs. "It's because we're so *connected*."

"I hate him," Vera says to the ceiling before giving her attention to me. "You *did* stop sleeping with Ezra though, right? You said you were going to after the last time."

"I"—I give my own tiny red straw a twirl, shrugging—"did say that. Yes."

"That's Dani-speak for 'We totally boned again,'" Nate says.

Vera cuts her eyes in his direction. "'Boned'? Really? You're thirty-five."

"What would you rather I say? 'Fornicated'? 'Made the beast with two backs'? 'The horizontal mambo'? I could just say they fu—"

"*Shh*," I hiss. I drop my head to the bar, ignoring the slight stickiness there and forcibly not thinking about when they might have cleaned it last. "I didn't mean to."

"You didn't mean to?" I catch Nate arching an eyebrow at me when I peek at him from the side. "Did you, like, fall on his dick?"

Vera's nose wrinkles. "Classy." She turns toward me curiously. "You didn't, right?"

"I swear to God." I close my eyes, expelling a breath. "*No*. I just . . . maybe he's a witch or something."

Nate leans in, lowering his voice. "I think they're called warlocks if they're dudes. Don't joke about that shit."

"Had someone hex you lately?"

Vera laughs. "That would check out."

"I just mean that even though he drives me up the fucking

wall, he's the best sex I've ever had." I raise my head, giving them both a pointed look. "I will deny that if it ever comes up again."

Nate crosses his heart. "Maybe tell him you want to gag him? You could say it's a kink of yours."

I don't tell him that the filthy words that spill out of Ezra's mouth actually *add* to the pleasure of our encounters; I refuse to admit that out loud to anyone. Ever.

"It's *outside* the bedroom that's the problem," I groan.

Vera cocks her head. "I thought you said you guys don't do it in bed?"

"What?" Nate looks confused. "Where are you doing it then?"

I shoot Vera a look of warning, then shake my head at Nate. "That's not up for discussion."

"Sorry," Nate says with a faraway look. "I'm just imagining the two of you in like a sex swing or something."

"Stop imagining us anywhere," I warn.

"Okay, but seriously," Vera starts. "You have to nip that shit in the bud. I know you've gone head-to-head with him before—"

"Pun intended," Nate deadpans.

Vera ignores him. "*But*, this is the biggest case of your career. I mean, you're looking at junior partner here. You don't need any distractions. Not to mention the shitstorm you'd be facing in conflict of interest if anyone else found out."

"Dick-stractions, one might say," Nate muses.

"*Shut up*," Vera and I say at the same time.

"Fine, fine," Nate acquiesces. He takes a sip of his drink, eyeing me. "Vera's right, you know." He notices Vera giving him a look of surprise and adds, "But I won't be admitting that again."

He eyes me thoughtfully. "Unless . . . are you sure that you don't—"

"Don't even finish that sentence," I warn.

"I'm just saying," he tries again. "Obviously you like *something* about him, even if it's just his equipment, maybe there's something more there."

"There is absolutely nothing more there," I stress. "I'm not looking for anything more anyway."

"Listen," he sighs. "We know better than anyone that products of divorce have issues, but maybe you—"

"Don't." I shake my head. The last thing I want to do tonight on top of everything else is end up wallowing over old shit. "This has nothing to do with my parents."

Vera's stare is piercing. "I hope it isn't about Grant."

"The mysterious Grant," Nate whispers in awe. "Do I finally get the story?"

"No," Vera and I say in unison.

"What?" Nate puffs out a breath. "Come on, I know he like broke your heart or something, but neither of you have ever said—"

"Nate," Vera warns, most likely noticing my frown. She gives me another searching look. "Dani?"

"Of course it isn't," I say too quickly. One of the hazards of being friends with Vera for so long is that she has intimate knowledge of the worst parts of me. There's nowhere to hide from her. I sigh, shaking my head. "It really isn't. I wouldn't be stupid enough to let myself get too close to someone like Ezra. Especially not after Grant."

"Well, then my point stands."

"I know," I sigh. "I need to end it. For good this time. It can't happen again."

"You said 'can't,'" Vera points out.

Nate nods. "Not 'won't.'"

"*Won't*," I correct. "It *won't* happen again."

My friends both stare at me in what I can only describe as pity, like I'm a foregone conclusion. I glare at both of them.

"It *won't*," I stress.

"Right," Vera says.

"Sure," Nate offers.

I shake my head. "I hate you both."

"Yeah, but you hate Ezra too," Nate says lightly, "and you let him bend you into a—"

"Do *not* finish that sentence."

Vera pats my shoulder. "I have faith in you. Mostly."

"Lovely," I mutter.

Vera and Nate start arguing about something or other that I can't help but tune out, slurping down a big portion of my drink and hoping a buzz will help loosen the tension in my shoulders. I know that today was just a preview of what will probably be a long and exasperating trial should it come to that, just like I know that my friends are right, that I need to shove Ezra into a "strictly professional" compartment of my brain and leave him there. My mind is completely on board with this plan. It's practically nodding in agreement, applauding this logical decision.

But unfortunately . . . logic never really seems to have anything to do with my decisions in regard to Ezra Hart.

DANI

TYPICALLY, THERE ARE two ways a mediation meeting can go. One, the couple remains amicable, having a predetermined plan for how to divide their assets and cordially move through the motions of doing that; or two, chaos ensues. I have seen women chuck vases at their cheating husbands. I have watched men devolve into toddlers, copying everything their wives say just to annoy them.

Sitting in the largest conference room here at our firm, I have no idea how this one is going to play out.

Mr. Casiraghi is exactly what I expected him to be. He exudes power; his suit probably cost more than my entire wardrobe, and his white hair is slicked back and combed over to hide the way it thins at the top. He hasn't said a word since he arrived with both Ezra *and* Eli Hart ten minutes ago, and as much as Bianca and I prepared for this meeting, I have to admit that Ezra's firm sending both brothers has me on edge. Especially since Eli rarely handles divorce cases, from what I've gleaned from the papers.

Bianca doesn't seem to be suffering any of my reservations. Her shoulders are squared and her spine is straight, and she hasn't taken her eyes off her soon-to-be-ex-husband in the entire time they've been in the same room. Her stare is confident and determined, everything about her showing no fear of what lies before her. God, I want to be her when I grow up.

My thoughts inevitably wander to my parents, as they often do during these proceedings. How easy had it been for them to divide everything up? How simple had it been to take my entire life and turn it on its head?

We did this for you.

"So," the mediator starts, tearing me out of the past, thankfully. "I think we're all here if we want to begin."

I shoot a glance at Eli, who is watching all of us from down his nose. "I wasn't informed you would be bringing cocounsel."

"It was . . ." Ezra clears his throat, frowning. "It was a last-minute decision."

Eli's eyes narrow slightly, not enough for him to appear outwardly rude, but enough to make me want to flip him the bird all the same. "Do you have some issue with my being here, Ms. Pierce?"

"No issue," I say as placidly as I can manage. "I just like to be kept informed."

"Well," Eli says with a smile that doesn't meet his eyes. "Consider yourself informed."

Wow, fuck this guy.

I catch Ezra's nostrils flaring slightly, his mouth in a tight line before he says, "We're ready to proceed if you and your client are, Dani."

Eli casts an odd look at his brother at the casual use of my nickname, but I ignore it.

"All right," the mediator tries again, sounding a little wary as he flips through his notes. "I see here that Mrs. Casiraghi is requesting a complete division of all shared assets?"

I nod. "That's correct."

"We aren't in agreement," Ezra adds.

"I see," the mediator says.

Mr. Casiraghi finally speaks up with a scoff. His accent is thicker than Bianca's, the inflection on his words making what he's saying sound harsher. "My *wife* has no grounds for such a thing. She signed the prenup, yes?"

"That's true," the mediator points out. He flips another page in his notes. "I have your signature right here, Mrs. Casiraghi."

"We have reason to believe the terms of the prenup have been breached," I say.

Eli makes an amused sound. "Circumstantial reason."

"I can handle this," Ezra says tightly, using a tone I'm not sure I've ever heard from him.

Eli shrugs as if to say "Whatever," lacing his fingers together over the conference room table and continuing to watch what's happening in front of him like some sort of bored spectator.

"My client has several exchanges between your client and your client's mistress suggesting an affair," I tell Ezra, pointedly not looking at his brother. "I gave you copies of these exchanges during disclosure."

"And again," Ezra says calmly, all business for once, thankfully. "This evidence is circumstantial. It can't be proven that it was our client that sent these emails."

"They were from his computer," I snort.

Ezra waves me off. "In an office that several people have access to. Any one of the employees working near him could have fabricated those exchanges."

"And what purpose would that serve?"

"For all we know," Ezra says, "those emails could have been sent at the behest of your client in order to frame her husband so that she could claim her prenup terms had been violated."

I rear back, feeling hot anger lick down my spine. "That's not a claim you can substantiate."

"It's nothing any of us haven't seen before," he answers softly, looking almost like he's trying to placate me. "You know that's true, Dani."

I hate that my name on his tongue *still* makes my stomach flutter, even now. Would it kill him to not use it in this setting? The last thing I need is to get flustered in front of his dick brother.

"That's something a judge would have to decide, I suppose," I answer stiffly.

The mediator clears his throat. "Perhaps both parties might be willing to discuss some sort of compromise to avoid trial?"

I'm opening my mouth to answer, but Bianca chooses this moment to enter the conversation.

"There will be no compromise," she says matter-of-factly, eyes still locked on her husband. "You have taken most of my life. Half of yours is a fair exchange."

"Don't be hysterical, Bianca," Mr. Casiraghi huffs. "You don't need the money, and you have no proof that there is anyone else. You can't admit to yourself that our marriage has run its course, so you fabricate lies about me in revenge."

"Lies," Bianca chuckles. "You think you're clever, Lorenzo. You always thought yourself to be clever. You forget who it was that helped forge the empire you are so greedy with. Who gave up weekends and holidays to help get your business off the ground. You may have beguiled me into signing a prenup with lies of it being for my protection, but I know now that it was never money that I needed protection from. It was your black heart."

"Always the actress," Mr. Casiraghi says with a roll of his eyes.

Bianca's stare is hard, the seconds passing in pregnant silence as everyone at the table waits with bated breath for her next words. She doesn't smile when she says them, doesn't show any sense of triumph or gleeful satisfaction—and given her words, I find that astonishing.

"Tell them about the account, Lorenzo."

Her husband goes still, his smug expression flickering with concern for a brief moment before he tugs down the mask again. "I don't know what you mean."

"You don't?" Bianca smirks. "You have so much money that you misplaced an entire account?"

Ezra's eyes meet mine from across the table, looking for answers that I don't have. I have no idea what Bianca is talking about. I reach to tentatively press my fingertips against her forearm, but she shakes me off, leaning in to hold her husband's gaze.

"Tell them about the account you share with this woman," she says pointedly. "Tell them how you put millions of dollars into it over three decades."

My mouth drops open, turning my head to watch as Mr. Casiraghi blanches, a tic in his jaw. "You know *nothing*."

Bianca's grin widens then, the look of it almost feral around her painted red lips. "I know enough, husband."

"I will not stand for this," Lorenzo seethes, pushing away from the table. He points a finger at his wife. "You will not like where this ends, Bianca."

She continues to give him the same sly grin. "I don't much like it now, Lorenzo."

His face is turning red now, and he makes a disgusted noise before he storms out of the room, leaving the five of us behind without another word. Eli frowns as he rises, not even bothering to bid anyone goodbye before he follows. The rest of us are left stunned in their wake, and I look from Ezra to Bianca to the mediator and back again, trying to rationalize what just happened.

Ezra speaks first. "What account are you talking about?"

"It seems your client did not disclose everything," I manage to say without portraying my shock.

"If there are undisclosed assets, I can assure you I don't know about them," Ezra tells me.

He looks genuinely surprised by this entire thing, and strangely, I find myself believing him. His brother, however, didn't seem ruffled in the slightest. Curious.

I clear my throat. "It seems like we won't be reaching a compromise today."

"No," Ezra sighs. "It seems like we won't."

I take a steady breath to collect myself, regarding the two men in front of me. "Could you give us the room? I'd like some time with my client, please."

The mediator immediately agrees, leaving hastily as if he wants no part of the drama unfolding in the room. Ezra is frowning at me, a little wrinkle between his eyes as if he'd like to say something, but he nods instead, giving me a lingering look before he leaves Bianca and me alone.

I immediately turn to face her in my chair. "What the hell was that?"

"My husband shares a secret account with his mistress. He has been adding money to it for almost thirty years."

I gape at her. "And you didn't think this was important information to give me *before* today?"

"I wanted to see his face for the first time when he knew that I knew," she says simply.

Goddamn it.

I sigh, pinching the bridge of my nose. "This is information I could have been digging into, Bianca. I get that you wanted to have a *gotcha* moment, but I can't help you if you don't keep me in the loop."

"I am sorry for not telling you sooner," she tells me sincerely. I feel her hand cover mine, and when I meet her gaze, her expression seems far less confident than it was moments ago. Right now she looks . . . worn down. "Lorenzo made a fool of me. For many years. I may never get the answers I deserve, but I want him to *feel* what he's done. Do you understand?"

"Is that what this whole thing is about for you?" I don't ask because I disagree, but I want to understand what I'm getting into, considering everything I have riding on this. "Do you even care if we win?"

"Oh, we will win," she says fiercely, curling her fingers around mine. "You are a powerful woman, remember? You will make him feel it."

I find myself nodding slowly, a small smile painting my lips. "I'm sure as hell going to try."

"That's my girl," she chuckles. "Do you forgive me?"

"I'm your lawyer," I say. "Consider it one of the hazards of the job."

Her lips tilt in a smile. "We will speak more of this."

I take a deep breath, my mind already spinning in the face of all the extra digging I'm going to have to do. Weirdly, it only makes me more excited.

I give her an answering grin. "Sounds good."

I ACCOMPANY BIANCA to the elevator before making the walk back to my office, my head buzzing with the various possibilities that might be tied to her husband's mysterious account. Having a mistress is one thing, but regular payments for almost three decades? Is their entire relationship transactional, or is he just too lazy to bathe her in his money in person? I don't notice there's someone else in my office until I've already shut the door behind me, my lips turning down in a frown at Ezra's broad back as he stands across the room studying the framed pictures on my bookshelf.

"By all means," I grumble. "Make yourself at home."

He glances over his shoulder at me, flashing me his panty-dropping smile (I wish I could say that was just a baseless metaphor) as he points to the photo of my dad and me at McKinney Falls. "This is sweet. You should go back to pigtails."

"I was eleven," I mutter.

"Must be why you're smiling. Your face had to have forgotten how to do it not long after."

I roll my eyes. "Cute."

"Your parents seem so happy in your pictures." His eyes move from the frames littered on my shelves in a way that feels almost . . . wistful. "Hard to believe they got divorced."

"Yeah, well," I snort. "When you're just pretending to enjoy being married so your kid can have a 'normal childhood,' I guess it's an easy decision to split." His eyes widen, and I feel my own mirror the action. "I don't know why I said that."

"They told you that?"

I hate the pity in his expression.

"Are you in my office for a reason, or did you just come to bother me?"

He eyes me for a moment longer, like he wants to press the issue, but it's gone as quickly as it came. He grins at me instead. "Well, I *do* love bothering you."

"Ezra."

"Fine." He raises his hands in apology. "I came to assure you I have no idea about any secret accounts. Whatever happened in that room was news to me."

I force my expression to remain passive, not wanting to reveal yet that I believe him. "Your brother didn't seem very surprised."

His face does something strange then, a bitter shade passing over it that I never see on him.

"I didn't know he would be here today," he tells me. "My father sent him."

"Doesn't trust baby boy to handle things?"

I mean it as a tease, but the shadow across his face deepens, and he cuts his eyes away from mine. "Wouldn't put it past him."

I wrestle with that for a moment. I don't think I've ever heard Ezra speak ill of his family. Is there more to the Heartbreak Prince than just some family lawyer royalty? I decide it's not my business.

"Well, considering Bianca is emailing me the records she found, I guess it will all be out there soon."

"Yes, I imagine so," he sighs. His eyes find mine again. "But I needed you to know I didn't lie to you or withhold information."

I won't pretend that his admission doesn't make my chest tighten, but I play it off with a shrug. "Why would it matter what I think?"

"Because . . ." His lips curl in a sultrier smile now. "I enjoy our . . . arrangement."

"Our arrangement," I echo.

He strolls to my desk, toying with the bronze scales of justice paperweight at the corner. Then he turns, leaning to rest his ass against my desk while his stupidly large hands slide down to grip the edge.

"Yes. I would hate to see it end because of a misunderstanding."

I purse my lips. "I already told you it was over."

"Yes, I know, but I wouldn't want to give you a reason to actually mean it, for once."

I glare at him. "You don't think I mean it?"

"I think you *want* to mean it, Dani," he laughs. "But no, I don't think you actually do."

"The sun doesn't rise and set on your dick, Ezra," I scoff. "I think you're putting too much stock into it."

"Maybe." He shrugs one shoulder with a sly grin. "I'd much rather be putting it somewhere else."

I groan. "Does that actually work for you?"

"I don't know." His eyes flick down the length of me with heat in them that has me suppressing a shiver. "You tell me."

I hate that it does. *Hate* it. There's no good reason for warmth to be filling my chest, no reason for me to be getting wet from such a stupid come-on. So why am I?

Why him? I ask my body for the thousandth time. *Why does it have to be him?*

I take a step forward, pressing my fingers into his chest with every intention of telling him off and booting him out of my office. "Listen here—"

His hand lifts to cover mine, his thumb rubbing lightly across my knuckles, sending a jolt of electricity down my spine. "Yes?"

"I . . ." My eyes drop to where his fingers graze the back of my hand in light touches, my mouth going dry. "You're . . ."

His voice feels closer now, and I can smell the mint of his toothpaste as his breath hits my cheek. "What am I, Dani?"

"Infuriating," I mumble as his lips graze my throat.

I can feel his laugh against my skin. "I think you like it more than you pretend."

"I'm not pretending anything."

"You're not?" I feel the warm weight of his palms sliding over my hips in a featherlight hold. "Then tell me to stop. Tell me not to touch you, and I won't."

Just say it, I chide myself. *Tell him to stop touching you.*

But I don't do that. Why don't I do that?

"Come on, Dani." His hands move slowly to slide against the fabric of my skirt, a barely there touch on my ass where he cups me. "Tell me you don't want me to touch you."

"I hate you," I groan instead.

His teeth nip gently at the sensitive skin below my ear, and much to my displeasure (figuratively, at least), a tiny moan escapes me.

"I know," he says.

I don't *mean* to press my hips further into his. I don't *mean* to zipper my body to the front of Ezra's like I'm trying to wear him. At least, I think I don't. My head is a little fuzzy right now. It's like when Ezra touches me, all the stress and the worry that is my life melts away, allowing me to focus on nothing else but his hands and his body and the sizzle of irritating pleasure he brings.

"You always smell so good," he murmurs, his nose skimming along the length of my throat. "But you feel better."

I gasp when he rolls his hips, feeling the hard length of him even through the layers of his dress pants and my skirt. Even with the way that little part of my brain is still screaming at me for giving in to this *again*—my body lights up like a Christmas tree at even this. He says that I feel good, but it should be *illegal*, how he feels. It should be a goddamned crime.

"I think about fucking you over this desk," he tells me roughly, nibbling on my earlobe as I shiver. "Or maybe mine. Every time I see you in one of these fucking skirts, making your ass look like a fucking *gift*—I think about inching it up over those pretty thighs of yours and filling you up."

He squeezes my ass for good measure, and an irrational urge to turn my face and press my mouth to his floods me, but I hold it back. Even if it's something I can't stop thinking about when he's this close.

"I could have you right now," he rasps, pulling me closer to the throbbing heat between his legs that I know will feel incredible inside me. "It would be so easy. So fucking easy." My head falls back at the soft kiss below my jaw. "And you'd let me, wouldn't you, Dani? You'd let me push you over this desk and take what's mine."

Everything inside me freezes. Isn't this the exact thing I said

I shouldn't be doing? Didn't I *just* resolve not to let myself get wrapped up in this anymore? That there's too much at stake to risk doing so?

What the fuck am I doing?

I wrench out of his grip, untangling myself from the heat of his body as mine screams in protest. His eyes are heavy lidded, dazed in his lust-drunk state, which no doubt matches mine, and I breathe deep through my nostrils to try to steady myself.

"I'm not *yours*," I say through gritted teeth. "I'm not your anything."

He blinks once, then twice, his hands still reaching slightly as if the fact that he isn't touching me anymore hasn't quite caught up to his brain. I watch him lower them slowly, running his palms over the tops of his thighs as his throat works in a swallow, his head turning to the floor for a moment as if he's thinking. When he looks back up at me, there's a small smile on his mouth, but it's not the one I'm used to. It's almost . . . sad.

"You're right," he laughs softly. "You're not. I got carried away."

I feel . . . flustered. Not just because I was practically humping his leg seconds ago, but also because I've never seen Ezra look anything less than assured. Which is not how he looks right now. He looks like he might be trying to figure out why he even said what he did in the first place.

I watch him adjust himself, and then that brief moment of uncertainty is gone, in its place the same collected, confident Ezra I know. "Just thought you might want a little stress relief after that doozy of a bomb your client dropped."

I'm still trying to catch up to whatever the fuck just happened, but I manage a snort. "I have a bottle of wine at home that will give me less of a headache than what you're offering."

"Right," he chuckles. "You really do make a habit of comparing me to activities involving your mouth."

"Get out of my office, Ezra," I growl, brushing past him to my desk, as if I wasn't four seconds away from letting him do *exactly* what he said I would. "Some of us have work to do."

He shoves his hands in his pockets, striding to the door as I drop down into my chair. He turns as he pulls it open, lingering in the doorway. "You have my number if you change your mind."

"I won't," I say a little too quickly.

He's still smiling, but I notice it doesn't quite meet his eyes. "Sure."

I tell myself I don't care why he was different just now, because I don't. Ezra Hart's issues are of no concern to me. That's not what we are, and it's not what we'll ever be. Still, I stare at the cracked door he left behind for far longer than I'd like to admit. I don't know how many seconds pass before I start tapping the end of a pen against my notepad. Even hours later, I can't escape the nagging idea that I might not have Ezra as figured out as I thought.

Seven

EZRA

THERE'S A CREEPING sense of unease along my skin as I step off the elevator and onto the landing for the offices back at my firm. The welcome desk is empty, Maggie having long gone home by the time I make my way back to hopefully get some work done without running into my father or brother. Based on the three missed calls from the former in the last few hours, I have to assume it's in my best interest to dodge his company entirely while he cools off. I'm sure Alexander is pissed that I didn't come right back after Bianca Casiraghi's revelation in mediation, but honestly, I needed a while to get my head on straight.

I'm not surprised in the slightest that the elder Harts are keeping things from me about the case, which I have to assume they are, given my brother's complete lack of reaction to hearing about Lorenzo's supposed secret account. It's laughable how within the realm of reason it would be. Regardless, I wasn't lying when I told Dani I didn't know anything about it.

Dani.

I pause my steps halfway down the hallway that leads to my office, frowning at my shoes. My encounter with Dani in her office is definitely another large part of my needing to think. What the hell was that anyway?

And take what's mine.

I hadn't been thinking when I said it. That's the most logical explanation I can come up with. Still. It's well outside the bounds of . . . whatever Dani and I are doing. I can only assume that I was just caught up in the moment. The lingering irritation with my father for announcing that Eli would be sitting in on the mediation today is still heavy in my chest—just another example of Alexander undermining me at every turn. Maybe that's why I wandered into Dani's office after leaving the conference room. Even with her sharp tongue, there's something . . . comforting about this thing between us. It's as if I can take solace in her complete lack of expectations of me, which is a foreign concept to me. All I've ever known are expectations. Mostly of the "you'll never live up to" variety.

"Are you just going to linger in the hall all night?"

My eyes snap up to find my brother standing only a few feet away; I was so lost in thought that I didn't even hear him approaching. I let the frown on my face dissipate, not wanting him to gain any sort of read on me. "I didn't know anyone was still here."

"I suspect that's why you're sneaking in so late," Eli muses flatly.

I move to walk past him. "Right. Well. I'd better get to work then, shall I?"

"Ezra."

Eli's hand reaches to wrap around my bicep, and I tense. Eli doesn't have my height, but there's a bulk to him that I don't quite have. He's built more like Alexander, which I guess makes sense. He has the same dark hair, the same bright blue eyes, the same high cheekbones—he's a fucking carbon copy of the man. Which really is just perfect, considering. I want to shake out of his grip, but I know it will only cause a fight I don't want to deal with.

I look down at his hand briefly before flicking my eyes up to meet his. "Yes?"

"Dad wants you to call him back."

"I'm sure he does," I answer coolly.

"Don't be a brat. You need to discuss what happened today."

I huff out a breath, his fingers loosening enough so I can finally slip away from him. "It might have been nice to have that discussion *before* we went into mediation. Since this is *my* case. Unless you'd like to save everyone the trouble and take over?"

"You and I both know I don't handle divorces, but that doesn't mean I want to let you fuck this up."

"I appreciate your concern," I say with obvious contempt.

"You seem friendly with Danica Pierce."

I rear back. "Excuse me?"

"It's an observation. There's a familiarity there."

"I don't see how it's any of your business."

"Have you fucked her?"

My lip curls in a sneer. "The fuck? What kind of question is that?"

"A valid one." Eli regards me like a parent scolding a child. I fucking hate it. It's something he's adopted perfectly from Alexander over the years. "Considering the importance of this case and the status of this client, it would be completely inappropriate for you to have some sort of sexual history with the opposing counsel."

I refuse to tell Eli a goddamned thing about Dani. I don't even want her in his head. I can't say why the idea of him considering her at all makes me want to hit something, but in this moment, I really could hit him. Something I haven't done since we were teenagers.

"Again, it's none of your business, but there's nothing going on that you should be concerned about."

"Good." He crosses his arms over his chest. "Keep it that way."

"I can't believe it bears reminding," I sneer, "but you aren't my father."

"I'm just someone who will have to be here when you fuck up."

"Do I need to remind you again of my win ratio?"

Eli shrugs. "It could be higher."

Right. If I stoop to levels you and Alexander are comfortable with. No thanks.

"Are we done here?" I straighten my suit jacket just to have something to do, turning away from him. "I have work to do."

"As long as you agree to call Dad," he tells me. "Sooner rather than later."

"I will see him in the morning. I'm sure whatever bullshit you two have been keeping from me can wait until then."

Eli shakes his head. "Always determined to be difficult, aren't we, Ezra?"

I grit my teeth as I walk away from him. I won't give him the satisfaction of an answer.

I don't stop walking until I'm slumping down into my desk chair, leaning back into the supple black leather, and closing my eyes. I'm sure I absolutely do *not* want to hear the story behind this whole secret account shit with Mr. Casiraghi, positive that it will only make me like the guy less. Hell, I knew he was a prick after our first meeting. The guy definitely strikes me as the type who would fuck someone over, most of all his wife, but unfortunately, I don't get the luxury of being choosy when it comes to my clients. No choice but to fall in line.

I'm still seething quietly over Eli's crassness in regard to Dani, wondering if an outsider might sense something between us that I might be missing. Sure, I like to tease her, to rile her to points I'm positive no one else can, but I try to reserve it for just the two of us. I would never *actually* jeopardize her reputation by goading her in public or making our personal relationship obvious.

I snort at that. *Relationship.*

You can't really call it that. I don't even know what you *would* call it. I can't even slap a friends-with-benefits label on it, since I'm pretty sure I'm the furthest thing from what Dani considers a friend. I just . . . can't seem to stop wanting to touch her. If she's in the room, my hands itch. If she's nearby, my eyes gravitate to her. Even when she's tearing into me, I can't bring myself to be annoyed. I just enjoy her talking to me at all. Most of the time I try not to analyze it. Most likely, it's something as simple as her being the best sex I've ever had. My body knows when it's found a good thing and is engaging in its own form of self-preservation so that it can keep it. That's all. So again, what the fuck was that back in her office?

I decide it's a problem for another day. Just another thing for me to push under the rug. If I can't see it, I don't have to deal with it. One of these days, I'm going to flip up that rug to a life's worth of rotting junk—but that's Tomorrow Ezra's problem.

Today Ezra has other shit to worry about.

DESPITE WORKING UNTIL almost midnight at the office, I still manage to drag myself out of bed at eight in the morning the following day to head to my parents' house. I woke up to Alexander practically demanding that I do so, and if I know anything about Alexander Hart, it's that absence definitely does *not* make the heart grow fonder. Delaying the inevitable will only make it that much worse when I finally face it.

I tell Rita good morning as she waters my mother's flowers in the foyer when I step inside the too-large house. It's always been too big for us, I think idly, following the marble tiles through the front of the house.

"Oh, Ezra," my mother calls from the kitchen. "I didn't know you were coming today."

I halt my steps toward my father's office to duck back into the other room, finding my mother at the kitchen table with her journal. I bend to press a kiss to her hair, which is a dark wheat color similar to mine, only just starting to gray at her temples. "Morning, Mom."

"Good morning, darling," she says with a bright smile. Her eyes look clear. This must be a lucid day. "I've missed you. You didn't come to dinner last week."

"Sorry . . . work has been busy."

She clucks her tongue. "You're just like Eli and your father. Always working."

I'm nothing like them.

"Well, someone has to keep the firm running," I tease.

Her green eyes crinkle at the corners, and for a moment everything is normal. There's no live-in nurse watering the flowers in the other room, no bastardized version of a father down the hall in his office. It's just my mother and me and her smile.

She reaches to pat my cheek. "Your hair is getting so long. You should let me cut it."

"Now, Ms. Hart," Rita interrupts, ruining the moment. "You know you can't have scissors."

The flash of pain is brief in my mother's face, but I see it. I wish I didn't, but I do.

"I'll make an appointment for a trim soon," I assure her. "I really have just been busy."

Rita comes up beside us to settle her hand against Mom's shoulder. "It's time for your morning meds, Ms. Hart. Do you want orange juice or tea?"

"Juice is fine," my mother answers softly, her eyes far away now.

I swallow against the lump in my throat, pressing another kiss to her hair. "Talk soon, Mom. Okay?"

She nods meekly. "Of course, dear."

I have to take a moment back out in the hall, the urge to stomp down to Alexander's office and cause him bodily harm ever present. But there are a dozen reasons why I can't do that, and one of them is sitting in the other room.

I find him just where I expected to, perched in his giant wing-back chair surveying documents on his desk as if he's looking at lands to be conquered. For all I know, he might be. Alexander Hart views everything as something to be conquered.

"Sit down," he says.

As far as greetings from him go, it could be worse.

I plop down into one of the chairs on the other side of his desk, lacing my fingers together in my lap just to have something to hold on to. I wait several minutes for him to finish whatever he's doing, knowing that interrupting will only spur him to make me wait longer. I can't say how much time passes before he gives me his attention, but his cold blue eyes find mine with that *look* he reserves only for me, as if I am a disappointment waiting to happen.

"So, yesterday didn't go as planned," he says dryly.

"Yeah, no shit."

He narrows his eyes. "Watch your tone. It's unfortunate that you didn't predict Bianca knowing about the account."

I actually balk. "I'm sorry? I was supposed to anticipate Lorenzo's wife knowing about a secret account that I wasn't even privy to? Is it your goal to have me try this case with one arm tied behind my back, or did it just conveniently slip your mind to tell me the man has been paying some woman for almost thirty years?"

"We didn't think it was information Bianca could gain access to, therefore we didn't deem it relevant to disclose."

"*We*," I snort. "Why did you even hand the case to me if you're going to micromanage things from behind the scenes?"

"Your brother's caseload is already too heavy as it is. I thought *surely* you could handle something as simple as a divorce with a signed fucking prenup."

"Is it *my* fault your friend seems to be an asshole?"

"Careful," Alexander warns.

I press my lips together to hold back another retort. I know this won't get me anywhere. There's no arguing with Alexander Hart. There's only doing whatever the fuck he says.

"So how do you suggest I proceed from here?"

He leans back in his chair. "The woman Lorenzo has been issuing payments to is a relative. The money is to cover her medical bills. She's chronically ill, you see."

"Chronically ill," I parrot dryly.

He nods. "That's right."

I close my eyes and count to three. "Are there any documents confirming the nature of this account? Medical bills? Discharge records?"

"Unnecessary, given that Bianca and the little lawyer Moreno's assigned to the case will never find any evidence refuting it."

"So you just expect me to give them that horseshit and assume they roll with it?"

He cocks an eyebrow. "Why would they not? It's the truth."

"Of course it is," I mumble.

"This case should be an easy win for you," Alexander says. "I would hate for there to be any more hiccups. If you can't handle something as simple as this, perhaps I should lighten your caseload entirely."

My heart starts to beat faster. I know where this road leads. The threats will not end with just me. They never do.

"I can handle it," I assure him. "It's fine."

"Good to hear," he says. "Be sure to tell your mother goodbye before you go."

And just like that, I'm dismissed. I know better than to press any issues, standing without argument. "Anything else?"

"Eli tells me you're friendly with Danica Pierce."

My jaw clenches, and I can only hope he doesn't notice. "She's an acquaintance. We've been opposing sides for a number of cases now."

"I see." He regards me for a long moment, my stomach twisting into knots the entire time. "See that it remains that way. A friend-ship with someone from a rival firm wouldn't do well."

I give him a stiff nod, quickly retreating from his office before he can think of anything else to discuss. Fucking Eli. Fucking Alexander.

This fucking family, I swear.

I *do* tell my mother goodbye before I leave, but she's less than before. Less talkative, less aware, just . . . less. It twists my insides to see her like that.

I sit in my car afterward checking my messages, and I only feel a *slight* tinge of desperate relief when I see Dani's name among them. I don't analyze it too deeply. I can't.

> **Sour Patch:** I've forwarded the documents Bianca shared with me for disclosure. We can do depositions on the 16th or the 26th. Do either of those dates work for you?

There's an overwhelming urge to call her, to ask to see her—if only to have a brief respite from the tumultuous emotions roiling inside me. Not that she would want it. Honestly, I think this might be a rare day where her barbs would be less than endearing. I think today they might actually cut. I tamp everything I'm feeling down, tapping out a quick reply.

> **Me:** I'll check my schedule, but the 16th should work.

I see the dots dance across the screen, disappear, pop back up, and then disappear again before she finally sends:

Sour Patch: 👍

Despite everything, it makes me laugh. In a world of uncertainty, Dani being prickly is a constant. It's oddly comforting. It even lifts my mood a little.

Me: Don't miss me too hard.

More dots. Then *more* dots. Then nothing. Then:

Sour Patch: 👍

I laugh out loud, feeling lighter. She really is so prickly. It's probably weird that I find it endearing.

I refuse to analyze that either.

Eight

DANI

"ARE YOU NERVOUS?"

Bianca arches one thin brow from her seat beside me. "No. You will ask questions. I will listen. What is there to be nervous about?"

I feel myself grin. I should have known better than to ask. I've learned in the weeks since I met her that there is very little that seems to ruffle Bianca Casiraghi. "I wanted to do this back at my firm," I tsk. "I should have known they'd push to do it here on their own turf."

"Does it matter?"

"Not in the grand scheme of things," I tell her, checking the time on my phone as we step off the elevator. "But I hate knowing that they're probably just trying to intimidate you."

"They can try," Bianca chuckles.

"That's the spirit." I wave to Maggie at the front desk as we pass her. "Remember, you won't be able to say anything unless you're being deposed, and when you are, you can answer all questions asked of you even if there's an objection. This is all preliminary. A judge will decide if they're admissible or not."

"I know the rules, Danica," she says primly.

I smirk over at her as we head down the main hall. "Just making sure there are no more surprises in store for me."

"You are being cute," she says, sounding amused. "I will be good."

"I appreciate it."

When we reach the chosen conference room, I open the door to follow Bianca inside. My eyes find Ezra immediately, not only because they seem to be hardwired to pick him out in a room, but also because he seems to be in a quiet but heated discussion with an older man that I haven't seen before. He's almost as tall as Ezra, his salt-and-pepper hair combed back and his mustache neatly trimmed.

His bright blue eyes land on me when we enter the room, piercing and calculating as they hold mine. I make sure to hold his gaze, having no intention of being intimidated. Ezra turns to follow the older man's line of sight, and where he would normally shoot me a playful grin that would make my stomach swoop in that frustrating way I've come to know—right now he looks almost pained. Apologetic, even. It's strange.

"Ezra," I say in greeting, my eyes flitting between him and the older man. "Cocounsel again?"

There's a thin-lipped smile on the older man's mouth, one that does nothing but stir a sense of unease. "My apologies, Ms. Pierce." He steps forward to close the distance between us, offering his hand. "I asked if I might sit in today. Alexander Hart. Managing partner."

Ah. I see it now. There really is a striking resemblance between him and his other son. Ezra must take after his mother, because the differences between him and the other men in his family are night and day.

I manage to keep the wariness I'm feeling off my face, the idea of Alexander Hart wanting to listen in not sitting well with me. Mostly because there's no good reason for it.

"Has something happened that I'm unaware of?"

Alexander waves his hand casually. "No, no. Nothing like that. Such a potentially high-profile case . . . we like to stay on top of things in my office." Another smile that more closely resembles a leer. "You understand."

"Of course," I answer tightly.

I notice Lorenzo sitting at the far end of the table then, pointedly not looking at us. There's a middle-aged man behind him setting up a camera and another man about my age on the other side, tucked away in another chair looking nervous. I have to assume that's my first witness.

"Ezra has had such nice things to say about you, Ms. Pierce," Alexander says sweetly. "'Capable' and 'headstrong' were the words he used, I believe."

I don't give him anything, keeping my expression passive. "Ezra is too generous."

"Oh, I don't think he is," Alexander answers. "I can always tell, you see. Always been able to sift out the sharp ones."

I'm not sure how to answer that, so I decide not to answer at all, the silence lingering between us with nothing more than my pursed mouth and Alexander's leering grin. I can't say what it is exactly that I don't like about Alexander Hart—but it's there.

"I guess we can begin now that we're all here," Ezra chimes in hesitantly. "Dani?"

I turn to regard him. Have I ever heard him hesitant before? He looks . . . withered, somehow. Like a caricature of his normal self. There are dark circles under his eyes, and his body language is tense, like he's too tightly wound.

"Of course," I tell him, grateful to be done with these threadbare pleasantries. It's surprising, but there's a fleeting urge to pull Ezra aside and ask if he's okay. I ignore it. "Ready whenever you are."

I lead Bianca to the side of the table opposite Ezra and his party, helping her into her seat before turning my attention to the nervous-looking man near Lorenzo. "Mr. Andrews?"

"Yes," he says quickly, sitting up straighter. His eyes dart to his employer, Mr. Casiraghi, for a brief moment, then back to me. "That's me."

I gesture to the chair at the head of the mahogany table we're all sitting around. "If you can just have a seat there, we can get started."

"Right," he says, shooting out of his chair and smoothing his tie in what definitely seems like a nervous gesture. I guess if I was being asked questions about the guy who paid my salary, I'd be nervous too. He points at the chair in question. "Here?"

"That's good." I glance at my notes, moving closer to Mr. Andrews. "Thank you for coming, by the way."

Another quick glance at Lorenzo. "Of course."

"You've worked at Casiraghi Development for"—I check my notes—"eight years now, correct?"

"That's right. I was hired in 2016."

"And what is your position there?"

"I work as Mr. Casiraghi's personal assistant."

I pretend to study my notepad, wanting to appear aloof. "And what are your responsibilities in that position?"

"I . . ." He licks his lips, flicking his gaze to Lorenzo briefly before answering. "I manage Mr. Casiraghi's schedule and his correspondence, mostly."

"So it's fair to say you have access to his emails, correct?"

"Objection," Ezra interrupts. "Speculation."

I don't look back at him, keeping my focus on the witness. "You can answer. A judge will decide later if it's admissible or not."

"Oh." Mr. Andrews nods, swallowing. "I . . . yes. I have access to his emails."

"Are you aware of anyone else having access to them besides you and Mr. Casiraghi?"

Mr. Andrews' lips form a thin line. "Not to my knowledge, no."

"So by the defense's own speculation, the lascivious emails suggesting an affair sent from his computer would have to have come from either you or Mr. Casiraghi himself, correct?"

He looks behind me. "I . . ."

"Objection," Ezra sighs. "Leading the witness."

"Strike that. I'll rephrase," I counter. "To the best of your knowledge, is it possible for someone other than Mr. Casiraghi or yourself to enter his office and gain access to his personal computer?"

"I . . . Maybe? It's not like he keeps it locked at all times."

"Does anyone else work on the floor where his office resides?"

"Well, no. Not on our floor."

"So for the most part, it's just you and Mr. Casiraghi on the top floor."

"That's . . . correct."

"I imagine Mr. Casiraghi's computer is password protected though, correct?"

"All company computers are password protected."

"And the only people with access to Mr. Casiraghi's computer are you and him, yes?"

"Objection," Ezra calls. "Asked and answered. We've already established that Mr. Andrews has access to Mr. Casiraghi's computer and email."

I grit my teeth, exhaling through my nostrils slowly. "Mr. Andrews, in your opinion, would it not be incredibly difficult for someone other than Mr. Casiraghi or yourself to gain access to Mr. Casiraghi's personal computer without the password?"

"Foundation," a voice other than Ezra's cuts in with a menacing edge. "Lacks foundation. Do you have any IT experience, Mr. Andrews?"

I turn to regard Alexander, who looks less collected now—giving me a hard stare from his seat at the table.

"Well, no," Mr. Andrews starts. "I—"

I raise a hand to stop him, still holding Alexander's gaze. "You don't have to answer that, Mr. Andrews," I say pointedly. "One riot, one ranger, Mr. Hart. Ezra is taking the deposition of the defendant. You have no grounds to speak here."

I see something dangerous flash in the old man's eyes, but he remains dutifully silent. I hope that my eyes say what I can't, that I'm not intimidated by him, however much he'd like me to be. I notice a quirk of Ezra's mouth that might be the beginnings of a smile when I spot him in my peripheral, but it's gone as quickly as it came. I hear his echoed objection after, but I've already got a redirect ready.

If Alexander Hart takes anything away from this little sit-in, I hope it's that I am not a woman to be fucked with. Regardless . . . he doesn't say another word for the remainder of the deposition.

———

IT TAKES FIVE hours for us to cycle through the list of witnesses we've lined up (most of them mine), and by the time we've reached the end of the agenda on which Ezra is to question Bianca, I don't feel half bad about the progress we've made today. Between the various employees speaking as character witnesses and household staff who came in for questioning, I've been able to make quite a few points in our favor.

Unfortunately, so has Ezra.

It's already been forty-five minutes of him pulling at various threads as he prods Bianca on everything from her honeymoon to her last fight with Lorenzo—but much to my delight, Bianca doesn't seem ruffled in the slightest. She really might be made of iron, this woman.

"Mrs. Casiraghi," Ezra says politely. "I just have one more thing to discuss, if that's okay."

She gives him a stiff nod. "Go on then."

"Just to be clear, we're here today because you are formally accusing your husband of breaching the infidelity clause in your prenuptial agreement, therefore entitling you to half of all marital assets, correct?"

"That's correct," she answers without any hesitation.

"Mm-hmm." Ezra nods thoughtfully. "Tell me, this isn't the first divorce petition you've filed against your husband. Is it?"

My heart rate quickens. What the fuck?

Bianca, to her credit, remains cool. "That's correct."

"But you withdrew that petition shortly after filing, correct?"

"That is also correct."

I'm staring at the side of Ezra's face with my mouth slightly parted. "Where are you going with this?"

"Is there an objection there, Dani?"

"Relevance," I force out, narrowing my eyes when they meet his.

He turns back to Bianca. "I'm sorry to ask about such delicate matters, but I assure you, Mrs. Casiraghi, it is relevant."

She says nothing, only nodding. "Ask what you want to ask, Mr. Hart."

"Isn't it true that weeks after withdrawing your petition for divorce back in 1994, it came to light that your trust fund suffered considerable losses due to bad investments?"

"Objection," I blurt out. "Hearsay. There was no evidence entered in disclosure to prove that claim."

Ezra moves to sift through the binder at his seat, pulling out two copies of a stapled document and passing one to me. "This was just brought to our attention today. I was going to formally submit it as soon as possible."

I skim the financial record he's given me, overviewing what appears to be the account housing Bianca's trust. Just as he said, there was a significant loss shown in late 1994. I look up to find Bianca's eyes. This is also something she should have told me. What the fuck is going on?

"Mrs. Casiraghi," Ezra goes on. "Is it correct that these two events occurred within the same month?"

I watch as Bianca looks past Ezra, following her line of sight as I notice her looking at Lorenzo. Her husband looks smug, but when I look back at my client, there's a spark of sadness in her eyes that wasn't there before. A crack in her armor that is entirely unlike her. She shakes it off before giving Ezra her attention again.

"It is true that these two things occurred close together. One has no bearing on the other."

Ezra nods, taking a breath before turning to look at me. I've already caught sight of his father, who looks pleased, but strangely, Ezra doesn't. If anything . . . he looks apologetic.

"Pass the witness," he tells me quietly.

Alexander pats Ezra on the back as he takes his seat as if offering congratulations, and I quietly seethe in mine, my teeth grinding as I just barely manage to keep my irritation in check.

"I'll reserve for trial," I manage.

"We are off the record at four thirty-six," the court reporter chirps from the corner, signaling the end.

I feel decidedly less confident than I did only moments before, this new information sure to raise doubt in a juror's mind. Everything in me wants to pull Bianca aside and grill her about what the hell just happened, but I know it will make us look unprepared, so I force myself to wait until we're alone. She leaves almost immediately, and I wonder if she will wait outside for me or slip away so that I'll have to chase her down. She's determined to make my job difficult.

"Well, that was exciting," Alexander says as he approaches me, his leering smile back in place as I pack away my things. "Good sport."

I narrow my eyes. "These are people's lives we're dealing with. I would hardly call it sport."

"It's all sport from where we're standing," he chuckles. "We're nothing but gladiators in another's arena, after all." I blink back at him with disbelief, but he's already turned away from me to give his attention to Ezra. "Good work today, Ezra. Come to the house this evening. Your mother would love to have dinner."

Ezra doesn't look up from where he's still scratching notes down in his seat, but he gives a tight nod all the same. Alexander leaves us alone after that, everyone else having already filed out, and I decide if I never have to see Alexander Hart again, it will be too soon.

"I'm sorry about what he said," Ezra says softly. "He can be . . . challenging."

"He can be a real dick," I snort. "No offense."

To my surprise, Ezra's mouth twitches in a smile. "None taken."

"I hope he's better to you than he is to everyone else, because fuck."

There's a flash of something across Ezra's face, but I can't place it. He finally packs his things back into his briefcase, pushing away from the table. "I was against him coming, by the way."

"Why? You're on the same team, after all," I grouse.

Ezra's lips turn down, a wrinkle forming between his brows like he's considering that and realizing that it doesn't suit, which I find odd.

"I assume it was for my benefit," I huff, changing the subject. I don't like the almost pained expression on his face. "Probably thought he could intimidate me."

There's a hint of Ezra's real smile, the tightness around his eyes lessening just a bit. "Are you saying I don't intimidate you, Dani?"

"I think you wish you did."

"Intimidation is at the bottom of my list of things I'd like to do to you," he teases.

I frown at him, my chest heating with both annoyance and

attraction. Two sides of one coin that's constantly being flipped inside me where Ezra is concerned. "Do you always have to make a joke out of everything? Is there anything you take seriously?"

"I . . ." He pauses, frowning again. "I take a lot of things seriously."

"Doesn't look like it from where I'm standing."

Ezra sighs, looking genuinely weary. It's another new side to him. I seem to be seeing a lot of new sides to him lately. "Do we always have to do this? This stupid game where you pretend you hate me? We both know you don't."

"What?" I splutter. "What are you talking about?"

"Things would be a lot easier if you would just acknowledge that you're attracted to me. You don't have to spit venom at me every waking moment just to try to convince yourself that you aren't."

My eyes go wide. "I'm not trying to convince myself of anything."

"Then why are you going to wind up back in my bed?"

"I . . ." I grit my teeth. I can't tell if he's genuinely annoyed, or if this is all just another game to get me riled up. I decide not to play into it. I take a deep breath to steady myself, blowing it out and willing myself to calm. "You're right."

Ezra looks surprised. "I am?"

"Yes. I'm attracted to you. Clearly."

"See?" He beams. "Was that so hard?"

"Which is why we really have to stop doing this."

His smile falters. "Stop doing what?"

"This." I gesture between us. "It can't go on. And I admit that I'm as much to blame for it going on as long as it did as you are, but it won't end well. Neither of us wants anything more than sex, and that's not worth the complications of keeping this up for longer than we already have."

"It doesn't have to be complic—"

"Sex is always complicated," I sigh. "Look at us right now! I can't even be in the same room with you without wanting to either kiss you or punch you in the gut. And you know as well as I do that any sort of . . . connection between us should be reported to each of our clients. Technically, without their written consent to continue, we're both playing at grounds for dismissal."

Ezra's eyes widen. "Did you just admit you want to kiss me?"

"I'm saying it doesn't matter if I do." I shake my head. "I have too much riding on this to add you in the mix too. We should just end things here and focus on the case."

"The case," he echoes.

I nod. "Yes."

He looks away from me, his eyes fixed on the opposite wall as his mouth purses in thought. I can almost see a dozen things running through his mind as he tries to decide which one to settle on, but I see the moment that he does. An expressionless mask comes over his features, and he nods as if to himself, eyes finding mine again.

"All right, Dani," he says flatly. "If that's what you want."

I eye him suspiciously. "That's it? It's that easy?"

"Why wouldn't it be?"

"Because this isn't the first time I've said we should end it, and you're usually much less inclined to just agree."

He shrugs. "I don't make begging a habit, and if you say you aren't feeling it anymore, then I guess that's that."

"Uh-huh." I continue to watch him as if he's going to laugh at any second, making this into another joke, but when he doesn't, I feel a flood of something coursing through me. I tell myself it's relief, but I can't be sure. Does relief make your stomach knot? "All right then. So we'll stick to strictly professional going forward?"

"Strictly professional," he repeats. "Can do."

"Well, I . . . huh. Okay." I rub the ends of my hair that have fallen over my shoulder, still eyeing him. "Thank you, Ezra."

"Of course."

I keep waiting for him to say something more, and when he remains silent, I'm struck with an overwhelming urge to put distance between us. As if it might be me who does something reckless if I stay here any longer.

"I'll be in touch," I tell him. "I have some additional interrogatories."

He gives me another brief nod. "Sounds good."

I allow myself one last look, realizing that he really is going to leave it at this, and I tell myself it is relief that I'm feeling as I turn from him to leave the room. That it's a smart decision, ending this thing between us. No good can come of it, it certainly isn't going anywhere, and I don't need the distraction. This is a good thing.

Bianca is already gone when I leave the conference room, but I think I expected that. I suppose that means I'll need to call her when I get home and try to sort through what happened back there. It's not a phone call I'm looking forward to. I realize too late that I'm still lingering outside the conference room, just standing in front of the door without any real reason as my thoughts swim. Pretending I don't know why I'm so distracted. Telling myself it has everything to do with the professional happenings that just occurred in that room and not the personal ones.

It's a good thing.

I tell myself that a dozen more times on the walk to my car.

Nine

DANI

IN THE WEEKS that follow depositions, Ezra makes good on his word to keep things professional. Gone are the random flirty text messages at least once a day I've become used to, and when we *do* text—it's curt, succinct, and completely centered on the case.

It's what I wanted, what I asked for, sure. So why have I been so . . . unsettled?

It's as if I'd gotten so used to his annoyingly constant presence that now that he's stepped back (like I *asked* him to), I feel out of sorts. It might be more annoying than Ezra is, feeling this way.

"Dani, you're crushing my nuts."

I jolt, dropping the pastry cutter I've been using to break up Mom's pecans for the bottom of her pie. When I look into the bowl I've been working with, it's clear I have in fact pulverized several of them into powder.

"Sorry," I mutter, dumping my work and grabbing another cup of shelled pecans to start over. "Spaced out."

She frowns at me from where she's icing her cake. "Everything okay?"

"Yeah, everything's fine."

She looks unconvinced. "Anything bothering you at work?"

"No, no. It's going well at work."

Well, mostly. Bianca's second omission about her previous divorce petition and trust fund woes was a setback, one she hadn't been too keen to talk about. When we discussed it, she more or less went Edna Mode on me. I could practically see her waving at me from over her shoulder saying, "I never look back, darling. It distracts from the now."

Which is frustrating. Since she refuses to dive any deeper into the withdrawal of her petition, I'm only left with the assurance that her trust fund quickly regained its lost assets, giving her ample reasoning to go through with her petition, if money had been the issue. She didn't have to stick it out with him for another thirty years if that had been what she was worried about.

"Good," Mom says. "No work stuff today."

"That might be hard considering half of your guest list are Dad's old work buddies."

"And if I hear anyone talking shop, there will be no pie for any of them."

A laugh escapes me. "You know, most people don't continue to listen to their spouses after the divorce."

"We respect each other," Mom answers casually. "We don't need nuptials for that."

I frown, giving my attention back to the bowl in front of me. I don't think I can handle letting my mind wander to the complexity that is my parents and stepparents today. That's never a fun time for my brain.

"Where is Bill anyway?"

"Oh, he and Patty are out back with your dad trying to get the grill going. Leave it to your father to buy the fanciest model they make without having any idea how to use it."

That makes me smile. It definitely sounds like Dad. I finish chopping the pecans for the bottom of the pie so Mom can add the filling, wiping my hands on my apron before pulling it over my head. "Do you need my help to finish this up? I was going to get changed."

"Oh, I got you a new dress," she tells me. "I left it in your old room."

"What? Why?"

"Do I need a reason to buy my daughter a gift?"

I roll my eyes. "Is this bribery? Because I already brought the apple pie."

"No," she laughs. "I just thought it would be nice to see you out of work clothes."

I glance down at my beige linen slacks, frowning. "What's wrong with my clothes?"

"Nothing at all," she assures me. "Just indulge an old woman, okay?"

"Fine, fine."

She pauses what she's doing, eyeing me from across the kitchen. "You sure you're okay?"

"Yes? Why wouldn't I be?"

"I just know how you get when we're all together . . ."

"Mom, stop." I have to shove down the roiling emotions bubbling inside. "You know I love Bill and Patty."

"I know, honey, but . . ." Her teeth worry at her lower lip. "I don't know. Sometimes it feels like you hardly ever smile anymore. I guess some days I can't help but worry that it's our fault."

Jesus Christ, the universe is really out to get me lately.

"Mom," I answer, trying to keep my tone even. "It's been years. I'm over it."

"I just wanted to make sure you knew that you could talk to me," she urges. "I don't care how long it's been. You're always working so hard, and I just worry about you."

"We don't have to talk about this at every family gathering," I say softly. "Honestly."

She nods slowly. "All right. Don't mind me. Just being a worrywart."

I can tell there's more she'd like to say; there's nothing new about my mother prodding at my emotions whenever we're alone as if she might somehow teach me how to suddenly open up to someone, and just like every other time, I'm determined not to give her much. I never want her to feel guiltier than she has to for the way our lives turned out. I carry enough guilt for the both of us.

"I'll just . . . go get changed."

Mom nods again. "Good idea. People should be arriving soon."

I leave her in the kitchen to head for the stairs toward my old bedroom; I've told Mom and Bill a hundred times that they should turn it into something useful, but Mom insists on keeping it as is. I think deep down she tells herself that keeping this one small thing the same might somehow make up for the childhood I still feel like I lost.

I find Mom's gift laid out over my bed—a bright red sundress covered in tiny little daisies that cinches at the waist. It's nothing that I would ever pick out for myself, but I can't deny that it's pretty. I move to the full-length mirror in the corner of my room, holding it against my body. It's weird, the last time I did this—my high school graduation, I think?—I agonized over which dress to wear, which seems silly now, given that it was going to be under that ugly gown the entire time.

The small smile on my face falters, my mind inevitably wandering to *after* graduation. To coming home and finding out my entire life was a lie.

We didn't mean for you to find out this way.

We were going to wait until you went to college.

We made this decision together.

We just wanted what was best for you.

This isn't your fault, Dani.

That last one echoes for a heavy minute, pinging around in my head like a stone puttering down a well. I keep waiting for it to inevitably fall to the bottom, to *settle*—but it never really does. Maybe it's because I still don't believe it.

My mother and father are the classic friends-to-lovers story; they went to middle school, high school, even college together, and what started as a deep friendship blossomed into something more. Until it didn't. After one night together, they realized they were better as friends.

They didn't anticipate me.

I'll never fully understand why they chose to sacrifice seventeen years of their lives in a phony marriage for some convoluted idea about giving me a "normal childhood." Finding out after so long that the people you thought wrote the book on love have been

lying to you your entire life . . . well. It shapes your ideas on relationships and love as a whole. It made me stop believing they
could even really exist.

Maybe that's why it hurt so badly when I let someone in. When
Grant decided that I wasn't enough.

I take a deep breath, pushing the thoughts away like I always
do. I wish I could stuff them in a trash compactor and get rid of
them for good, but I know that if they've stuck around this long,
there's most likely nothing that will chase them away. I shuffle out
of my clothes, slipping the dress over my head and smoothing it
out to inspect it. It really does look good on me, complementing
my fair skin and dark hair. Not that there's anyone to impress,
given that most of the people coming to this stupid party will be
over fifty.

Not that there's anyone I *want* to impress, I amend internally.

I have to squash that line of thought before it turns against
me. I know where that one leads. It leads to tall, blond, and a
handful.

I run my fingers through my hair, sighing again.

Let's get this over with.

MOM AND DAD'S backyard—or rather, *Mom's* backyard now, I
guess—is practically full within the hour. Dad finally got the grill
going, which means there is a slight scent of burnt hot dogs in the
air, and based on the level of laughter I can hear happening all
around me, I have to assume that Patty's spiked punch is a hit.
These things usually end the same way, with my parents *and* stepparents passed out in various rooms of my childhood home, as
well as a few of their friends, more often than not. They really do

act like teenagers sometimes. I guess because they missed out on so much when they were younger, they're determined to make up for it now.

Dad's friend Howard, a tax attorney from a smaller firm here in town, currently has me cornered on the porch to regale me with a tale about saving some company from bankruptcy after they got into trouble over back taxes, and let me tell you—there is nothing more boring than tax law. Seriously. I can practically feel my eyes glazing over, but I'm trying my best to nod when it's appropriate, to smile where it's warranted, however infrequent that might be.

"—and then after negotiations, they decided that it would be more beneficial for us to move forward, as you can imagine."

He chuckles as if he's said something that's actually funny. I have to force a smile onto my face, but in my head I'm wondering how much longer I have to hang around before I can escape without my parents noticing. Not for the first time, I wonder why I even came. It's not like there's anyone here my age. I suspect that after another half hour, my parents will be so blitzed that they'll be in no condition to argue with me tomorrow when I tell them I was totally here until cleanup.

"Dani!"

I turn my head to see my dad's hand raised high over a sea of salt-and-pepper heads, trying to flag me down. Thank God.

"Sorry, Howard," I offer without feeling particularly sorry at all. "Duty calls."

Howard nods around his punch glass. By the hazy look in his eyes, I suspect he'll already have another victim for his case recounting shortly after I'm gone. I have to push through a small group of people who have started up their own little dance floor where they are attempting to do the hustle just off the deck, almost getting caught by Mom's friend Harriet and dragged into the fray before I can untangle myself.

I finally spot my dad over by the tire swing that's been hanging on the giant oak in the backyard since I was five—my mom, Patty, and Bill all huddled together under the sprawling limbs overhead. They're laughing at something someone's just said, and based on the decibel of it, I'm thinking it's almost time for me to work on my out. And I'm planning to do just that.

Until I see who's standing there with them.

I pause only a few steps away, my feet seeming to be rooted in the grass as my brain tries to make sense of him being here. *Here.* At a family party. In the backyard of my childhood home. If the way I can feel my mouth gaping is any indication, I can only surmise that I am nowhere near close to catching up to what's happening in front of me.

"Dani!" my dad says again, practically shouting even though I'm standing right next to them. "Look who showed up."

As if I haven't already noticed. After not seeing him for two weeks, it feels like every nerve ending in my body suddenly perks up, almost as if trying to reach out and touch him. Because there, with my dad's arm slung around his shoulders as if they're old friends, is Ezra Hart.

Fucking Ezra Hart.

Ten

DANI

I CAN FEEL myself gaping at him.

Ezra looks entirely unfazed by my obvious shock at him being here, his smile natural and his eyes giving me absolutely nothing. I can't help but take in his appearance; it's unfair that he can make faded jeans and a threadbare tee look just as good as a three-piece suit, but of course, this is Ezra Hart we're talking about.

However, the most surprising thing that I feel as I gawk at the person I've been trying not to think about for the last two weeks—because again, it's what I *asked* for—is the flood of overwhelming relief that washes over me seeing Ezra standing there. Like a breath I've been holding. Like suddenly someone let all the air back into the room.

And that feeling fucking terrifies me.

"What the hell are you doing here?"

My mother smacks my arm. "Dani! Don't be rude."

"I'm sorry." I try to let some of the harshness leach out of my tone even as my heart thuds against my ribs. I shouldn't be *relieved* to see him. Not in the slightest. I take a calming breath. "Can I ask how my opposing counsel—who you barely know—ended up here?"

"I saw him at Frank's last week," Dad says with a wave of his hand. "We got to talking. Did you know that he was captain of the football team back in high school?"

No idea how that's relevant, but: "I didn't, but that makes sense."

"I told him all about the touch football games we have out here," Dad says.

I roll my eyes. "You guys haven't played that in three years. Not since Lou fractured his tibia."

"We could play again," Dad argues. "Whatever." He squeezes Ezra's shoulders. "This guy told me he planned to spend the holiday by himself at home! I couldn't have that."

"Of course you couldn't," I mutter.

Ezra is uncharacteristically quiet through this exchange, watching me curiously as if waiting to see how this will play out. Is that why he came? To get a reaction from me? Was the whole "we'll keep things professional" a crock of shit? The thought is . . . disappointing. It shouldn't be, but it is. And I need to pack those feelings right up into a tight little box where they'll never see the light of day.

I grab Ezra's arm, tugging at it as I keep my tight smile plastered on my face. "Can I talk to you for a second?"

"Oh, let the man have some fun," Dad protests. "You're the one always saying no work stuff here."

I have entered another dimension. That's the only explanation. I am currently in another reality where my worst nightmares have all come out to play, and my dad is suddenly best friends with my work nemesis who—up until a few weeks ago—I was sleeping with.

"Ezra?"

His eyes flick down to my hand that is still wrapped around his bicep, and all at once I am overly aware of how warm his skin is. I'm acutely aware of the time that's passed between us since I last touched him. In this moment, I can feel every second.

Finally, he gives me a slow nod. "Sure," he says casually. "We can talk."

My dad grumbles the entire time he releases Ezra from his hold. "You come back in a while, yeah? I want to hear how that Petrovsky case turned out."

"I said no work talk!" I toss over my shoulder as I drag Ezra closer to the shed a few yards away, where there are fewer people.

He follows me easily, and my hand is still clutching his arm, the muscles bunching under my fingers in a way I am doing my best not to think about. It stirs up too many memories of those same muscles tightening and stretching because of the way he was touching *me*. I don't stop until we're both hidden in the shadows just beyond the shed door, releasing my grip on him and giving his chest a light shove.

"What are you doing here?"

"Hello, Dani," he answers flatly. "Nice to see you too. How's the weather? You look nice in that dress. Are you enjoying the party?"

Don't you dare get fluttery. Don't you do it, Dani.

"Don't play with me. Why in the world are you here?"

He shrugs. "It's just like your dad said. I was having lunch at Frank's this week and ran into him eating alone. He invited me to sit with him, and we got to talking. There's no evil plot here."

"But you knew I would be here," I huff.

I can only hope that the slightly needy edge to my voice is unnoticeable. I'm sure Ezra would find it hilarious to think that I might have missed him. Not that I did.

Even in the dim lighting, his gaze is thoughtful, something there I can't quite read. "I did."

"And you didn't think that would be awkward?"

"Why?" He crosses his arms over his chest, the material of his T-shirt stretching. I refuse to let myself linger on it. In fact, I blame his arms for the weird things running through my head. It's definitely their fault. And maybe his neck too. It's entirely too corded. Like it's begging for me to put my mouth there. "We agreed we were just going to be professional with each other from here on out. Why would it be weird that we're at the same party?"

I blink, trying to remember what we were talking about. What is *wrong* with me?

"My *family's* party," I manage after a beat.

His lips twitch. "That I was *invited* to."

I throw up my hands in frustration. "You're impossible."

"I really don't see why this is a big deal." He bends a bit, and by doing so, allows the sun, which has just started to sink behind us, to make his green eyes almost gleam. Not to mention the way I can smell his cologne—a subtle hint of citrus and sandalwood that makes me want to lean into it. "Unless . . . does it bother you to be around me, Dani?"

"No," I splutter immediately. "I don't care."

I hate the way he studies me, like he knows I'm lying. He doesn't know that I'm lying. Hell, *I* don't even know if I'm lying.

"All right." He leans back, flashing me an easy smile. "Then I see no problem here. Just two professional colleagues at the same gathering, right?" He looks back over his shoulder. "If you'll excuse me, you interrupted a conversation."

My mouth drops open as he turns to just *leave*, and I feel hot all over from anger and—no. *Just* anger, I tell myself. That's *all* it is.

"Oh, and, Dani?"

It takes me a second to realize he's spoken over the wild rush of blood in my ears. "What?"

"You really do look nice in that dress."

I DIDN'T LEAVE the party early like I planned. I keep telling myself that it's because I want to make sure my parental party of four don't get too drunk and do something that will embarrass themselves, something Ezra can add to his arsenal, but even in my head it's flimsy at best. I've been lurking by the snack table for the last hour, watching his perfect head of dark blond hair weave through the crowd as he charms everyone he meets. Literally, he's spoken to every single person here. I'm almost positive.

Well, except me.

He hasn't said a word to me since our argument by the shed. If I can even call it an argument. I guess if I'm being honest, it was more of an interrogation on my part. One that completely blew up in my face, since it seems Ezra really *did* just come to hang out because my dad invited him. There's no way he came here to mess with me somehow, considering he can't do that while actively avoiding me like he has been.

And I should be grateful for that. I *am* grateful for that. Mostly. Sort of. I don't know. I doubt grateful people sip punch as aggressively as I have been for the last twenty minutes. I doubt a grateful person would keep unconsciously homing in on Ezra's movements as he socializes like he was born for it. A *grateful* person wouldn't be secretly miffed that he hasn't even tried to speak to them again, and they certainly wouldn't be utterly flummoxed that they would feel that way in the first place. That is, if they *did* feel that way.

I rub my temple, my head starting to hurt in the third person.

I'm not drunk, not even tipsy, even though I kind of wish I was—but I'm feeling just loose enough to allow myself to really dissect the complicated things Ezra's presence here is making me feel. Seeing him interact so easily with my family and their friends, like he belongs here—it's weird. It's almost like he fits in here more than I do. I don't know what to make of that. I know I shouldn't care, that it shouldn't make me feel an odd sting in my chest watching him fit in so easily, and for a moment I allow myself the fantasy of what it might have been like if it was *me* who had invited him here. Would he have wanted to come? Would he be having as good a time as he seems to be right now?

But that's ridiculous, because I *wouldn't* invite him here—I didn't—because that's not something we did. Definitely not anything close to what we were.

I take another sip of my drink, watching him bend to laugh at something Mrs. Liechman is whispering in his ear. It's preposterous for me to be jealous of his laugh, since the woman is in her sixties, and he's not my damned boyfriend—so why the hell is my stomach twisted into knots? It's easier to just blame Ezra. It's always easier to blame him rather than admit anything that I might regret later, even if it's only to myself.

I can't help but wonder if he's been with someone else these last few weeks. It's not like we ever said we were exclusive, even when we were . . . whatever we were, and it's also not something I ever really allowed myself to dwell on. But what's more surprising than me pondering Ezra's love life since the time we parted ways, I think, is the sheer gut punch that is imagining him touching someone else. My head fills with images and whispered words and soft touches that are for someone else, and I realize with stunning clarity that I . . . hate it. I shouldn't hate it. I can't *let* myself hate it. Ezra Hart is the fucking Heartbreak Prince, and that's *exactly* what's waiting for me if I don't get my head on straight and remember just what it is that he and I are—*were* to each other.

His eyes snag mine from across the yard then, and my entire body freezes, my hand gripping the cup that is still suspended in the air. It's magnetic, the way he looks at me. If I were a more honest woman, I might even say it has been since the first time. Even if he opened his mouth a moment later and ruined everything by revealing just how big of an ass he can be. Even from this distance, I can see when his gaze dips to my mouth, and I can't fathom what possesses me to choose that moment to let my tongue swipe along my lower lip to lick away the excess punch, but I can't even begin to pretend that the answering tightness of his jaw isn't a little satisfying. Even if I can't fully puzzle out why.

Yes you can, you fucking liar.

It feels like it takes hours for him to pull his gaze away from mine to answer something Mrs. Liechman has just asked, but in reality, it can't be more than a few seconds. I watch as he gives her a polite smile and a nod before separating himself from the little group he was mingling with. My eyes follow him as he finds my dad a few yards away and says something to him before my dad gestures back toward the house. Ezra doesn't look back at me as he stalks over to the deck, climbing the stairs and weaving through the crowd before disappearing through the patio doors, but I'm looking at him. Hell, I'm tracking his every move. Why am I doing that?

I can feel my heart thumping in my ears, can feel my skin warmed by the punch in my belly and the goose bumps erupting all over from the breeze washing over me, and I blame all of these things for what I do next. It's just easier that way.

Especially since I'm already heading toward the deck.

Eleven

DANI

ON A SCALE of one to ten of "how bad of an idea is the thing you're currently doing"—I'd have to say that following Ezra to the guest bathroom of my parents' house and knocking on the door is a solid eleven. I can hear the water running from the sink, so I know he's in there, and for a moment I am frozen on the other side with my fist suspended in the air asking myself what in the hell I'm doing. But I'm here, and I know if I go back outside right now, the thoughts in my head will just drive me crazy.

So I knock.

"Are you decent?"

I hear his answering chuckle just as the water shuts off. "I guess that depends on who you ask."

"Ezra."

There's a soft *snick* as he turns the lock. "It's open."

I push open the door just as he's drying his hands, amusement in his eyes as he watches me step inside and close the door behind me. I admit that I hadn't given much thought to what I was going to say when I came in here, so hopped up on the adrenaline of following him that the *after* hadn't fully occurred to me.

"Do you always follow your party guests into the bathroom?" Ezra asks with one arched brow and the barest hint of a smile at his lips. "Not the best host protocol."

I scowl at him, pressing my fists to my hips. "I just needed to talk to you."

"You could have talked to me outside."

"There's too many"—I wave my hand aimlessly—"people out there. Besides, I don't know how I would have done that with the way you were ignoring me."

I immediately regret letting the words slip out. Ezra's face flashes with surprise just before it morphs into something like delight, his mouth tilting at the corners until it settles into an impish grin. "Were you feeling lonely?"

"Shut up." I cross my arms over my chest. "I'm just trying to figure out what game you're playing."

"Who said I was playing a game?"

"Because there's no other valid reason for you to be here."

"It sounds like maybe you *want* to play a game with me," he teases.

I flush at the once-over he gives me, crossing my arms over my chest and huffing indignantly. "See? That right there. We agreed we were going to keep things professional, and it hasn't even been three weeks and you're here trying to . . ." I frown, not really sure *what* Ezra is trying to do here. I want to say that's what has me so worked up, but I'm not sure that's true. "It's just weird. You being here."

"I'm still having a hard time understanding why it's weird. Especially since I was invited."

"Right," I snort. "As if you'd have jumped at the chance to come to my family's party three weeks ago when we were still fucking if I'd asked you to."

"Who's to say I wouldn't have?"

I narrow my eyes at him. "Don't be cute."

"One," he says, holding up a single digit. "We've established that I'm adorable." He adds another finger. "And two, I'm not being anything, Dani. I'm just saying, how would we know if I would have come? Would you have actually asked me?"

"I—" My lips open, close again, and then press together for a moment. "Why would I? We're not even friends. We were just . . ."

"People who fucked," he says quietly, helping me when I'm clearly floundering to put a word to what we were.

I swallow. "Yes. That." I chew at the inside of my lip, feeling those unfamiliar goose bumps creeping over my skin once more. "And we ended that. Which I thought you were adhering to, since you haven't so much as texted me in the last few weeks, but then you show up here—"

"Did you want me to text you?"

"No," I say too quickly, practically spitting the word in a way that doesn't sound that convincing. "Of course I didn't."

"Hmm. Well, that's twice now you've mentioned me not reaching out. Not texting you . . . ignoring you at the party—your words, by the way. I don't know, Dani. It almost sounds like maybe you really *did* miss me."

I have to clench my jaw to try to compose myself, hoping that the heat in my cheeks isn't evident on my face, even as I feel it spreading down to my chest. I will my expression into one that I hope comes across as brusque. "You'd like that, wouldn't you."

He surprises me when he answers, "And what if I said I would?"

I feel my lips part on an unsteady inhale.

"What?"

"What if I said I liked the idea of you missing me?"

"Ezra . . ." I practically growl in frustration, running my fingers through my hair. "What are you doing here? Seriously? Are you just trying to fuck with me? Is that it?"

"So you really think," Ezra says with humor in his tone, "that coming to your family's party and not talking to you after you *explicitly* said that you wanted to end whatever we were doing is some sort of ploy to make you . . . what? Upset? Jealous? What is it that you're feeling right now, Dani? Because by all accounts, it doesn't sound like a very well-thought-out ploy. I would think you would give me a little more credit."

I feel silly after hearing it said out loud, my cheeks heating. "Then why the hell are you here, Ezra? Coming to my family's house? Prancing around the backyard and making friends with everyone here and pretending I don't exist? Why are you *here*?"

I can see his jaw working as he considers the question, and the way his eyes trace along the planes of my face make me want to shift on my feet. I do my very best to keep still. I won't let him think he's unnerving me with his stare, even if he is.

Something shifts in his gaze that is hard to read, something . . . soft. Almost worn down. Like whatever Ezra is thinking is enough to leave him weary. "Maybe I came here to see you."

I feel the blood rushing to my head so quickly it makes me dizzy, the room spinning for half a second while I try to determine whether he's just said what I think he's just said.

"What?"

"I didn't stutter, Dani."

"But you haven't said a word to me since we talked by the shed."

"Because you told me you had no interest in being anything more than professional with each other."

"That still doesn't explain why you would come here."

"Because I just . . ." He huffs out a breath, frowning as he looks away from me. "I don't know, okay? I just know I want to text you every fucking day, and I don't, because you don't *want* me to, and I just . . . fuck. How stupid is it that I miss you busting my balls as often as you possibly can?"

I blink, trying to process this, and then my nose wrinkles. "I don't do that."

"*That's* the part you're focusing on?"

"I don't know what to make of the rest of it. None of what you just said makes any fucking sense."

That weary look rests heavier on him now, and he shakes his head. "Trust me, Dani. It doesn't make any sense to me either."

I can't do anything except stand there uselessly, my heart thudding in my chest in an unsteady rhythm that I can practically feel in my throat. He missed me. He *missed* me? What am I supposed to do with that information? He can't miss me. That's not what this is. It's not what we have *ever* been.

So again, why do I feel so . . . relieved?

"You can't miss me," I say softly, not at all what I wanted to say but what comes out regardless. My throat feels like it might be closing up. It feels like it's getting harder and harder to catch my breath.

I gasp softly when he takes a step toward me, his finger coming to rest just under my chin as he tilts my face up to meet his. "Why?"

"Because—" I swallow around the giant lump in my throat, panic churning in my stomach. "Because I shouldn't have missed you."

There's a hint of relief on his face as well, slight but there. "But you did."

I don't answer, because I can't. I physically can't. I don't even know what's happening right now, but I'm terrified that I'm going to regret it tomorrow. I should know better than this. If Grant taught me anything, it was to be careful not to let my guard down. I should *know* better.

"It's okay," he says softly, saving me the need. "I missed you too."

I feel his other hand gliding down my bare arm, leaving goose bumps everywhere he touches. It's terrifying, how good it feels. That panic inside is clawing its way into my chest; everything in my head is screaming at me to run, to get out of this room, that this is dangerous territory that will leave me in uncharted waters until I'm drowning—and maybe that's why I try to pull away.

"I didn't miss you," I say too loudly. "And you didn't miss me." I try to untangle myself from his grip, his fingers wrapped around my arm a little tighter than they were moments ago. "This is stupid. It was just sex, Ezra. That's all it's ever been. There's no way that you—"

His hand cups my jaw, squeezing gently, the words dying on my tongue as he forces me to meet his gaze. "Tell me you want me to go," he says carefully, each word slow and deliberate. "Tell me that, and I will. Tell me to let you go, and I'll walk out of here and leave."

I open my mouth to do that, but the words won't come. Why won't they come?

Because you don't want them to.

I shut my eyes tight, pressing my lips together as I try to make my tongue form one simple sentence that will put a stop to all of this nonsense.

"Tell me to leave, Dani." Ezra's voice is quiet now, and I can feel the warmth of his breath only inches from my mouth. "Or I'm going to kiss you. Tell me to leave, or you're going to *let* me kiss you."

I make a sound that might embarrass me on any normal day, something like a muted whimper that's caught in my throat. I'm trembling all over—from nerves or anticipation I'm not sure—and I know all it would take is a few simple words to send him away. A few words, and that would be the end of it. It's what I *should* do.

I kiss him instead.

It's always been frantic with Ezra, this thing between us. Every time I've ever touched him, it's felt like some race to a faraway finish line. Like a short burst of something with an inevitable end. And that frenetic energy is still there when my arms wind around his neck, when his hands cup my face as if he might somehow pull me impossibly closer—but that finish line seems . . . more distant at this moment. Less of a race. For once, it feels like it's okay to just take my time.

I know that later I will pick apart that feeling, analyze it until my head hurts, but right now . . . Right now I let myself focus on the warmth of his mouth against mine, on the weight of his hands as they slide down my throat before roving over the front of my dress.

"Remember when I said you looked nice in this dress?"

It's hard to think with his tongue dipping past my lips, but I do my best. "Yeah?"

"I lied." I barely have time to process if he's insulting me or not, because his arm wraps around me, molding me to the front of him before one heavy palm cups my ass through my dress. "You look fucking beautiful."

I make that sound again, the embarrassing one, but I don't feel a scrap of embarrassment, miraculously. My head falls back as his lips wander, down my jaw and my neck and lower still as his tongue lightly flicks at my clavicle, which peeks out over the neckline of my dress. Distantly I register the sound of the lock clicking on the bathroom door, and even *more* distantly I know this should be setting off alarm bells, that I should be pulling away, but I don't do any of that. I can't physically make myself pull away from him.

I gasp when he spins me, pushing me against the vanity and smoothing his hands over my hips as his lips brush along my shoulder. His voice is low, making me shiver. "Do you know how crazy you make me?" His fingertips tease at the hem of my skirt, drawing it upward slowly. "I haven't been able to think about anything else but the way your skin feels since the first time I touched you."

"Ezra—"

Whatever I'd been about to say morphs into a moan when his fingers curl over my thigh to slide over the fabric of my underwear, teasing my slit through the material. "Already wet," he sighs. "Always so fucking wet for me. Even when you pretend to hate me, your body can't lie."

I should be telling him to fuck off, or at least, I think I should—it's hard to think when he presses his hard length against my ass, thrusting slightly as he continues to trace a slow back-and-forth over my underwear.

"Tell me how you want me," he breathes against my ear, his teeth nipping the lobe. "I'll give you anything you want if you tell me, Dani."

Tell him you don't want anything. Tell him that you—

"Hard," I rasp. "I want to feel it tomorrow."

"Perfect," he groans, tongue tracing the shell of my ear. "You're fucking perfect."

I feel his palm flatten against my spine as he bends me over the vanity, and vaguely I recognize the ruffling sounds of him digging in his pockets, catching sight of his wallet from the mirror as he pulls out a familiar foil packet.

I manage to cock a brow at his reflection, but the sarcasm is lost to the throaty tone of my voice. "Someone was confident."

"Just wishful thinking," he says with a lazy smile. I almost swallow my tongue as I watch him rip the packet open with his teeth before he spits the excess foil away. "Always wishful thinking when it comes to you."

I have to avert my eyes just to try to slow the racing of my heart, but I can *hear* everything. The metal grinding of his zipper as he slides it down. The crinkling of foil as he removes the condom. The soft sound he makes as he slides it on. It's almost worse somehow. Hearing it without seeing it. It means my head is full of nothing but him.

I bite my lip as he shoves my dress over my hips, bite it harder when he drags my underwear down to let them pool around my ankles before I toe them away—and where there should be discomfort at him pausing to stare at me, to take me in, strangely I find there is only pure *thrill* from the almost tangible vibration of raw need I can sense from him. It almost matches mine.

"Fuck, Dani," he mumbles, his fingers pressing against me

before slipping inside with one fluid movement. "Look at you. You're soaked."

I wait for the embarrassment to come, but still it doesn't.

"Do something about it," I whisper harshly.

I hear his soft chuckle, and I gasp when his lips press gently against the curve of my ass as he twists his fingers deeper inside me. "You want me to fuck you? Right here?"

Really? We're playing this game right now? With me bent over my parents' guest bathroom vanity while his cock is wrapped up and ready to go?

"I swear to God, if you don't—*fuck*."

My head lolls forward at the loss of his fingers, a whine lingering in my chest when I feel something thicker, *hotter* pressing against me instead. He eases inside slowly, letting me feel every inch, and not for the first time I wonder how it can possibly be so *good* every time. How every time with Ezra is somehow better than the last. It's always been infuriating.

"This what you need?" His palm rests against the base of my spine, rubbing soothing circles there as he sinks deeper, bottoming out. "Did you need my cock, Dani?"

My mouth falls open when he draws back just to rock back inside, the friction of it making me tingle all over and making it impossible to lie. "*Yes.*"

"Fuck, you feel good," he groans, thrusting into me again with a little more force. "Always so hot and tight and perfect. How is it so fucking perfect?"

I don't have the answer for that. Hell, I can barely formulate a coherent thought right now.

I should probably be concerned about where we are, that at any moment another party guest could come knocking on this door and discover us here, but somehow that only makes everything feel all the more delicious. What we're doing is nonsensical, it's *ludicrous*, it's the most un-Dani thing I've ever done in my life.

I have no idea why that thought has me *flying*.

"Harder," I manage, my voice sounding too rough.

His hand grips my hip, pulling me back onto his cock in a rough jolt that has the sound of skin on skin ringing throughout the small space. Every thrust hits me just right, the weight of his cock dragging across that place inside that pulls that embarrassing sound from me over and over again. It's still frantic, still a rush, but it's also . . . different. Or maybe it's just me.

He stops suddenly, making me whine for another reason. I'm opening my mouth to protest, when I feel his hand sliding up my front until his palm can grip my jaw again, forcing my head up as my eyes fly open to find him watching me over my shoulder.

"I want your eyes this time," he murmurs, his fingers holding my chin so that I can't look away. "I want you to watch me make you come. I want you to know it's *me* doing this to you." I suck in a breath when he starts to move again, slowly. "I don't want you lying to yourself for one more fucking second about how badly you want this."

He snaps his hips, and I watch in the mirror as my mouth widens in a gasp. I suddenly wish I could see more of him—hungrily taking in the sharp definition of his wide chest as it strains across his T-shirt, letting my eyes track the corded vein running down his arm as he holds me tight, keeping me still so that I have to take everything he gives me. Everything I *want* from him, if I'm being honest with myself.

"That's it." His thumb slides over my bottom lip to press against my tongue, and a moan tumbles out of him when I instinctively close my mouth to suck it deeper. "Look how well you're taking me." Another sharp thrust that pushes me deeper into the vanity. "You want this just as much as I do, don't you?"

My eyes try to drift closed, but a sharp smack across my ass has them going wide.

"I said I want your eyes," he reminds me. "You're going to watch yourself come on my cock."

I can feel that steady pulse building deep inside, a race of a different kind. I whimper around his thumb when his hand slides over my hip to force my thighs wider, his fingers gliding over my already swollen clit to rub a slow pattern that builds and builds with every frantic thrust inside me. I can only do what he says, can only take it, only *watch* myself take it—and there's a rush coursing through me that seems to thrum beneath my skin, building to a crescendo that feels like it might be devastating.

"*Ezra*. Ezra, I'm—"

"Come for me," he begs hoarsely, his fingers working my clit expertly with just the right amount of pressure. "*Please*."

"Fuck. *Fuck*."

The desire to shut my eyes is strong, so strong that I have to make a conscious effort to keep them open, but if I'm being honest with myself . . . I *want* to see. I want to see what Ezra looks like when he takes me apart like this. I want to see if he looks as wrecked as I feel. My body starts to tremble as my orgasm washes over me like a wave; I feel it in my toes and my head and everywhere else. There's a hazy quality to his green eyes that is captivating, and they stay locked with mine in the mirror even as a hiss escapes him when I start to come undone.

I can barely keep myself upright, leaning on my elbows as

Ezra's thrusts grow messy and unsteady—only seconds passing before his big body curls over mine, his hips pushing as close as they can to keep him deep inside me when he comes. Even still I can just make out one hooded eye peeking at me from over my shoulder, watching me. I can feel the warm huff of his breath against my neck as we come down from it, feel his arm curve around my belly to hold me tight as his heart races against my back. We stay like that for a moment, and I wait for that familiar panic to settle, the one that tells me to get away from him as fast as I can as soon as we're done, but for once I feel . . . calm. Even with the way we're still watching each other. Like now that I've allowed myself to go there, I'm finding it difficult to stop.

He presses open-mouthed kisses to my shoulder lazily, and I don't know who is more surprised that I lean into it slightly. "We're in your parents' bathroom," he says.

"No one is more aware of that than me," I huff.

"This is . . ." I feel his smile against my skin. "Not how I saw this night playing out."

I turn my head to smirk at him. "It isn't?"

"No." He feathers another kiss against my skin. "I told you. I just wanted to see you."

The fluttering in my chest is as confusing as it is alarming. I clear my throat, moving subtly so that he might separate himself from me. Ezra takes the hint, both of us wincing as he slips out of me.

"Don't throw that in the garbage," I tell him pointedly, shooting a look at the used condom he's still wearing and then at the open trash bin.

He cocks his head. "What do you suppose I do with it?"

"Flush it?"

"Do you want to risk it stopping up the toilet? I don't know about you, but that's not something I want to explain."

I frown. "Guess it's going in your pocket then."

"I . . . Shit." He grimaces, pulling it off and knotting it, then wrapping it up in some toilet paper. I look away while he works, straightening my dress. "I cannot go back out there and talk to your dad with a used condom in my pocket."

"No one asked you to get all chummy with my dad," I snort.

I can hear the rustle of denim, and I turn back just as he starts to button his pants, wearing a sly grin. "I can't help it that everyone finds me so charming."

"Right," I deadpan. "Sure they do."

He leans in, and even though my first instinct is to pull away, I find myself rooted to the spot as his lips brush against mine. "I think you find me charming, Dani."

"As if I would—"

We both startle as loud popping sounds begin to go off outside, jolting apart as I try to place them.

"Fireworks," I say after a beat. "I'd better go check on them before Dad blows a hand off." Ezra is still smiling that shit-eating grin, and I shoot him a wary look. "What?"

"You and I make sparks fly," he says, looking proud of himself.

I groan. "That was awful."

"You'll laugh about it later."

"I absolutely will not." I frown at the floor, fussing over my dress. "Where's my underwear?"

It takes me a second to look up and catch his grin, and only seconds more to follow the line of his arm to see my underwear hanging from his finger. "These?"

"Give them to me," I grouse, holding out my hand.

"Mm. No." He winds them around his fingers, haphazardly folding them into a little square. "I think I'll keep these."

"You will not."

"Need a memento," he says slyly. "Otherwise I'll wake up tomorrow thinking I dreamed this."

I could protest harder, probably, as I watch him stuff my panties into the same pocket he just stowed the knotted condom in, I know that. I'll never admit that watching him do it sets off a flood of warmth in my belly.

"You're an ass," I mutter instead.

He leans in when he has my underwear tucked safely away, pressing a kiss to my cheek that leaves a tingling behind in its wake. "I know."

I clear my throat as I pull away from him, checking myself over in the mirror. My dress is straight and my hair looks less sex-mussed, and I realize I don't know what else to say. I'm not stupid enough to pretend that something didn't . . . happen here, I just don't know yet exactly what it was. So, like a coward, I reach for the door.

"Dani," he says, stopping me.

I turn with my hand on the knob, biting my lip as his eyes meet mine. "Yeah?"

"You didn't say this was the last time," he points out, his voice uncharacteristically soft.

I swallow, my mouth dry. "I . . ." I take in a breath just to let it out. "I didn't."

His answering smile only elicits more fluttering beneath my ribs, so much so that it threatens to steal my breath. I wait for him to say more, no idea what I'll do if he does—so maybe it's a gift from Ezra that he doesn't. That he just nods and lets me leave through the bathroom door to escape. If I stay, we'll have to talk about what just happened, what it *meant*—and I'm not sure I can do that. At least not yet.

We don't talk for the rest of the party—in large part because of me, I think—as Ezra seems content to give me space while I work through the conflicting feelings I'm experiencing. But I feel his eyes on me the rest of the party, our gazes catching too many times to count as he mingles and I chaperone my increasingly hammered parents.

When I spot my dad laughing loudly at something Ezra says at some point, I do my very best not to think about the fact that Ezra is talking to my father with my panties in his pocket. Even if the heated look Ezra gives me over the crowd makes it almost impossible not to, especially considering how . . . breezy it is under my dress.

And when Ezra leaves sometime later, I watch him as he goes, casting me one last lingering look before he disappears through the wooden gate that leads out of the backyard toward the front of the house. It only takes moments after that for a buzzing in the pocket of my dress to make me jump, and that one text ensures that I will be thinking about Ezra for the *entire* night, if not well into tomorrow.

> **Asshole:** Next time I want you in a bed, and I want you for the whole night. Maybe it will be enough time to do the things I've been thinking about doing to you.

Twelve

EZRA

Sour Patch: If you don't stop
bothering me, I'm going to block
your number.

My entire face splits into a wide grin as I read her text. At first glance, one might think I've lost my mind, to be so elated by it, but those people wouldn't know Dani like I do. Her texts in the week following the Fourth of July party have been both the same and yet vastly different from the ones we've exchanged in the past—that same prickly edge to her words but with less . . . bite than before. I would never point out such a thing to her; she'd probably run for the hills if I did, but still it makes me smile to know it.

Me: I miss you too. 🫣

I tuck my phone in my pocket before she can reply, still grinning as I imagine her flushed expression when she reads my message. I can picture her sitting at her desk in her office as she reads it—her teeth pressed against her soft lower lip and her dark brows pulled tight—but I know that she won't actually block my number. Just like I know something shifted between us last weekend. Not that either of us have discussed it, since I know that this too would most likely have Dani bolting. Almost like a rabbit that senses it's being hunted by a fox, and I can't pretend I haven't always loved to chase her. Even more so now that she's slowing down enough to let me close the gap.

"Why are you smiling like that?"

My expression falters as I catch sight of my brother leaving his office just down the hall from mine, effectively making it impossible to duck inside and avoid speaking to him. I smooth my features into something more passive.

"I was just imagining what it would be like to buy out the floor above us and move my office away from yours."

Eli rolls his eyes. "Cute. Have you finished those briefs I emailed you about?"

"I have," I tell him. "Still not sure why you're checking in on my case. One you aren't assigned to."

"I don't keep an eye on your cases," Eli responds coolly. "I keep an eye on you."

In a family that was less fucked up, one might think this was a nice thing for Eli to do. That he was being a good brother by looking out for me, but I know better. Eli is too much like Alexander. Everything he does is for his own benefit.

"I can handle myself," I say tightly. "I've been doing it for years."

Eli shrugs, as if it's debatable. God, what I wouldn't give to *actually* move my office. Hell, to quit this fucking firm altogether. Even if it's not possible, it's nice to fantasize about.

"Dad wants to see you," he tells me, effectively ending our conversation. "He's in his office."

"I'll go see him after—"

"He made it very clear he wanted to see you the second you got in."

I clench my teeth. Every fiber of my being wants to argue, to tell the both of them that they can fuck right off into next week for all I care—but again, it's only something I can fantasize about. It's not something I can actually do.

"Fine," I manage. "I'll head that way."

"Good." Eli nods. "I'll check with you on those briefs later."

He strides off before I can remind him yet again that this is not his case—leaving me fuming in his wake as he often does. It's amazing how quickly my family can shift my mood; it was only minutes ago that I felt almost like I was floating, and now my stomach feels sour.

I steel myself for more fuckery as I tread down the hall to the corner office Alexander occupies, almost running into someone stepping out of it as I'm reaching for the doorknob. I feel hot anger licking at my chest when a familiar woman nods her head at me in greeting, and a quick glance down the length of her reveals obviously mussed hair and one too many undone buttons of her blouse.

"Ezra," Bridgett greets me demurely.

I don't offer her any pleasantries, settling on a nod. I refuse to make nice with the woman my father is sticking his dick in on a regular basis. A woman who isn't my mother. He doesn't even try to hide it. Quite the opposite, it's like he *wants* me to know.

I take a fortifying breath as I listen to the fading sounds of Louboutins that I'm sure Alexander bought for Bridgett clicking against the tile, and let it out shakily before wrenching the door to my father's office open and stepping inside.

"Finally," Alexander says with a huff. "Where have you been?"

"Working?" I shut the door behind me, moving further into the room and pointedly avoiding the love seat by the wall, opting for one of the leather chairs across from Alexander's desk instead. "I wish I could say the same for you."

Alexander shoots me a steely look. "Something you'd like to say, Ezra?"

"There's plenty I'd love to say," I seethe. I jerk my head back toward the now-closed office door. "Would it kill you to be discreet? Why don't you just fuck her in reception next time?"

"I would watch my tone if I were you, boy," Alexander says in a carefully measured way. "What I do is none of your goddamned business."

"Mom—"

"Your mother is happy and taken care of," he cuts in. "I suggest you remember that. You wouldn't want to break her heart, would you?"

My teeth clench so hard I fear they might crack, but I remain dutifully silent.

"Now," Alexander says dismissively, as if I didn't just walk in on the tail end of his latest tryst. "Lorenzo tells me that Bianca's lawyer is attempting to file an injunction over the inclusion of Bianca's trust."

"I can't exactly stop them from filing," I point out. "It wasn't agreed upon in the preliminary discussions."

"This whole case is becoming a pain in my ass," he says with a scowl. "I didn't expect Bianca and her little lawyer to fight us so hard."

I want to tell him that his first mistake was underestimating Bianca's "little lawyer," but I keep quiet. I imagine he'll realize that soon enough.

"What do you want me to do?"

"Maybe you should pay a visit to Bianca," he ventures. "You could . . . remind her how much she stands to lose when we win this."

My lip curls. "You want me to *threaten* her?"

"That isn't the word I'd use."

I make a disgusted sound. "But it's the one you meant."

"Sometimes you have to make the hard decisions for the greater good."

"Whose greater good? Yours?"

Alexander narrows his eyes. "The greater good of this firm. Our *family's* firm, remember?"

Our family. It takes everything in me not to laugh. I push up from my chair in a rush, shaking my head. "I'm not threatening Bianca. I can win this case without that shit."

"You'd better," Alexander warns. "I don't need to remind you of what I expect of you here."

As if I could ever forget.

Alexander waves his hand, dismissing me. "Go. I have work to do. See what you can do about blocking that injunction."

"Sure thing," I practically spit.

I spin on my heel, desperate to get out of the room, but my father's voice stops me at the door.

"Your mother's been asking to see you."

I'm reminded of how much I hate him at this moment. Reminded of the way he owns me, the way he can break me with a word. I rush out of his office, feeling my heart thud behind my ribs at a rapid pace as I move down the hall, bypassing my office entirely. I pull my phone out to call my mother's nurse, pausing midstride when I notice an incoming text.

Sour Patch: I plead the Fifth.

If I wasn't teeming with rage and frustration, I'm certain this text would make me smile. Even though it doesn't, it still offers a splash of calm in the midst of the raging storm inside me. Dani might be the only person alive who could do even that. Later, I'll wonder what that means.

Right now, I need to see my mother.

"LET ME GET that for you," I try, stopping my mother from getting up from her chair.

She clucks her tongue in protest but settles back into the rocking chair she loves so much, allowing me to add honey to her tea.

"Thank you," she says, taking the cup from me before blowing on it gently.

I drop down into the chair that matches hers—one I imagine she purchased with visions of sitting out on the back porch with Alexander like we are now. I highly doubt it ever happened.

"So tell me about work," Mom prods, offering me a small smile.

"Work is work," I answer flippantly. "Nothing new there."

"I heard your father talking about some big case you were all working on at dinner the other night."

I clench my jaw at the mention of Alexander. I want to argue with her, but I know it won't do anything but upset her, so I don't.

"It's nothing I can't handle." I pick a piece of lint from my slacks aimlessly, scrambling for a topic other than work. Something that won't end with her being upset. "How are the roses doing?"

She puffs out a sharp breath. "Found black spot on my tea roses the other day. Had to have Rita prune down half the bush to get rid of it all."

"I'm sure they'll be fine. You've always had a green thumb."

"I used to," she says softly. "On away days . . . sometimes I forget to look after them like I should."

Away days.

It's how she's come to refer to the days when her mind retreats into that place that never really healed. She has good days and bad days, but ever since her . . . incident, there are times when it's like she isn't here at all. I'm just happy that today isn't one of those days.

"Have they been getting worse?"

She takes a slow sip of her tea, not looking at me. "No, I don't think so. No more so than usual. It's better when Rita is here. It's easier not to . . . go away when someone is here."

A familiar wave of anger washes over me, knowing that Alexander gives her the bare minimum of attention. Eli is no better—poisoned by his own father to the very idea of Mom. Everything about her situation makes me sick to my stomach, more so because there isn't a damned thing I can do about it. Nothing except being here as often as I can and doing whatever bullshit thing Alexander asks of me.

I study her then—taking note of the slight slump of her shoulders, shoulders that used to hold me up for piggyback rides. She was always so much larger than life, and now she looks . . . frail.

Less of herself. If I could take her away from here, I would, but even if I could somehow fight Alexander and his hold on her, a part of me worries that his hold on her extends further than just a legal document. Part of me worries she wouldn't *want* to leave him, and knowing that might actually break my heart for her. Even more so than it already does. It's why I'm too chickenshit to bring it up.

"I don't want to talk about my nonsense," she huffs after a moment. "Tell me what's new with you. Are you seeing anyone?"

My lips part in surprise—not because it's the first time my mother has ever asked me this, but because it's the first time I'm not sure how to answer. I can't exactly say that the woman I've been fucking obsessed with and obsessed with fucking for months might finally be caving to the idea of tolerating me outside of sex.

My pause gives my mother the inch she needs, and she jumps all over it.

"Ezra Hart," she says with a grin, reaching to smack my knee before setting her teacup on the little table between us. "Are you? Who is she?"

"It's nothing, Mom." I clear my throat, looking away from her guiltily. I don't want to get her hopes up. "Just a casual thing."

That's safe, right?

"Casual is far more of an answer than I usually get out of you," she chuckles. "Tell me about her."

I know I shouldn't; telling my mother about Dani only for this entire thing between her and me to implode in a matter of days or weeks as it most likely will is just setting her up for disappointment. Still, the smile on her mouth is so reminiscent of the *old* her—the Jackie Hart before the incident and the medications and the entire fucking family falling apart . . . it's enough to have me opening my mouth against my better judgment.

"She works at another firm," I tell her. "She's actually my opposing counsel on the Casiraghi case. She's incredibly smart and
probably the only person on the planet who takes as much joy as
she does in putting me in my place. Honestly, she's the only person I don't mind losing to, as weird as that is. I kind of like it when
she's smug."

"She sounds like a real keeper," Mom laughs.

I can't help the chuckle that escapes me, staring down at the
stained wooden deck as I think about Dani's personality, which
reminds me of a feral cat that I can't stop trying to make like me.

"Dani is . . ." I shake my head. "She's something."

"When can I meet her? You should bring her to dinner sometime."

My smile dissipates. "I can't bring her here."

I don't mean it to come out as harshly as it does, and I immediately regret my tone the second the words are out. My mother's
happy expression wavers, and I know just from looking at her that
she'd almost allowed herself to forget just how fucked up this
house is.

"Right," she answers quietly. "Maybe some other time."

"Mom, I'm sorry, I—"

"Don't." Mom shakes her head. "Don't apologize. It isn't your
fault, sweetheart."

"It isn't yours either," I urge. "He can't punish you forever. You
shouldn't be *letting* him."

Mom says nothing as she reaches for her cup, staring thoughtfully into her tea for a moment before bringing it to her mouth to
sip. She holds it after, staring out over the backyard as she considers this.

"It's not that simple," she says finally.

I can't help the snort that escapes me. "It could be. We could fight him. You know I would do anything I could to—"

"Let it go, Ezra."

I'm breathing too hard, staring at my mother with my mouth hanging open. "Tell me why."

"So many reasons," she sighs. "But mostly . . . I won't let my children suffer for me. Not any more than they already have."

"But—"

Her head turns, her eyes capturing mine, and her smile is sad now, weighted down by years of heartache that I can't help but feel a little responsible for. "I love you. You know that. But this isn't a fight you can win. I'm not going to let you put yourself at risk just to try."

My hands clench the arms of the rocking chair, and I have a strong urge to stand and throw it across the yard. Everything about her situation makes me feel so fucking helpless. I relax my grip instead, reaching to cover her hand with mine and giving it a much gentler squeeze.

"I'm sorry," I tell her.

I don't say for what. There's no point. We both know exactly what I mean. We both know how much there is to be sorry for, and how much neither of us can change it.

I feel her thumb brush against the side of my hand in a slow back-and-forth. "So am I, sweetheart."

Not for the first time, I ache with a desire for things to be different. For my mother to be happy and whole, for my family not to be so fucked up, for something to go *right* for a change.

My mind wanders to Dani unwittingly, and part of me wonders if this is why I push her so hard. Do I want her the way I think I do? Or do I just need something that I chose to go the way I chose it for once in my life? They're questions I don't have the answers to.

Just like I don't have a good answer for why I want to see her so badly at this moment.

Thirteen

DANI

"HAVE WE ALREADY looked into her spending?"

I hear Nate hum absently from the speaker on my phone that lies a foot away on my bedspread, listening to him rifling through a stack of papers. "Pretty standard mistress stuff, if you ask me. Christ, the amount of money this woman spends on La Perla. How many pairs of underwear do you women need?"

"I'd say it's preferable to wearing the same four pairs until holes form," Vera remarks dryly from our three-way call.

Nate laughs. "Been going through my underwear drawer, have you?"

"Not without a hazmat suit and thick gloves," Vera deadpans.

I rub my temples. "Guys, I'm meeting with Bianca tomorrow to prep her for trial. I need some good news for her."

"Right," Vera snorts. "You could just ask her if she has any other bombshells tucked up her sleeve. Maybe Lorenzo has a secret dogfighting ring she can drop at the last second."

"Yeah, what's up with that?" Nate asks. "Have you talked to her about all the cloak-and-dagger shit she's pulled?"

"As much as she'll let me," I grumble. "She's not making any of this easy."

Vera makes a disgruntled noise. "I get the feeling that all of this is just Bianca having her public revenge against Lorenzo. Does she even care if she wins?"

"Let's hope so," I sigh. "Since my career is literally riding on it."

"Just keep looking," Nate encourages.

"I can't believe they're really going with 'sick relative,'" Vera chimes in.

I roll my eyes. "I mean, can't you? It sounds exactly like something Ezra would say."

My gut clenches at the thought of him; I haven't seen him since the party, and the conversation between us has been . . . different. Since that night, his stupid texts seem to irritate me less than before. Even if only a little. There are even times when they've made me smile—not that I will ever admit that to Ezra. And complaining about him now feels less . . . scathing than it might have a few weeks ago. Almost like my heart isn't quite as in it now.

"This could be something," Nate cuts in, drawing me out of my thoughts. "She's paying two mortgages."

I perk up. "The mistress?"

"No," Vera says flatly. "My hairdresser."

"Shut up," I huff. "Where are you seeing the second mortgage?"

"Page seven," Nate says.

I start backtracking to see what he's seeing, noticing multiple mortgage payments being made to the same bank.

"That's strange," I note. "Do we know of a separate property?"

"Haven't gotten word back on the subpoena we filed for her financials. All we have is Lorenzo's shit."

"Hmm." I highlight the page. "Well, make a note of it. It could be their own little honeycomb hideout. It's worth looking into."

"Okay, but," Vera says. "Why would they need two houses to fuck in?"

"I mean, he has already decided he needs two women," Nate scoffs. "Maybe he just likes to do everything in twos?"

"How neat of him," I remark dryly. "I can ask Bianca tomorrow if she has any ideas on this. How is it coming with Lorenzo's emails?"

"Wonderfully," Vera answers with a quickly following sound of disgust. "If you like to imagine cyber-sexting in emails like we're back in 2008."

"You were sixteen in 2008," Nate points out. "Who were you cyber-sexting?"

Vera *hmphs*. "None of your business."

"Guys," I practically growl. "I swear to God, if you two don't just fuck already, I'm going to—"

A knock sounds outside my bedroom at the same time that Vera and Nate both start talking over each other about how ridiculous the idea of them fucking would be, and I sit up straighter and peer through the open door into the living room. Another knock sounds at my front door, more insistent this time, and I frown at the time on my phone. Who the hell is coming by after nine?

"Hold on," I tell Vera and Nate on the other line, who are still arguing about how ridiculous the idea of them fucking is. "Someone's at my door."

"—rather fuck a sentient sea cucumber than touch him—"

"—hate to ruin her expectations for all other men—"

Yeah. They're not listening.

I carry their still-arguing voices into my living room, opening the peephole and peering out into the hall to see who in the hell could be coming by this late.

I almost drop my phone when I see who's on the other side. I'm so surprised that I forget I'm actively on a call, wrenching the door open with entirely more force than necessary.

"What are you doing here?"

Ezra leans against my door, one arm propped against the frame as his long body fills the open space. He's still dressed for work—fitted, navy blue slacks that hug him in all the right places and a matching jacket that's tailored just right over a white button-down with the collar undone—and it's really unfair that he could look so good in his *work* clothes. Seeing him again for the first time since the party is like an actual blow; I can feel the air rushing out of me just as my heart starts to race.

"Hey," he says casually, as if it's completely normal for him to be standing outside my door. "Can I come in?"

"What are you doing here?"

He arches one golden brow, his lips twitching. "You already asked me that."

"Normally, when someone asks a question, the other person answers them the first time."

He sighs, running his fingers through his hair. "I'd be perfectly happy to talk about it." He looks down the hall on either side of him. "Maybe just not out here."

Before this past weekend, I would have shut the door on him. We don't do things like this—surprising each other at home. Or at least, we didn't. I don't really know what we do now. It leaves me slightly addled. Maybe that's why I move to the side to let him in.

"Thanks," he mumbles, stepping past me as I close the door behind him.

I remember much too late what I'd been doing before he knocked.

"Shit," I mutter, bringing my attention to my now suspiciously quiet cell. "Guys, I need to call you back."

"Is that Ezra?"

"Is he at your *place*?"

"I thought you were done fucking him?"

"Does this mean you—"

I can't even tell who's asking what, with the way they're talking over each other. I know I'm going to have a lot of questions to answer when I see them again. That's a problem for tomorrow's Dani.

"Okay, talk soon," I say loudly into the phone, hanging up on both of them mid–barrage of questions.

Ezra has already made himself at home on my couch, his head leaned back against the cushions and his eyes closed. I walk around the couch in a daze, watching him trace idle patterns into the microfiber material.

"You still haven't answered me," I say finally.

His eyes open lazily, and I notice how tired he looks. There are dark circles under his eyes, and his usual frustrating air of playfulness is nowhere to be found.

"Would you believe me if I said I just wanted to see you?"

My heart does a strange flip-flop maneuver in my chest. I open my mouth, then close it, then open it again—realizing I look like a goldfish as my neck heats. "Why?"

"You know," he chuckles, "I honestly couldn't tell you. I had a shitty day, and for some reason, the idea of coming over here so you could most likely lay into me about whatever asshole thing I've done today sounded like a nice change of pace."

There's a flash of guilt that passes through me at his casual admission, one I brush away just as quickly as it comes. It isn't *my* fault Ezra is such an insufferable ass almost one hundred percent of the time.

I stare at him for a moment, his bronze skin practically glowing in the soft light of the lamp on my end table, all too aware of the fact that the last time he was on my couch, he was inside me. I cross my arms over my chest, my nipples pebbling under the faded University of Texas T-shirt I like to sleep in. His eyes sweep down the length of me—goose bumps erupting over every bit of skin they pass over.

Something about the haunted look in his eyes makes it impossible for me to resort to my usual tactics of keeping him at arm's length. Add that to the confusing encounter at my parents' party last weekend that I still haven't sorted through completely, and maybe it could almost explain why I sink down onto the couch only a foot away from him. Still trying to keep my distance.

"Why did you have a shitty day?"

He looks as surprised by the question as I am to have asked it. His eyes widen a fraction, his lips parting, and he studies my face for a beat before answering, "The same reason for all my shitty days."

It's a cryptic answer, one I can tell he doesn't want to elaborate on. Weirdly, that makes me want to push him. To force the answers out of him. Whether that's because of the desire he sets off in me to win or genuine concern, I can't be sure.

"Gonna have to give me more than that."

His lips purse as he turns his head to scrub his hand down his face, his palm lingering on his jaw as he considers. "Family drama. I promise it's nothing you want to hear about."

"What, are we not getting along with dear old daddy Alexander?"

His laugh is humorless. Dark, even. "There's nothing dear about Alexander Hart."

That gives me pause. Sure, I've never heard Ezra mentioning his dad, but I mean, they *work* together. There's nothing to suggest there's bad blood between them.

"You'd think he'd be over the moon with all the cases you're always winning for him."

Ezra's lips twitch. "So you are acknowledging my win rate now?"

"Abstractly," I answer flatly. "Without any interest whatsoever."

"Of course not," Ezra murmurs with actual humor now. He eyes me from the side, the amused look fading over the course of the next few seconds, his eyes losing focus as he seems to get lost in his thoughts. "Do you ever feel like . . ." He shakes his head. "Forget it. I don't even know why I'm here."

For reasons I can't fathom, I am infinitely curious about whatever he was about to ask me.

"No," I urge. "What? Do I ever feel what?"

"Like . . ." Ezra sighs, letting his head drop to the back of the couch. "Like you're just going through the motions? Like nothing you do matters because everything is always going to be just as shitty tomorrow as it was today?" He huffs out another blast of air that I think is supposed to be a laugh but comes out like more of a scoff. "Like your entire life has already been decided, and there's nothing you can do about it?"

His questions leave me gaping, his voice raw and pained and unlike anything I've ever heard from him. It makes me feel unsettled, with no idea how to answer. Especially since I know *exactly* what that feels like. It's a feeling that's been embedded in my bones since I was seventeen years old, sitting across from my parents and hearing that my whole life was a lie, and it was *entirely* my fault. It's a feeling that was solidified only a few short years later when I realized that the only person you can count on is yourself.

But I can't tell him any of that. Even with the way things have . . . shifted between us, I can't bring myself to be that vulnerable with him. Even if he's choosing to do so with me. I'm in unfamiliar territory here. I don't know what to *do* with a vulnerable Ezra, which is exactly how he seems right now.

"This is about your father?"

"My father," he snorts. "God. My father . . ." He shakes his head, and I have the strangest urge to reach out, to soothe him. It's confusing as hell. "Everything comes back to him."

"I'm sorry," I tell him, simply because I have no idea what else to say.

He shakes his head again. "No, I'm sorry. I'm sure this isn't at all what you'd like to be doing right now. Especially with me. I just . . . Today was such a goddamned nightmare, and I just needed . . . *something* that felt normal."

My heart trips in my chest. I ignore it.

"And you came . . . here."

He looks at me then, his eyes studying my face as if he's still slightly confused about why he did so. "I did."

"Still having a little bit of trouble with that part," I tell him honestly.

"I thought we were admitting when we miss each other now?"

My stupid heart flip-flops again. Maybe I should see a cardiologist.

"Ezra," I start warily, my first instinct to push him away. "I think maybe that was—"

He shifts his body, bringing himself closer to me. "You didn't miss me, Dani?"

"I—" His face is too close to think. His fingers reach to trail along my jaw, and my traitorous eyes flutter at the sensation. "No."

"You're such a liar," he laughs softly. "But that's okay." His finger ghosts ever so gently along my lower lip, tracing a slow back-and-forth. "I'll let you keep pretending. For now."

"Ezra," I manage huskily, hypnotized by the way he's still tracing my lip.

His thumb replaces his finger, applying a barely there pressure. "Open your mouth for me?"

And I do—without hesitation or question—and I should probably be angry at myself for it, but all I can focus on is the way his thumb dips inside to press against my tongue.

"Suck," he murmurs.

As much as part of me wants to tell him to fuck off, another—admittedly a much *larger* part—shivers at the quiet command. I close my lips around his thumb, sucking gently, feeling a strange sort of power seeing his pupils dilate as he watches. As if I'm the one in control, despite following his order.

"Do you know how often I imagine this pretty mouth of yours wrapped around my cock?" He slips his thumb deeper inside my mouth, keeping it pressed against my tongue. "Every time you cut into me, I imagine how quiet you'd be with your mouth full of me.

Maybe you'd glare at me the entire time. Why does that get me so fucking hot, Dani?"

An involuntarily whimper escapes me, and I press my legs together, feeling my pussy start to get slick. Why does the picture he's painting make *me* so hot? I've never dared get on my knees for him; it's something I've always thought would give him too much leverage over me, but right now, the soft way he's looking at me, like the sight of me on my knees could bring him to *his* . . . it doesn't feel like leverage at all.

I pull back to lick the pad of his thumb, smirking. "Is that why you came over here? You hoped you'd get your cock in my mouth?"

"No," he says matter-of-factly, still staring at my mouth. "I came over here because seeing you was the only thing in the world that I could think of that might make this day *less* of a god-damned nightmare."

My breath catches at the blatant admission, seeing nothing but complete sincerity in his eyes. It makes me feel . . . strange. Like I want to kiss him and throw him out all at once. It's terrifying but also thrilling. It's something entirely new.

I do my best to reel things back into more comfortable territory as I nip the pad of his thumb. Something I can actually handle. "So you're saying you don't want my mouth on you?"

"Wrong." His fingers grip my jaw then, hard enough to let me feel it but gentle enough that it doesn't hurt. "I want your mouth anywhere I can get it, Dani. It's all I fucking think about."

And even as something inside me screams that it's a bad idea, I don't move when he leans in to kiss me. He holds my face, leaving me helpless to the press of his mouth against my lips, the tease of his tongue which slips past to touch mine, and I can't seem to do anything but reciprocate. I close my eyes as his lips move in a way that seems meant to explore, not conquer, almost as if he could do this forever. Like he has all the time in the world for just this.

It feels too real, too soon. It feels like something I'm not ready for yet.

I break away to let my mouth wander, pressing kisses to the slight stubble at his jaw, lower still to trail down his neck. Ezra makes breathless sounds with every graze of my lips, his hands sliding around my waist to tug me into his lap as my fingers work open the buttons of his shirt. I let my hands press inside to explore the warm, firm skin underneath, raking my nails down his abdomen as he hisses in pleasure. When they stop at his belt buckle, my thumb flicking at the clasp, I think he stops breathing altogether.

"Maybe I've thought about it too," I whisper against his throat.

It's the truth, just one I've never permitted myself to voice.

I slowly pull his belt out from the buckle, moving to the button of his slacks next. "Maybe I've wondered what your cock would feel like in my mouth."

"*Dani*," he groans as I plunge my hand inside his underwear, letting my hand wrap around his already-hard cock. "Fuck."

I slide down his body as I pull him out, but being on my knees doesn't feel as daunting as it did before. How can it, with the way Ezra is looking at me like I'm some sort of fantasy come to life? Has he always looked at me like this when we're together? I've always made it a point not to look at him if I can help it. It makes it feel less personal.

But I'm looking at him now.

His chest heaves as his teeth press into his lower lip, his green

eyes dark and his pupils blown wide as he watches me slide my
fist lazily up and down his length. I squeeze the flushed head,
rewarded with a deep rumble of satisfaction from above, pressing
my thumb into the sensitive little V just underneath and rubbing
a slow circle. His throat bobs with a swallow when I pull him close
to rub the crown against my lower lip, and he releases a shaky
breath as he watches his precome paint me there.

I pull away only a little, just enough to swipe my tongue over
my lip to collect what he's left, and Ezra's hands fist in the material covering his thighs, like he's trying to keep from grabbing
me. It's intoxicating, having this effect on someone like him.

"Still an asshole," I chuckle before flattening my tongue in a
broad sweep up the underside of him. "But fuck if your cock isn't
pretty."

He practically shouts when I close my lips over the head, suck-
ling for a moment before pushing him deeper inside only to drag
my mouth back up slowly. I keep the pace steady and teasing,
wanting to watch him come as undone as he's constantly making
me feel. I trace my tongue against the vein that throbs against his
velvety skin, closing my eyes as I swirl my tongue over his tip before doing it all over again.

I pause when I feel his fingers pushing into my hair, my eyes
flying open to meet his. There's something entirely too gentle
about the way that he lightly pushes the hair from my face, combing his fingers through the strands as he watches me with hooded
eyes. It's more of that . . . something. That something I'm not
ready to face yet.

I pull off him with a wet sound, flicking my tongue just under
the flared head of his cock. "Stop being so careful with me," I tell
him, holding his gaze. "That's not what we do."

His tongue darts out to wet his lips. "You want me to use you, Dani?"

"Maybe I do." I give another broad sweep of my tongue against him. "Maybe I want it hard."

His eyes flare with heat, his lip rolling between his teeth again. "Then open that pretty mouth," he says roughly. "I want to dirty it up."

Everything between my thighs tingles, begging for me to touch, but I hold off. I open my mouth wide just as Ezra's fingers tangle in my hair, jerking my head back as he sits up straighter so he can slide his cock back and forth over my tongue.

He does this a few more times, getting himself slick, and his voice is a quiet rasp when he repeats the same command from earlier: "Suck."

I close my lips around him, but it's immediately clear I'm no longer in charge of the pace. He pulls me close so that his cock can slide deeper into my mouth, and I have to breathe through my nose as it pushes far enough to almost slip into my throat. I will myself not to gag, to prove that I can take whatever he gives me, like this too is some sort of competition between us—but I can't be sure who's actually winning when Ezra is making those animalistic sounds above me.

"Fuck," he grates, working me over his cock in a deep, slow slide that seems to build with every press of his hand against the back of my head. "You were made for my cock, Dani."

His praise spurs me on, and I tug against his grip on my hair to take him to the root, my nose brushing against the coarse hair at the base.

"*Fuck*," he moans. "So good for me, baby. You're so fucking *perfect*."

There's that sensation in my chest again at the endearment, like my heart is doing a barrel roll. That paired with his praise has me preening beyond all reason. It's something I've never admitted to anyone, even myself—but his praise in moments like this touches something inside me that rarely sees the light of day. Something that makes me feel like I'm *not* someone who ruins lives and messes everything up. Something that makes me feel like maybe I *should* trust someone else again. Something only Ezra has ever made me feel. Maybe that's why I never allow myself to acknowledge it. If I get used to it . . . it's going to be that much more devastating when it ends.

He's still fully clothed with only an open shirt and unbuttoned pants, and seeing him so done up and yet so *undone* has my pussy throbbing and my skin humming with want. I can't resist slipping my fingers under my leggings and underwear, rolling the swollen bundle of my clit in quick circles that I know won't have me lasting very long.

I'm still letting him move me how he wants, letting him drag my mouth up and down his cock like his own personal toy, and I should feel degraded, should feel used by the way I'm *allowing* him to use me, but all I feel is his desperation for me, his *need*—and that in turn makes me feel like all the weight I've been carrying around, the guilt . . . It makes me feel like it belongs to someone else. Even if just for this moment.

"Are you touching yourself?" His grip on my hair tightens, my scalp stinging slightly, but strangely, I like this too. "Are you going to come for me, baby? Gonna come with my cock in your throat?"

I can't help it, moaning around him as he lets out a guttural groan from the sensation. My fingers work faster, working my slick clit fervently as he thrusts deep into my mouth. My eyes flutter closed, and the minute darkness takes me, there's a sharp tug at my hair as everything stops.

My eyes fly open to meet his, his breath ragged and his gaze dark as he stares down at me with his cock still half in my mouth.

"Your eyes," he says shakily. "I want your fucking eyes when you come."

Later I'll analyze why I don't fight him on it. Maybe later I'll dissect why the walls I've built so carefully seem to be tumbling around me brick by brick. Right now though, all I can focus on is the slip of my fingers against my clit, the heavy weight of his cock as it slides against my tongue.

"That's right," he coos. "So good for me." His lids droop with pleasure as his hips lift from the couch, thrusting into my mouth at a brutal pace that has my eyes watering and my pussy clenching around nothing. "Just for me," he breathes. "You're going to take it all, aren't you? Every fucking drop."

I nod mindlessly as that pressure between my legs expands to unbearable levels, teetering on the precipice of something mind-blowing as my vision blurs and my thighs shake.

"That's it," he exhales roughly. "That's my girl." His hips stutter and his body shakes. "Oh, fuck. Oh, *fuck*, baby, I—"

I feel the warm gush of him in my throat just as I feel something similar against my fingers, my entire body trembling as I continue to touch myself wildly just to prolong the sensation. Ezra is still moving erratically in and out of my mouth, making sounds that are almost inhuman as he empties deep inside. And through it all his gaze holds mine, forcing me to watch every flicker of emotion that passes through them as I swallow everything he gives me.

I wait for the regret to come, the shame, anything, but all I feel as Ezra stills in my mouth—his cock growing soft even as my tongue continues to move gently against it to make him shudder—is a boneless bliss that courses through every part of me, my mind deliciously blank. Even when he pulls out, his palm cupping my chin and his thumb rubbing my lip in that slow, sensual way that started all of this in the first place—I can't rustle up even an ounce of remorse. It's something else I'll analyze later, I'm sure.

Ezra says nothing as his hands move to slip under my arms, pulling me up from the floor gently and tucking me against his chest as he falls back onto the couch, leaving me sprawled over him like a human blanket. His palm covers my hair until my face is buried against his throat, his fingers starting up that slow path through my hair that felt so overwhelming before. I wait for him to say something, or maybe for me to say something—but the silence that stretches on isn't unbearable, like I feel it should be. It's almost . . . comfortable.

Ezra reaches above his head and turns off the lamp to plunge us into darkness, all the while brushing his fingers through my hair in a soothing way that has my eyes growing heavy. Somewhere inside I know I should move us, that I should tell him to leave before we tangle ourselves up more than we already have—but I don't do any of that. I know if either of us speaks, this moment is over. Maybe Ezra knows it too. Maybe that's why he stays as quiet as I do. I press my face deeper into his throat, letting the remnants of his cologne soothe me in time with his still-combing fingers, choosing to say nothing at this moment, to just be and see where it leads.

As I drift off to sleep, I think that it's just one more thing I'll pick apart tomorrow, probably.

Fourteen

DANI

"YES, I'M DANICA Pierce. I'm here to see Bianca?"

I'm pressing the button at her gate much harder than necessary, letting my frustrations seep into the little plastic bit like it's
personally offended me. Which is completely unfair of me. It's not
the *button's* fault I woke up this morning to an empty apartment
and a cold couch and not even the bare minimum of a text explaining why the hell Ezra ghosted me. Last night was odd
enough, but to wake up this morning *alone*—no note, no explanation, no nothing—stings. Which in turn just makes me angry.
What the fuck was last night, and what the fuck was this morning?

I'm being stubborn and refusing to text him about it, waiting
to see if he will first, but he doesn't. Which has done nothing for
my mood this morning. I'm not sure if I'm irritated or relieved to
have the distraction of meeting with Bianca at her place for lunch;
part of me is still considering marching down to Ezra's office and
demanding what the fuck happened, but it's a *small* part. One that

is greatly overshadowed by another one shouting *Not in this life-time* and *He can choke*.

I ignore my traitor brain whispering *But who was doing the choking last night?*

My cheeks heat as I finally let up on the button, sure that if it were alive, it would be screaming by now.

"Mrs. Casiraghi is expecting you," a rough, male voice says through the gate speaker in a clipped tone.

The gate creaks as it begins to open, and I inch my car through as I pull into the well-manicured drive that circles in front of the large, stately house perched on the hill.

"Damn," I say to no one, eyeing the perfectly trimmed hedges and the ornate front door that looks like it was some kind of custom job. Clearly, I'm in the wrong line of work.

I step out of my car and smooth my pantsuit, grabbing my briefcase from the passenger seat before making my way up the stone steps to knock on the massive oak door with the frosted glass windows. It opens only a moment later, and at this point part of me was expecting to see some menacing butler with a scar running down his face glaring at me from the other side, so I'm relieved to be met with Bianca's staple red lips and sharp eyes instead.

"Danica," she greets, gesturing that I come. "So glad you could make it."

"Right," I say. "Sorry. You really didn't need to feed me. I would have been happy to do this at my office."

She waves a hand in front of her face. "I sit in this house all day by myself. It is good to have company now and then."

"Sure," I agree, letting my eyes take in the massive entryway with the sparkly chandelier overhead. "Your house is beautiful."

"Yes, well," she scoffs, closing the door behind me. "Thankfully, Lorenzo's taste in decor is as bad as his taste in women, so I picked everything out."

"Current company excluded, of course," I say with a grin.

She nods, her lips curling. "Of course." She wraps her hand around my forearm. "Come in, come in. We're going to have lunch on the veranda. It is such a nice day, after all."

Sure, if you're not carrying around your own personal rain cloud because you went down on a guy and fell asleep with him just for him to ghost you.

"It is," I say instead. "That sounds great."

"Let me just check on the food, yes? Look around. Enjoy my good taste."

I laugh softly as she disappears into another room, doing as she says and wandering around the wide sitting room. There is a chaise longue that looks too nice to sit on, and a wall of shelves just behind it that boasts books and pictures and little trinkets that sparkle in a way that makes me suspicious of their carat count. I step closer to browse, noticing several books on real estate law that make me feel sleepy just reading the spines.

There are several framed photos here though, and I feel a twinge of sadness for Bianca to notice so many of a younger version of her and Lorenzo looking very happy in most of them. I imagine she hasn't gotten around to putting them away, or maybe, deep down, it's still too hard for her to do so even with all her bluster.

It just proves the real deal isn't so real.

One frame at the end of the shelf catches my eye, tucked beside a dusty old book and a heavy bookend. I pick it up, frowning, studying the two men smiling back when I hear Bianca's footsteps reentering the room.

I hold up the photo for her perusal. "How long has Lorenzo known Alexander Hart?"

"Eh?" She steps closer, plucking the frame from me. "Ah. Terrible man, Alexander. I never liked him much."

"So they've known each other for a long time?"

"Many years, yes," she says with a nod. "I don't know what it is about him that I do not like, but there was always something . . ." She frowns as her gaze lingers on the photo, finally shaking the thought away before placing the frame back on the shelf. "Perhaps some part of me knew he would be helping Lorenzo hide his wrongdoings."

"I'm sorry," I offer. "I wasn't trying to dredge up bad feelings."

Bianca laughs. "I am old, and my husband is giving his cock to some puttana under my nose. I live in bad feelings."

"Sorry," I say again.

She shakes her head. "Do not apologize. Bad feelings make us strong. If there are no bad feelings, we would not appreciate the good ones. Understand?"

I nod dumbly. Bianca doesn't even look upset as she says it, and I think idly that I'd definitely like to be her when I grow up. Maybe sans the whole cheating-husband thing.

"Anyway," she says. "The food is not quite done. We will have tea while we wait."

She turns on her heel, not leaving room for argument, and I take one last look at the photo of a young Lorenzo and Alexander, frowning.

There's nothing dear about Alexander Hart.

I immediately brush off the thought. *We are not thinking about Ezra right now,* I tell myself for the dozenth time. I follow Bianca instead, putting all the Hart men far from my mind.

"RIDICULOUS QUESTION," BIANCA scoffs.

"But it's one they're going to ask," I sigh.

This entire exercise has been less than fruitful. Given all the surprises that Bianca has sprung on me thus far, prepping for our first day in court seemed prudent. Getting caught off guard in mediation is one thing; having egg on my face in front of a judge is quite another.

"I don't see why it is so important to talk about something from so long ago," Bianca says stubbornly.

I frown. "You filed for divorce before, Bianca. A judge is going to be curious why you didn't follow through. Especially given the inconvenient timing with the issue of your trust fund taking such a hit."

She takes a slow sip of her tea, looking thoughtful. So far when we've talked about this, she's been less than forthcoming. I've gotten nothing but vague answers and brush-offs regarding her first filing and withdrawal so many years ago. I know that "I changed my mind" is not going to satisfy Ezra or anyone else in the courtroom, I just need to drive that home to the stubborn woman sitting in front of me.

"I believe you when you say that withdrawing your petition had nothing to do with your trust," I go on. "I really do. But you have to understand, the opposing counsel is going to paint a very specific picture. One that does not cast you in a flattering light. It won't look good to a judge."

"What is the point of having all Lorenzo's disgusting emails if I still have to broadcast my business for strangers?"

"Because as *disgusting* as those emails are, they're going to say it's circumstantial, because unfortunately, it is. At least in the eyes of a judge. We can't prove without a doubt that someone *didn't* use Lorenzo's computer to send them, even if you and I know it's ridiculous to even consider."

"No one will believe such nonsense," she snorts.

"Again, unfortunately, it's not what you believe, it's what you can prove in court." I lean to set my saucer and cup on the patio table between us, giving her a sympathetic expression. "I don't want to lie to you, so I won't. They're going to say this is all about the money. Yes, we know that your trust is fine, but with a preestablished history of it being in jeopardy in the past, they're going to say that you're just trying to make sure you're taken care of. Maybe even that you're vindictive. That you and Lorenzo had grown apart, and this is your way of taking your revenge. Honestly, there are a dozen ridiculous things they could say to sway things to their side. I want to make sure we're prepared for all of them. Starting with the *real* reason you filed for divorce and then changed your mind shortly after."

Bianca turns her head to stare out across her yard, eyeing the flower beds that line the tiled space we're currently lounging in. There is an array of white tulips swaying gently in the breeze, and Bianca's gaze is far away as she regards them.

"Do you know what white tulips symbolize?"

I flick my gaze to where she's still watching them, shaking my head. "I don't."

"They mean 'I'm sorry,'" she tells me. "Lorenzo gave me such a large bouquet when he first broke my heart."

"Bianca, I—"

She holds up a hand, meeting my gaze. "I will tell you everything, but you must promise me that you will find a way to keep it from the courtroom, yes? I will not be shamed further. Promise me, Danica."

"I . . ." I don't know if it's something I can or should promise her, but it's the first time I've seen this strong, confident woman look vulnerable, and the crack in her normally solid demeanor makes me want to try. "I'll do my best."

She nods, taking another slow sip from her cup, thinking. "I can't have children."

"You can't?"

"No." She shakes her head. "I found out only two years into our marriage."

I sense there's more to the story, but I want to be patient. To let her tell it in her own time.

"When we were younger, Lorenzo was . . . different. Before the money, he was doting. He was kind. I was smitten after our first meeting. My father did not approve; Lorenzo was not the sort of man he saw me marrying. Lorenzo came from a family with nothing to their name, and where I come from, your name is everything."

"But you married him."

There's a flash of that same wistful smile. "I have always been stubborn. We married in secret. My family almost shunned me for what I did, but eventually, they came around. Lorenzo was charming, after all. They saw the drive in him. It was always known Lorenzo would be successful."

"This was in Italy?"

She nods. "We moved here in 1992. Lorenzo always said our future was here, and I always believed everything Lorenzo said. When we first came here, we lived in a tiny house with almost no money. My trust was not to be touched until I was twenty-five, since my father wanted to make sure Lorenzo was not with me only for the money."

"How old were you then?"

"Only twenty-two," she says. "Too young to be in a strange, new place, but I believed Lorenzo when he said he would take care of me." She looks thoughtful then. "He did for a while."

"But something changed," I venture.

She nods solemnly. "Lorenzo always wanted children, as did I, and we were excited to start a family. We tried for many months, but after so long it become clear something was wrong."

My stomach tightens at the palpable grief etched into her tone, knowing there is no happy ending here. Without thinking, I reach across the table to place my hand over hers, squeezing it lightly. Bianca gives me a brittle, sad smile.

"Lorenzo's business was still small, just beginning to grow," she goes on. "He was always so stressed—stretched so thin trying to shake the right hands, to make friends with the right people. He was so desperate to be who he believed he was meant to be." She swallows thickly. "When we learned I could not have children . . . it drove us apart."

She goes silent, her eyes glassy with unshed tears, and it breaks my heart, seeing this strong woman in obvious pain from such an old memory. "Bianca," I say gently. "What happened?"

"I came home to them. In our *bed*, Danica. The shame I felt . . . the *grief*, knowing he had strayed from me because of the failure of my own body."

"Bianca," I choke, my voice tight.

"I realized then that Lorenzo was not the man I thought he was. *My* Lorenzo would never touch another. Not when I still grieved what would never be for us. I did not know this Lorenzo."

"So you filed for divorce."

"Yes." She nods, still trying to collect herself. "I couldn't look at him. He begged for my forgiveness, but it was too hard. I could not forget." She lets out a laugh that sounds bitter, shaking her head. "But as I said . . . Lorenzo has always been charming. Somehow . . . he convinced me to stay. That things would be different. That he loved me. That it was a *mistake*." She turns her head, staring out at the tulips again. "I was young and foolish. I should have never stayed. Maybe things would be different for me now."

"Bianca, I . . ." I don't think there are words I can say that will make her feel better; I'm sure if there were, she would have already heard them a dozen times over by now. I can't imagine what it would be like to forgive someone for such a thing only to realize so many years later they never stopped hurting you in secret. "I'm sorry," I settle on.

"It is the past," she tells me. "It is my mistake, and I will live with it." She meets my eyes then, her gaze harder. "But I will *not* live with him making a fool of me, do you understand? Not again. Not after everything he has already taken from me. This time, I want it to be *him* who is made to be a fool."

Her secrets and her dodginess make so much more sense now; I can't imagine being faced with reliving a pain like that in front of a room of strangers. I resolve that I will do whatever I can within my power to make sure she never has to.

I give her hand another squeeze. "I'm going to do that for you," I promise her, still unsure if it's a wise move. "We're going to make sure he is the fool this time."

Bianca nods, her mouth tilting at the corners, but only just. "Like a powerful woman."

"Exactly," I tell her with a grin.

This earns me a real chuckle, and she slips her hand from beneath mine, patting the back before reaching for her teacup. "I hope you would never let a man make a fool of you like I have," she tuts. "You are much too smart."

"You'd be surprised," I mutter, remembering this morning when I woke up alone on my couch.

Bianca cocks an eyebrow at me. "You have man troubles?"

"No." I wave her off. I'm not about to get into this . . . thing between Ezra and me after hearing her story. They can't begin to compare. "Nothing worth talking about."

"Danica," she laughs. "One thing I have learned about men— if it is worth thinking about, it is worth talking about."

"I'm . . . not very good at that," I tell her honestly. "Talking about things."

Bianca shrugs. "If you cannot talk about it, then you should not do it."

She says it so simply, as if it *is* simple, even when it feels so far from it. I want to tell her that this back-and-forth game I've been playing with Ezra isn't worth talking about at all, but then I realize how much I've been plagued with thoughts of it since the moment I woke up alone on my couch, and it makes me wonder if she's right. If the fact that I can't stop thinking about it somehow means I should talk about it. Not to her, obviously. She has enough on her plate. But maybe . . .

I shake away those thoughts. It's not something I should be worrying about right now.

"We have more questions I'd like to go over," I say, changing the subject. "We'll circle back around to your petition of divorce. We'll think of a diplomatic answer. I promise."

"This is why I hired you," she says matter-of-factly.

A grin spreads across my face. "Yes. Yes, it is."

Bianca excuses herself to check on lunch then, and the weight of my phone in my pocket feels heavier after her words, almost impossible to ignore. I wrestle with the idea for what feels like a long time before I work it out of my pocket, biting my lower lip when I notice *his* name on my screen for the first time today.

Don't open it, I tell myself. *It's just going to upset you.*

Which has me spiraling about *why* Ezra has the power to upset me. What a fucking mess.

I open the damned thing anyway.

Asshole: Are you going to ignore me all day?

I feel my chest heat in anger, my fingers already tapping across the screen.

Me: Ignoring you implies you've said something to me, which you haven't.

Asshole: I was waiting for you to text me.

Me: Oh? Was I supposed to glean that from you sneaking out of my apartment this morning?

Asshole: I didn't sneak out.
I wanted to give you space
to process.

> **Me:** There's nothing to process. It
> was an accident. We just fell
> asleep. It wasn't a big deal.

Asshole: Dani.

> **Me:** Ezra.

There's a pause as I watch the dots pop up and disappear over and over again, and I am loath to admit how tightly I grip my phone, how closely I watch them as I wait for his reply. It takes him a full minute to finally respond.

Asshole: Let me know when you're
home. I want to call you and talk
about it.

> **Me:** I don't have anything to say.

Asshole: Don't be stubborn.

> **Me:** I'm not being anything.

Asshole: Fine. Let me know when
you're home, so I can call to go
over the list of interrogatories.

I clench my teeth. He really is an asshole, pulling this. He knows it's not something I can refuse. Not with our first court date looming. Now it's me typing and erasing a dozen times before settling on:

Me: Fine. Work only.

Asshole: Sure thing, Dani.

I'm just starting to seethe at his blasé tone, one I can sense through text, can practically hear the sigh following, but Bianca's voice interrupts what was surely going to be an incoherent response.

"I hope you're hungry," she says kindly, holding a tray of something that smells delicious.

I stow my phone back in my pocket, but not without squeezing it too tight for the briefest of moments. "Starved," I tell her.

"But no work while we eat," she tells me sternly. "We will practice your questions after."

I can't help the quiet laugh that escapes me. "Fine, fine. You're the boss."

"Powerful woman," she teases.

My smile is bright, even if thoughts of Ezra are still lingering at the back of my mind. "You're goddamned right."

Fifteen

EZRA

Sour Patch: Fine. Work only.

I sigh while reading her response. It's clear she's pissed, but I had no doubt she would be.

Waking up with a boneless, snoring Dani sprawled over my chest had been an experience like no other, one that had filled me with elation and confusion all at once. I've never seen her like she was last night—with none of the biting tones or snarky retorts. Last night, she seemed . . . Well. She seemed different. Which I'm grateful for, because I *feel* different.

Maybe that's why I'd been so terrified when I woke up. There was such a strong chance that in the morning light she would revert to the Dani who hides, the Dani who pretends she doesn't want this thing between us, and after last night . . . I don't think I could have stomached watching her expression change to that cold, closed-off look that she reserves for me. Maybe it makes me a coward, leaving before she had the chance.

I know there's nothing I can say to her right now that will quell her anger, telling myself there will be time for that later. That Dani's walls are something to be chipped away at slowly, not broken down all at once. With that in mind, I shoot off a complacent text, telling myself we'll talk more later.

Me: Sure thing, Dani.

She doesn't respond, but I didn't actually expect her to. Tonight, when she's home and ready to talk, we can discuss last night. I've already decided that I'm not going to let her keep running from me, even if that means following her at a slow, steady pace. I can be patient, I think. I know, with Dani, I'll have to be.

A knock on the doorframe of my office jerks me out of my reverie. My eyes narrow at the sight of my brother. "What?"

"Stop with the scowling," Eli warns. "I just came to tell you that you're supposed to be at dinner tonight."

"Pass," I say immediately, giving my attention back to my phone. "Thanks for the not-quite invite though."

"It's nonnegotiable," Eli stresses. "Dad wants you there."

"Well, you can tell Alexander that I'm very busy trying to win his stupid case for him."

"He said you'd say something like that," Eli laughs. "In which case he told me to tell you that Lorenzo will be joining us. So will Mom."

I straighten, tensing. "Why is Lorenzo coming to dinner?"

"They're friends," Eli says with a shrug. "Why wouldn't he? I think they're discussing some charity gala Dad is hosting soon."

I resist the urge to roll my eyes. It's ironic that Alexander would do anything so selfless, considering how selfish he really is. I have to assume it's all for his precious image.

"Still not hearing why the fuck I should care to or need to be there for it."

"Does it fucking matter? Dad wants you to come, and we both know this back-and-forth is pointless. Just make sure you're at the house by six."

My neck heats with irritation as I think of all the things I'd rather be doing than sitting at the same table as Lorenzo, Eli, and Alexander. Eli is right though; it really is pointless to act like I have a choice in the matter.

"Fine," I huff. "I'll be there."

"Of course you will be," Eli says, like there was never any question. "When are you prepping Lorenzo and his assistant for court?"

"Tomorrow," I mutter. "They're coming by the office."

"I'd like to sit in."

My eyes flash to meet his. "That's not necessary."

"Too fucking bad," Eli snorts.

"Honestly, just take the fucking case, Eli. If you're going to hover over every goddamned part of it, then why don't you just—"

"Stop being dramatic," Eli cuts me off. "I'm just making sure there aren't any snags."

I grit my teeth. "How thoughtful of you."

"Just make sure you're not late to dinner," Eli says flippantly as he pushes off the doorframe.

I don't answer as I watch him disappear, contemplating getting a very strong lock for my office door. One that neither of my family members have a key to. It's a nice fantasy. I scrub a hand down my face as I imagine the disastrous night looming ahead of me, knowing that there will be nothing appealing about sharing a meal with possibly three of the worst humans in existence while my mother sits quietly like some sort of living doll, not allowed to speak. And then I still have to talk with Dani at some point.

It's going to be a long fucking night.

I ARRIVE AT my parents' place fifteen minutes late just to piss off Alexander; I know he's unlikely to say anything with Lorenzo present, and the irritated look he'll most likely give me will make it slightly worth it. I can already hear subtle laughter from the dining room when I step through the front door, steeling myself for a night of bullshit as I traipse through the cold hallway toward the brightly lit room.

The four of them are gathered around the polished wood table that sits under the crystal chandelier, each holding a glass of red wine, save for my mother, who is tucked in her chair with her hands sitting demurely in her lap. Alexander looks up at me as I walk through the door, his eyes narrowing for a second before he schools his expression.

"Ezra," he says blandly. "I thought for a moment you might not be coming."

"And miss all the fun?" I paste a fake smile on my face as I pull out a chair next to my mother. "You know how much I love family dinners."

"This one is funny," Lorenzo chortles, his cheeks already flushed in a way that tells me this isn't his first glass of wine. "Chip off the old block, eh?" Lorenzo barks out another laugh. "Not really though, I suppose."

I see my mother flinch from the corner of my eye, and I curl my hands into fists under the table. "Always good to see you, Lorenzo."

"Lorenzo was just telling me that the little lawyer representing Bianca is asking questions about the bank account he and his cousin share," Alexander says offhandedly.

"Cousin," I remark dryly. "Right."

Lorenzo arches one thick brow. "You have something to say, little Hart?"

"Nothing at all," I answer blithely. "Knowing the intimate details of your personal life is well outside my need to know, isn't it? It's not like I'm trying to keep you from having to shell out millions. Why would I need to be privy to all your dirty little secrets?"

Lorenzo stares at me for a moment, his red face blank and not giving any evidence of how he might react, but surprisingly, another sharp laugh escapes him. "That is funny," he chuckles. "Someone like you speaking of dirty little secrets."

My jaw clenches. "Is there something *you* would like to say, Lorenzo?"

"Let's not talk business," Alexander says drolly, like this entire conversation is boring him. He taps his fingers on the table near my mother. "Jackie. Go check on dinner, would you?"

"She's not your fucking maid," I seethe.

Alexander narrows his eyes. "It's not your fucking business, boy."

My mother's hand pats my knee gently under the table, and when I turn to look at her, she gives me a slight shake of her head, already rising from her chair. One of Alexander's *actual* maids enters the room from the galley door, holding a fresh glass and a bottle of wine, just as my mother disappears through it. The maid sets the glass in front of me, presenting the bottle.

"Wine?"

Normally, I would say no, but a little liquid courage feels necessary if I'm going to get through this dinner. "Please."

She fills my glass as Alexander and Lorenzo delve into quiet conversation about the event Alexander is apparently hosting here at the house in the coming weeks, occasionally bringing Eli into the fold as I nurse my glass, effectively ignored for the moment. I'm used to it, but I fail to see why it's something I'm still forced to subject myself to. Part of me thinks it's for Alexander's entertainment. I think he enjoys reminding me just how firmly under his thumb he has me pressed.

My mother returns a short while later with people bringing in dinner behind her, and Lorenzo gushes loudly about the food as Alexander laughs at his antics. Even from here I can see that his laughter is fake, that the amusement in his features is calculated. His eyes tell a different story, glaring at Lorenzo with thinly veiled disgust when Lorenzo isn't looking. Almost like he actually can't stand to be in the other man's presence.

Interesting.

"So, Jackie," Lorenzo says at some point. "I hear you are doing well these days, no? Must be nice to have your husband take such good care of you after everything."

My fingers close around my fork, gripping it tight. "Maybe you've had enough wine, Lorenzo."

"It is not a secret," Lorenzo snorts. "You should be grateful you are even here. That Alexander still gives you a place at his table. It is much more than I would have done."

"It's not something we like to talk about at dinner," Alexander says, surprising me. I would think he would love an opportunity to remind me. I suspect it's just that he doesn't like Lorenzo knowing his business, which raises the question, why does he? "Why don't you tell me about the merger instead. Have you finalized?"

"I'm feeling tired," my mother says softly, causing everyone to turn and look at her. "Would it be all right if I went on up to bed?"

"You'll stay until we're finished," Alexander says, his tone leaving no room for argument. Then he ignores her completely to give his attention back to Lorenzo. "Anyway, the merger?"

Maybe it's the wine in my system, or the stress of this fucking case paired with Alexander and my brother constantly breathing down my neck, or maybe it's even a bit of the mess with Dani—I can't be sure. All I know is that my blood is boiling under my skin, and there are tinges of red in my vision that form when I see my mother shrivel down into her chair.

"She said she's tired," I manage tightly. "I'm going to take her to bed."

"She will stay until we are finished," Alexander warns, fixing his gaze on me. "And so will you."

I look to Eli, who is watching this unfold with a bored expression. "She's your mother too," I say, my tone accusing. "How can you let him treat her like this?"

"She stopped being my mother the day she got knocked up with you," he says cruelly.

My mother sniffles, and I see full-on red. "Fuck you, Eli. I should feed you your fucking teeth for—"

"Sit *down*, Ezra," Alexander bellows, slamming his fist on the table.

"No, I'm sick of both of you treating her like some kind of—"

"Sit down right now," Alexander continues darkly, "or you will deeply regret continuing this little tantrum."

Even with my heart beating a tattoo against my ribs, my blood pulsing in my ears with anger—I recognize the threat is not for me. Alexander knows that there's nothing he can do to me. That it's not *me* he'll make suffer.

I gulp down a breath, feeling like my chest is too tight, my eyes flitting from Alexander to Eli to my mother and back again before finally letting out a frustrated sound and sinking down into my chair. I could kill them both at this moment, I think. I could bury them both in the backyard and never lose a night's sleep over it. But even that seems like too easy an end for monsters like them.

Lorenzo, having been quiet through all of this, lets out another annoying laugh after the dust settles, only fueling my rage. "You have quite the leash on him, eh?" He flashes a grin at Alexander conspiratorially. "If it had been *my* wife who had gotten herself saddled with a bastard baby, I would have tossed them into the streets." He fixes his gaze on me, leering. "You are very fortunate your father is such a giving man."

"He's not my fucking father," I hiss.

The entire table goes silent.

It's a truth we all know, one that has been the fucked-up glue to this broken dynamic that we've been suffering since the day my life changed and my mother practically lost hers—but I don't think I've ever dared to say it out loud like this. Not to Alexander, at least. His response is immediate, his blue eyes turning frigid as he laces his fingers together, leaning toward me from the other end of the table.

"I think maybe you *should* go," he says darkly, his voice menacing. "Go home and reevaluate your priorities, and how much you stand to lose by falling from my good graces. I didn't toss you out in the street like Lorenzo said, and you would do well to remember that."

I wish you had, I practically scream in my own head. *I wish you'd just let us both go.*

I turn to my mother, and her gaze is pleading, searching mine and begging me not to make things worse. I feel like shit then, knowing that she'll be the one he takes his anger out on. Not physically, since he's never put his hands on her—I'd kill him if he did—but mentally. I know that he'll twist and abuse her guilt until she's more broken than she already is. It's an art he's perfected over the years.

"Go," she says softly, squeezing my knee. "I will call you later."

I push away from the table, my chair scraping loudly against the wood floor as I spin on my heel to leave. I don't even spare a glance at the other men still at the table, wishing more than anything that I never had to look at them ever again. Wishing that I would have just skipped this farce of a family gathering in the first place; it would have been better to take Alexander's chewing out tomorrow than put my mother through what I just did. I know how much it kills her to be reminded of what she did, even if I'm sure Alexander fucking deserved it.

I'm in my car when I feel my phone buzzing in the pocket of my suit jacket, and I tear it out and swipe it unlocked. The breath that escapes me upon seeing Dani's name on the screen might be the first full one I've taken since I arrived here.

Sour Patch: I'm home. If you still
want to go over things.

I even smile at the text that follows, which seems impossible.

Sour Patch: Work things. Work
things only.

I drop my phone into the cup holder, suddenly desperate to get
home.

Amazingly, despite the shit show I just suffered . . . all I can
think about right now is how much I want to hear her voice.

Sixteen

DANI

I STARE AT my phone for a few minutes after telling Ezra that I'm home, chewing on the end of my thumbnail as I wait and see if he'll respond. When it's clear that he won't, I get angry at myself for even worrying about whether or not he would in the first place.

How in the hell did things get so mixed up in such a short time?

I shake it off, stomping down the hall to my bedroom and dropping my phone on my bed as I start to undress. I change out of my work clothes, briefly considering the University of Texas shirt I love before kicking it away and grabbing another one from my dresser drawer. I can only hope that Ezra hasn't ruined my favorite shirt and that I'll eventually be able to wear it without remembering last night.

My brain actually aches from the day I've had; between last night and this morning and Bianca and Ezra—it literally feels like there is nothing left but a puddle in my skull, one that throbs. I grab some Tylenol from the medicine cabinet over my sink, using a bit of water from the faucet pooled in my hand to swallow them before straightening to regard myself in the mirror.

I could be imagining it, the slight redness of my lips that looks deeper than normal, but part of me thinks that with the way I let Ezra use my mouth last night . . . it would be entirely feasible to say they're still a little swollen. The thought makes me as hot as it does angry.

I sweep my dark hair into a messy bun on top of my head, grabbing my toothbrush from the holder by the sink and slathering it with paste before aggressively going after my teeth in a series of rough passes. I'm trying *not* to think about the fact that it was *Ezra* who wanted to talk, that it was him who had asked me to reach out when I was home only to treat me to radio silence; the entire thing only brings back the memory of this morning, of waking up alone and confused just for those feelings to morph into a bitter, cold feeling in my stomach that I would rather never repeat again, if at all possible.

I spit in the sink before rinsing the brush, only hearing the slight buzzing from the other room when I turn off the tap. I would like to say that I *don't* drop my toothbrush in the sink and sprint back into my bedroom, but that would be a lie.

Which means I'm all the more disappointed to see it's my mother calling instead.

"Hey," I greet her, trying not to sound like Eeyore.

"Dani," she says in her ever-chipper tone. "I was just calling to see if you wanted to have lunch tomorrow. Your dad and Patty heard about this new tapas place downtown, and we thought you might like to—"

I blame the stress. That has to be the cause of the choked sob that escapes me.

"Dani?" My mom immediately sounds worried. "Sweetheart? Are you okay?"

I wipe my eyes, traitorous bastards starting to leak. "I'm fine."

"You don't sound fine."

"It's just been a very long day."

"Well, tell me about it."

I puff out a breath. There is no way I can tell my mother about this morning, because it would mean I would have to tell her about last night. Which is *not* happening. And legally, I *can't* tell her about my discussion with Bianca and how raw it had left me.

"It's nothing," I tell her. "Work has just been stressful."

"Work is always stressful," she presses. "It's never made you sound like this."

"I—"

I shut my mouth immediately. I have no idea what to say to her. No way to encapsulate whatever it is I'm feeling right now. I just know that the thought of sitting across from her and my dad and their respective spouses and pretending for one more damned day that it doesn't kill me to know that they sacrificed half their lives for me is the straw that breaks the camel's back.

"Mom," I say quietly. "Did you ever consider telling me the truth? I mean . . . sooner?"

My mother is quiet for several moments, and I know she's taken off guard. It isn't even what I meant to ask her, and I already feel guilty for letting it slip out.

"Of course we did," she says finally, her voice strained. "So many times."

"Then why did you wait so long?"

"Because your father and I both came from broken homes, Dani. When we had no one else, we had each other. Sometimes, each other was *all* we had. We never wanted that for you. We wanted you to have a better childhood than we did. One that you didn't have to spend years getting over."

But I'm still getting over it regardless, I want to say. *How can I trust anything when my entire life was a lie?*

But I don't say that, because I can't. After everything my parents sacrificed, I can't bring myself to give them anything more to hurt over.

"Is that what this is about?" My mother's voice is soft, searching. "Are you . . . Do we need to talk about this? You've always said that you were fine, but I've often worried that—"

"No," I cut her off. "It's not about that. I *am* fine. I promise." *As fine as I can be.* "It's just been a long fucking day, and there are things I learned today about the case that are eating at me. That's all. I didn't mean to upset you."

"You didn't upset me, sweetheart," she urges. "I always want to know what you're feeling. Even if it's hard. *Especially* if it's hard. I want to be there for you no matter what." She's quiet for a moment, and then: "Sometimes I think that if we'd talked about this more, maybe you wouldn't have locked yourself away like you did after Grant—"

"I don't want to talk about Grant, Mom." My voice is tight. "He left. He chose a job over me. That has nothing to do with me or you or Dad. It has everything to do with him. I just want to fucking *stop* talking about him, okay?"

"I'm sorry," Mom says quietly. "You're right."

For the millionth time since they sat me down and changed my life, I wonder how I can still be so bitter, with parents as amazing as them. It only further cements the truth that *I'm* the problem.

"I really am fine," I stress, trying to make her believe it even if I don't. "Promise. Just a bad day."

She's quiet for entirely too long, like she wants to press the issue, but maybe she can sense how at the end of my rope I am. Maybe that's why she blessedly doesn't. "Okay, honey. But remember, you can talk to me about anything, okay?"

"I know, Mom. I promise."

"Go get some rest. You sound like you need it. If you decide you want to do lunch, text me in the morning. But no pressure if you're still not feeling well."

I already know I'll be going, no matter how much it will mess me up inside.

"Okay," I manage. "Good night, Mom."

"Night, hon. Talk soon."

I close my eyes and sink down on my bed as I hang up, flopping back against the mattress as I swallow another sob. I'm usually so good at keeping it all together, but lately . . . lately it feels like I'm coming apart at the seams. It bothers me that I can't even pinpoint one thing that's the cause of it.

My phone begins to vibrate again on my stomach where I've dropped it, and I reach for it, frowning when I see the name there.

He's definitely a *large* part of it, if I'm being honest with myself. I consider not answering for all of three seconds before I swipe to answer, hitting the speaker button and setting the phone on my chest.

"What do you want, Ezra?"

"So many things," he says cryptically, sighing after. "But for now, I'd like to talk about this morning."

"I already told you," I mutter bitterly. "There's nothing to talk about."

He's quiet for a moment, and I can practically hear his brain recalibrating. "Then we'll talk about work. We still have your interrogatories to go over."

"That easy?"

"I can't force you to talk to me about your feelings," he says simply.

I scoff. "That implies I have feelings on the matter to begin with."

"You're the one still pressing the issue right now."

I scowl at the smile in his voice. Asshole.

"Fine," I say tightly, rolling over my bed to my nightstand to grab my laptop. I open it up to his last email, snorting when I'm reminded of his ridiculous objections as I set my phone back on my chest. "We'll talk about work. Starting with how ridiculous your objections are."

"I don't know how you mean," he answers, still sounding amused.

I shut my eyes, sighing. "For starters, you have *eight* general objections."

"So?"

"We both know that the state of Texas doesn't allow for general objections."

"I would venture to say that they're just frowned upon."

I rub the space between my eyes. "You're going to have to revisit and revise. You can't object to *every* single one."

"Just wanted to make sure we had plenty to talk about," he says, his tone slightly teasing now. It makes my stomach flip in a way that makes me scowl. "Besides, I think what I've provided is more than adequate barring any *general* objections."

"Ezra."

"Fine. I might be willing to make you a trade," he says nonchalantly. "I could be persuaded to remove a few."

"And what, pray tell, would you want in return?"

"I want to talk about this morning."

My nostrils flare with an exasperated exhale. "Of course you do."

"You do too, if you would just be honest."

"I don't know what you want me to say. We fell asleep, and then you were gone when I woke up. I think it speaks for itself."

"We both know if I'd been there when you woke up, you would have freaked out. You would have overanalyzed the entire thing, and then we'd be right back to the insufferable game we've been playing where you pretend you don't want me, and I pretend it doesn't make me crazy."

"Well, I guess we'll never know," I tell him blandly. "Since you left."

Ezra sighs. "Let's play a game. Answer my questions, and I'll trade each answer for an objection." He pauses for another moment. "Save for a select few."

I let out a heavy sigh, leaning my head back against the headboard as I look up at the ceiling. I wonder if it was always inevitable, us having a conversation like this. I wonder if it was ever possible that we could just get through this thing we've been doing scathe-free.

I focus my attention back on my laptop, resigning myself to a conversation I'll probably regret.

"Fine," I say tersely. "You objected to Request Number Four on the basis that it is *vague, overly broad, and unduly burdensome*, and that it *seeks information that is proprietary and confidential.* Surely you understand what material is sought by this request, otherwise, how could you determine that it seeks information that is proprietary and confidential?"

"Fair enough," he assents. "I can omit that one."

"For a price," I mumble bitterly.

"I'm a lawyer, Dani," he chuckles. "All I do is counter."

"Fine. Ask your question."

"What would you have done, really, if we'd woken up together this morning?"

I blanch. "I . . . how would I know? There's no way for me to know since you—"

"Be honest, Dani. After everything that's happened between us, how do you think you would have reacted?"

I go still, thinking. If I were being truly honest with myself, there's no doubt in my mind I would have freaked out. Fucking each other is one thing, *sleeping* together is something completely different. I hate that he apparently knows me well enough to call me on this.

"I can . . . admit that I might have reacted poorly."

"You would have flipped shit and kicked me out," he snorts.

I will not smile at his teasing tone. I won't.

"Guess we'll never know for sure."

"But you enjoyed last night, didn't you?"

Uncomfortable awareness creeps up my spine. "That's more than one question."

"Sorry. Go ahead."

"Number Six." I find the line on my screen. "You objected on the basis that *it exceeds the scope of expert discovery under Rule 194.1.*"

"And?"

"Rule 194.1 governs the production of statements given by parties or witnesses—*not* the scope of expert discovery. Even if you meant to refer to Rule 192.4, which does address expert discovery, you are still wrong, because the law requires the production of *any written report made by the expert* concerning the expert's findings and opinions."

"Someone's getting technical," he laughs softly.

"Someone has a lot at stake," I counter. "We *have* named experts now. They have to answer."

"Okay. You're right. Omit it."

"Fine. Ask me another question."

"What do you mean you have a lot at stake?"

Fuck. I walked right into that one.

"I just meant that it's an important case."

"I don't think that's all you meant. We had a deal, Dani."

I know giving him this information will probably come back to haunt me, and I can't even say why I'm compelled to give it in the first place. All I know is that my mouth is opening before I can stop it.

"My boss has agreed to put me up for junior partner if I win."

"Wow."

"But that doesn't mean I want you cutting corners or babying me," I stress.

"I wouldn't dream of it," he says, a smile still in his voice. "That's not who we are."

"Right. So just forget I even said anything."

"I'll do my best," he answers softly. "Do you have another?"

"I think your objection to Request Number Seven is plausible, so I'm not going to contest it, but you objected to Request Number

Nine on the basis that *the request potentially seeks attorney work product and attorney-client privileged information.* You then go on to state that *no documents are being withheld pursuant to these privileges.* If there are no documents subject to these privileges, why are you objecting?"

"Can't argue with that," he says. "Feel free to omit."

"Good."

"Why don't you like me?"

I blink in surprise, taken completely off guard by the question. "Excuse me?"

"I mean, I don't think you *actually* dislike me, not anymore," he says, setting off a flicker of annoyance in me before he goes on. "But the night we met, you decided I was some asshole within one conversation. Why?"

I can't help but remember the night in question, thinking back to the moment I saw him laughing at the open bar of the party we were both attending—the memory of his smile fixing me in place still vivid after so many months. I knew who he was; how could I not, with him and his stupid Heartbreak Prince nickname floated around by other lawyers, but being that he'd only just moved back to Austin after a stint in New York for the last few years, I hadn't actually run into him before.

"You were talking to another woman," I say, remembering. "Smiling and laughing while she ate it up."

He makes an indignant sound. "Wait, so I'm being punished for talking to other women before I even met you?"

"Don't be ridiculous," I huff. "It was just . . . clear how into you she was. She was hanging on your every word, Ezra."

"I'm still not following."

"You looked up and saw me, and you just . . . walked away from her. You barely even gave her an excuse. You just came over to me and started flirting with me. It was clear to me how little you appreciate a woman's attention, even then, so why would I be excited about the fact that I can't seem to stop being an idiot enough to stop giving you mine?"

He doesn't say anything for a long time, so long that I almost feel like *I'm* the one who's done something wrong.

"Well, say something," I urge.

"I never thought about you seeing it that way," he says, almost like he's only just considering it for the first time.

"Of course you didn't," I scoff. "Because that's all women are to you."

"Is that what you think?"

"What the hell else was I supposed to think?"

"Dani," he laughs, actually *laughs.* "I walked away from that woman whose face I can't even remember because from the second I saw you, for every fucking moment *since*—there hasn't been anyone in my head but *you.*" He laughs again. "You might as well live there now."

I feel the air rush out of my lungs, anything I might have been about to say spilling out of my head to leave me with no thoughts. Of all the things I thought Ezra might say, they hadn't even come close to *that.*

"Well," I say finally, my voice thick. "That's a good line, I'll give you that."

"No," he sighs. "It's just the truth. As exhausting as you are, I can't seem to stop chasing you. Even if I wish you'd do a bit of the chasing every once in a while."

I don't know what to say to that, and like the coward I'm beginning to suspect that I am, I change the subject.

"It's my turn," I say shakily.

"Right," he answers wearily. "Sorry. Go ahead."

"I just have one more," I tell him. "Request Number Seventeen. You objected on the basis that it *seeks information protected by attorney work product, attorney-client privilege, and/or materials prepared in anticipation of litigation.* You need to give me a privilege log if you're holding something back."

"Of course. I can do that."

"Good. Well."

I reach for my phone then, holding it close and feeling caught by the way I'm slowly becoming uncomfortable with the idea of this conversation ending like it's so obviously about to, without any real answers and still a wide void between us. One I'm not even sure I want anymore. Everything in my head is so messed up.

"Actually," I say quietly, unable to help myself. "One more thing."

Ezra sounds almost eager for it. "Yeah?"

"Has there been anyone else? Since we started doing this?"

I've never asked, and he's never offered. I know it makes me sound weak and needy, just like I know how much I've wondered about it does the same thing. But I can't help it. With everything he's told me tonight . . . I have to know.

Ezra's sigh is long and loud, and my fingers are shaking, holding the speaker close to my ear so I can't possibly miss his answer. "I told you, Dani," he says carefully. "I haven't been able to see anyone else but you since the night I laid eyes on you."

There's fear bubbling in my chest at his words, at the implication of them, but there's a giddiness there too. One that's foreign. One I don't know what to do with. "Yeah?"

"How could I?" His voice is lower now, and I close my eyes as it washes against my ear where I'm holding my phone close. "Everything about you is a fucking dream. You're so smart. Even when you're using that big brain to kick my ass, I'm in awe of you. You're so beautiful it damn near hurts to look at you. All I think about is touching you, tasting you. I can barely get anything done most days without thinking about it."

I swallow thickly, feeling a slow throb building between my legs despite everything. "What do you think about?"

"I think about the sounds you make when I'm inside you; they're so soft, like you don't want to let them go. It drives me crazy knowing you can't help it. That I'm the one making you lose that carefully crafted control you cling to."

I want to argue with him, it's always my first instinct, but surprisingly, there is an even more overwhelming urge to hear more.

"What else?"

"Your mouth. Not even about how soft it is, how good it feels on mine—although I do think about that a lot too—but just . . . you're so damned sharp, Dani. I've never met anyone who could go toe-to-toe with me like you do. I *never* know what to expect from you, and I fucking love it. Even when you're scowling at me, or cutting into me, all it makes me want to do is get closer to you. Honestly, I feel like maybe I'm some sort of masochist at this point."

I can't help the laugh that bubbles out of me. "Maybe you are."

"I think it's just you," he utters, breathy and soft. "You're in my head, and I don't know how to get you out. I don't even think I want to."

I suck in a breath; that throbbing between my legs is an allover sensation now. Especially in my chest. I would be afraid of it if I could feel anything outside the steady *thump thump* of my heart.

Neither of us says anything for a long time, and I suspect it's because neither of us knows *what* to say.

But it's Ezra who finally breaks the silence. "I should let you go."

"Oh." Why do I feel disappointed? "Right."

"I have an early morning," he explains. "Unfortunately."

Get a grip, Dani.

"Okay."

"What are the chances I could see you tomorrow night?"

"Slim," I tell him honestly. "I have dinner with my boss and the other partners."

"Sounds like a fun time."

"Mm-hmm."

Another long beat of silence before, "I guess I'll see you in court Friday?"

"I guess so."

I can't even tell if the long silences are awkward or not at this point.

"Okay," Ezra says. "Well—"

"Ezra," I blurt out, my voice tight.

His tone is expectant, eager again. "Yeah?"

"Me too," I fumble before clearing my throat to try again. "You're . . . in my head too."

This time the pause is a pregnant one, and I hold my breath waiting for an answer.

"Don't worry," he says, his voice warm and light. "I won't tell anyone."

I smile in spite of myself. "You'd better not."

"Good night, Dani."

"Night, Ezra."

I hang up first, before I say anything else that I might regret tomorrow. I wait for the embarrassment of my admission to come, but strangely, even several minutes after hanging up, it never does. Even stranger, the feeling that lingers long after I've tucked myself into bed, having replayed Ezra's and my conversation over and over in my head before succumbing to exhaustion—is dangerously close to anticipation.

And I have no idea what to do with that.

Seventeen

DANI

I TELL MYSELF that the nerves that have taken up residency in my belly are because of our first session in court this morning and *not* because it's the first time I will see Ezra since I fell asleep in his arms. It's not as true as I'd like it to be, but it keeps me from actively dry heaving into the umbrella holder outside the courtroom.

"Are you all right?"

I give Bianca a tight nod. "I'm fine."

"It does not inspire confidence for my attorney to appear more nervous than I am," she chuckles.

"I'm not nervous," I assure her, inserting false confidence into my voice. "I just want to make sure I have all my ducks in a row."

Her brow quirks with amusement as I flip through my notes. "I have faith in you, Danica." She peers into the open double doors to the courtroom where a few people are starting to shuffle in. "I think I will take my seat. Come inside when you have sorted your ducks."

Cool as a cucumber, Bianca Casiraghi. I could take several leaves out of her book. She breezes into the courtroom like the queen she is, and I watch her glide to her seat at our table at the front and sink into it with infallible grace. Despite the fluttering in my stomach, I can't help but smile.

"Thinking about me?"

I jolt when I find Ezra standing just beside me. "Don't do that."

"Do what?"

"Sneak up on me."

He cocks his brow, his mouth twitching. "In public?"

"Shut up," I mutter.

I can't help but let my eyes sweep down the length of him. His gray suit hugs him in a way that should be illegal, and I allow myself only a brief moment to appreciate it before I meet his gaze again.

"Where's your client?"

His lips purse. "Late."

"You didn't tell him that being fashionably late to your own divorce trial isn't looked upon favorably?"

"Tried." He shrugs, offering me a grin. "Guess there was a bit of a language barrier."

His smile makes the fluttering in my stomach spark up for reasons other than nerves. Has he always been this beautiful, or have I just never really allowed myself to appreciate it?

"You ready for today?"

"As I'll ever be," he muses.

"I'm looking forward to your cockamamie opening arguments."

His grin widens. "That's a ten-dollar word."

"I'm happy to give you a dictionary if it escapes you," I deadpan.

It doesn't hit me immediately that we're just standing outside the courtroom doors smiling at each other, but I can't pretend that this more familiar banter isn't comforting. Which is a word that I never thought I would use in regard to Ezra Hart in any capacity.

"We should go in," I say after a beat, clearing my throat and breaking eye contact to peek back into the courtroom. "I imagine we'll be starting soon."

"Probably," he agrees, even though he makes no move to go.

I catch him still looking at me when I turn back toward him, his gaze a caress. I suppress a shiver at the intensity of it, my chest feeling tight.

"About the other night . . ."

He perks up, seeming almost eager. "Yeah?"

"I just . . ." My teeth worry against my lower lip, and I don't miss the way his eyes flick there. "I just wanted to say that—"

"There you are," a gruff voice interrupts.

We both turn to catch Lorenzo striding up toward us, his lips turned down in a frown. He looks back and forth between us for a moment, finally deciding to ignore me completely as he gives me his back to face Ezra instead.

"We should go in," Lorenzo grunts.

Ezra's brow knits. "We should have gone in ten minutes ago, but you're late."

"I had business to attend to. I am here now. Shall we?"

He turns and saunters inside, and Ezra shares a look with me that says he thinks his client as much of an ass as I do, which I find very interesting.

I twist my face into a caricature of Lorenzo's expression, lowering my voice. "Shall we?"

It's not like me to be silly, but the beaming smile Ezra gives me makes it worth it. A revelation that takes me completely by surprise.

Who the fuck even am I lately?

"After you, Ms. Pierce," he says with a gentlemanly wave of his hand.

I feel him close behind when we enter the courtroom, and for the first time since I've known him . . . the thought doesn't irritate me.

"ONE HUNDRED AND twelve million dollars in assets, Your Honor, and yet Mr. Casiraghi is trying to hold my client to a parsimonious prenuptial agreement that we have more than enough evidence to prove is suspect. Mrs. Casiraghi is entitled to half of the assets as well as a reasonable continuing percentage of profits in his company."

We've been at it for nearly an hour, our opening arguments bleeding right into *actual* arguments that seem like they might never end, despite how badly I would like to end this session so that I can pick it back up later.

I hear the scrape of Ezra's chair as he stands from their table. "I'm sorry to interrupt, Ms. Pierce, but the evidence you're referring to is circumstantial at best." He turns to face Judge Harding, a stern woman in her sixties who delivers edicts like she's reading the weather. "Your Honor, there has been no solid evidence presented that my client has breached the terms of the prenuptial agreement that was set when he and Mrs. Casiraghi were first married. An agreement that *she* signed, I might add."

There's always been something slightly appealing about the air of confidence that Ezra projects, one that even the me before these past few weeks couldn't help but appreciate. Now though . . . Now it feels more charged. Like every authoritative word zings through my bloodstream, leaving me with an urge to give him my attention, to lean into his voice so that I can hear more of it.

Not exactly prudent for his opposing counsel, to be sure.

I tuck those feelings away, rolling my eyes at his assertions of a lack of evidence to prove Lorenzo's infidelity. I *know* that he knows it's bullshit, anyone with a working brain can see that, but I also know that it would be too easy for him to not drag me through the ringer, to not make me work for it. It just wouldn't be Ezra if he didn't.

"With all due respect," I counter sweetly, "I would venture to say that pages upon *pages* of salacious exchanges between Mr. Casiraghi and another woman can't be called anything less than solid evidence."

"As we've already discussed, Ms. Pierce," Ezra says calmly, tucking his hands in his pockets as if he's readying to take a leisurely stroll. "Those emails did not originate from Mr. Casiraghi. We have been conducting our own investigations in regard to who might have been using Mr. Casiraghi's computer without his knowledge."

"I'll bet," I scoff.

"Regardless," Ezra says smoothly. "Inconsequential exchanges that can't be proven in origin do not entitle Mrs. Casiraghi to over five hundred million dollars."

"Mrs. Casiraghi has offered over thirty years of moral support in regard to her husband's business," I argue. "One might even say that she is the reason that Mr. Casiraghi is where he is today."

"That is *outrageous*," Lorenzo growls suddenly, slamming his fist on their table. "Bianca had nothing to do with my success. This is just a silly game."

"I didn't?" I turn to catch Bianca's raised brow. "Who listened to your complaints night after night? Who hosted your silly parties for your terrible friends? Who was there, Lorenzo? Certainly not the woman you have been giving your tiny cock."

"Ma che *stronza*—"

Judge Harding bangs her gavel, silencing Lorenzo's insults. "Order!" She points at Ezra. "Mr. Hart, get your client under control." She shoots me a look. "Yours as well, Ms. Pierce."

"Yes, Your Honor," Ezra and I say back simultaneously.

"Now." Judge Harding nods at me. "You may continue, Ms. Pierce."

I try not to feel gleeful when I catch Ezra casting a chastising glance back at Lorenzo, keeping my attention on the judge instead. "Your Honor, it has also come to our attention that the account that Mr. Hart claims is shared by his client and an ailing relative has no concrete ties to anyone in his immediate family. Furthermore, we've discovered that the funds within that account are being used to pay for not one but *two* mortgages—one of which was not listed among Mr. Casiraghi's assets during disclosure."

Judge Harding laces her fingers together, turning her attention to Ezra. "Is that true, Mr. Hart?"

"Mr. Casiraghi holds the account in question so that he can deposit funds to be used at the discretion of his relative. It is not his responsibility to keep up with every purchase made with those funds."

"How convenient," I mutter. "Your Honor, it is our belief that this 'relative' mentioned is not a relative at all. In fact, we were just granted a subpoena to obtain financial records from the woman in question as well as a DNA test."

"A DNA test will be circumstantial at best," Ezra chimes in. "She is a relative by marriage. A close friend from childhood."

I cut my eyes to him, frowning. His answering smirk has me suppressing the urge to smile, weirdly enough. I can tell by the glint in his eyes that he's enjoying the back-and-forth between us.

"I'm sure," I say. "Nevertheless, we are confident that Ms. Kinsley, the woman Mr. Casiraghi claims is an ailing relative, will reveal that she has undergone no medical treatments. Not only that, but we believe there will be adequate proof within those records that will offer the 'solid evidence' that Mr. Hart mentioned. That they will substantiate our claims."

Judge Harding cocks her head. "Are you asking for a continuance, Ms. Pierce?"

"I am," I tell her confidently. "I ask that we reconvene in one week's time, which will give both parties ample time to review this new evidence once it is disclosed."

I don't look at Ezra while the judge considers, but I can feel his eyes on me. I am certain that he would like to argue with me, to find a reason as to why I shouldn't be granted this continuance, but for reasons I can't fathom, he doesn't. I can see him from the corner of my eye, still standing tall just outside my line of sight with his hands tucked in his pockets, watching me.

"All right," Judge Harding says finally, and I release a pent-up breath. "I will grant you your continuance. We will reconvene next Thursday to resume." She bangs the gavel. "Court is adjourned."

I peek over my shoulder at Bianca, and her red lips twist into a smile that oozes pride, which warms me in turn. I like making someone like Bianca proud. It feels monumental. I keep my eyes off Ezra as I return to our table to quietly discuss a meeting with Bianca the following day to talk through the evidence that was just relinquished to us this morning, giving myself the night to review it with Nate and Vera before corroborating with what Bianca might know.

I'm still gathering my things when Bianca leaves me, and when I get the opportunity to glance at the opposite side of the courtroom, I'm mildly surprised to find Ezra already gone. I close my briefcase as I peer over my shoulder, catching sight of him just outside the courtroom with a stoic expression as Lorenzo points a finger at his face. Ezra doesn't outwardly show his displeasure, not in a way anyone else might notice, but I do.

I can see it in the way his jaw is flexing subtly, the way his arms are crossed tight over his chest and his spine remains rigid. Everything about his posture screams discomfort. I move briskly between the rows of seats to close the distance between them and me, noticing Ezra's eyes flicking to mine as I approach.

"Counsel," I say blandly. "I was wondering if I might discuss something with you about disclosure?"

Lorenzo looks annoyed to have been interrupted, his face brightening with a flush of scarlet that makes me worried for his blood pressure, but he seems to drop the issue. He points a finger in Ezra's face once more, his voice tight. "Remember what I said, boy. Do better."

We both watch him stalk off, and I wait until he's well out of earshot before I blow out a breath.

"Wow, he seems like fun."

Ezra chuffs a dry laugh. "He's . . . something."

"You didn't fight me on the continuance," I point out. "Why?"

His brows raise. "Should I have?"

"It's not like you not to fight me on every little thing," I answer. "You're not taking it easy on me because of . . ."

His mouth quirking makes me scowl and sweat simultaneously. "Because of what, Dani?"

"You know what," I huff in exasperation. "I told you I don't want you acting differently."

"And I told you I would never," he assures me. "I admit I'm . . . curious about your new evidence. I would like the chance to review it as well before we dig into the meat of things."

Now it's my turn to raise my eyebrows. "You're not suggesting that you don't already have access to Lorenzo's mistress's finances, surely."

"Now, Dani," he teases. "Innocent until proven guilty, remember?"

I roll my eyes. "That doesn't answer my question."

"I'm sorry, I didn't actually hear a question."

"You're infuriating," I groan.

He leans in slightly, lowering his voice. "But you like it."

I step away instinctively, looking around us to make sure no one saw him whispering to me and only breathing in relief when I notice that the hall outside the courtroom is mostly empty.

"You don't have access to her finances already?"

His smile dissipates, leaving behind a pinched expression. "I don't think it's something I should be discussing with you."

Part of me is hurt by the assertion, but the more logical part of me knows that's ridiculous. First and foremost, we're here to do a job.

"I'll be sure to forward you everything when I'm finished compiling."

"Great," he says.

We both linger for a moment, and I shuffle my weight from one high-heeled foot to the other as I struggle for something more to say. Which only serves to make me chide myself for even feeling the need to find more to say in the first place.

"Big plans this weekend?"

I want to suck the words back in as soon as they leave my mouth. Could I *be* any more desperate? I don't know what the last week has done to me, but it's making me more and more disgusted with myself.

"My father is hosting a charity gala at his house," Ezra says with a flat tone.

"Ah. That sounds . . . fun."

"It sounds excruciating," he grumbles.

I find myself curious again as to what the story might be with the Hart men. The more clues left intermittently in conversation with Ezra, the more I suspect there are other pieces to the story than just a legal dynasty.

"At least the food will be good," I offer. I try for teasing. "I doubt there will be anything as good as my stepmother's party punch though."

Ezra laughs quietly. "I sincerely doubt it."

I can tell the moment his thoughts shift to the same place mine do, my cheeks heating as his eyes grow warm, no doubt remembering the last party we attended. If I'm being honest, I haven't *stopped* thinking about that party since I left it.

"You know . . ." He trails off, looking unsure. It's not something I'm used to seeing on him. "You could always crash it."

I bark out a laugh. "What?"

"You know." He shrugs. "Pay me back for crashing *your* family's party."

"Who said I wanted to pay you back?"

"Don't you always?"

Damn it. He has me there. It's very rare that I allow him to keep the upper hand if I can help it. Still.

"Something tells me *your* family's party won't be nearly as entertaining as mine," I chuckle.

His smile falters a bit, his gaze heavier. "No," he says quietly. "Definitely not. But . . . it could be. If you came, that is."

My pulse quickens at his thoughtful expression, and I have to swallow around the growing lump in my throat. "I swear to all that's holy, if you make an innuendo right now—"

"I would never," he insists, breaking out into an actual smile. It loosens something in my chest.

I consider for a moment, wondering what it would imply if I were to go like he's asking. There have been so many lines blurring between us lately . . . half the time I don't know which way is up. That alone tells me it's probably not a good idea.

"I don't know . . ." I frown at my feet. "I might be busy."

Ezra says nothing while I stare at my shoes like a coward, and when I finally chance a glance back up at him, I notice his expression is teeming with disappointment.

"Right," he says. "Well. If you change your mind . . . I'll make sure you're on the list."

We're standing still again, space between us that feels wide and yet too close, and I struggle for words, any words, that might cut the tension. But they never come.

"Anyway," Ezra says finally, beating me to the punch. "I have a meeting. I'll text you the details, yeah?"

"I didn't say I would come," I argue feebly.

Ezra's grin is warm and bright, and I feel it lighting up parts of me that have long been in the shadows, leaving me feeling exposed. "I'm learning that it's the things you *don't* say that I should be paying attention to, Dani. That's usually where your real feelings are."

My mouth gapes at his back as he casually turns to walk away, and I can't help but feel that for all the ground I gained in the courtroom today, I just lost a much larger battle outside of it.

The strangest part is how little I seem to mind.

Eighteen

DANI

"ARE YOU SURE we were invited?"

I catch Nate gaping at the crystal chandelier and open my mouth to answer, but Vera is one step ahead of me. "Technically, *you* weren't. You invited yourself."

"As if you didn't want me here," Nate huffs. "We're a threesome."

"Don't call us a threesome," I groan.

His brows knit. "A posse?"

"Not better," Vera sighs. "Also, inaccurate."

"I don't even know why *I'm* here," I hiss, linking my arm with Vera's to keep her close as we weave through a sea of crisp suits and idle chatter. "I must be insane."

"Pfft. We all know why you're here," Nate snorts. "And his name is—"

"If you like your balls," I warn, "I wouldn't finish that sentence."

"Testy," Nate tuts. He whips his head around, searching the area. "Isn't there supposed to be an open bar at these things?"

"I hope so," I mutter.

Nate tugs on Vera's other arm. "Let's go get our baby bird some liquid courage."

Vera arches her eyebrow. "Why do I have to go?"

"I only have two hands," Nate points out. "I can't carry everything."

She narrows her eyes suspiciously, but eventually unwinds her arm from mine before giving me a look. "Stay here. We'll be right back."

I watch them go, Nate already teasing Vera about something that's making her scowl. Her midnight-blue dress complements his navy suit perfectly, almost like they planned it, but I know if I were to point that out, they'd both kick me, most likely. Well, Vera would.

Stay here, I scoff internally. As if I know anyone here. It seems all of Alexander Hart's guests are over sixty, and none of them look nearly as friendly as my parents' work friends. Most of them look like they haven't smiled in years. It's daunting, and it makes me wonder again why I came.

When Ezra texted me details about the party as promised, my immediate urge was to blow it off, to assert again that I wouldn't be attending. But something about his expression when he'd told me about it, the almost eager tone of his messages when he asked . . . I couldn't seem to find it in me to say no to him. Which is nothing new, if I'm being honest. I'm just having a harder time pretending the urges aren't there now.

"Champagne?"

A pretty brunette in a vest and tie offers me a flute and a smile. I take one gingerly, returning her smile with a nod. "Thanks."

"Of course," she says back before continuing through the crowd.

I take a sip as I scan the groups of people littered about the wide ballroom, looking for signs of Nate and Vera. Knowing them, they're probably arguing at the bar over what to bring me. I'm *not* looking for golden-brown hair or a teasing grin, that's for sure.

Seriously, what am I doing here?

"Ah, Ms. Pierce," a dry voice says behind me.

I bristle as I turn, recognizing it. "Mr. Hart."

Alexander Hart looks the same as I last saw him—completely put together and just as cold. "I wasn't aware you were coming tonight."

"Neither was I," I answer coolly. "My invitation was last minute."

His grin isn't at all friendly, and I don't like the way his gaze travels down the length of my clingy, red dress. "Well, the more the merrier, I say. Anything for charity, am I right?"

"For charity," I echo. "Right."

"I assume Ezra invited you?"

"He did."

His eyes are calculating, and I keep my expression carefully blank.

"I hear you have been doing well representing dear Bianca," he remarks, bringing his own glass to his lips, his blue eyes still on me. "But you have always given Ezra a run for his money, haven't you."

"I try," I answer tightly.

"He must really . . . respect you," Alexander says with that same unkind smile. "It is rare for him to invite friends to these functions."

"I don't know if I would call us friends."

"Oh?" Alexander leans in closer, enough that I can smell his too-strong cologne. "What would you call yourselves then?"

"Dani."

I take a step back from Alexander to put distance between us, finding a very irritated-looking Ezra standing beside us. "Ezra."

He's gorgeous in his tailored black suit, his golden skin and hair seeming richer against the dark color. Even angry, his green eyes are hard to look away from. It's why I've always done my best not to look too deeply. I've always been afraid I might get lost there.

"I was just complimenting your . . . friend on her efforts with the Casiraghi case," Alexander explains. "Ah." He flashes me that creepy smile again. "But you said you are not friends, correct?"

"Senator Wilson is looking for you," Ezra tells his father evenly.

Alexander nods before winking at me, and I have to fight back the urge to shudder. "Duty calls, I suppose. It was good to see you, Ms. Pierce." He levels a stare at Ezra, clapping him on the shoulder. "Come say hi. The senator and his wife are big supporters."

"Sure," Ezra mutters sullenly.

I wait until he's gone to speak. "I know he's your dad, but that guy gives me the creeps."

"Yeah." Ezra's smile doesn't reach his eyes. "I didn't think you were coming."

"Neither did I," I tell him honestly.

Like his father's, Ezra's eyes sweep down the length of me, but this time, it fills me with heat instead of the chilled sensation Alexander left. "You look . . ." He pauses, working through a swallow, and I feel goose bumps creeping across my skin as he takes in my red silk dress. "You look amazing."

"Thanks," I say quietly. I clear my throat, looking past him at the room we're standing in. "This place is . . . something."

"Alexander has never been one for subtlety," Ezra tells me.

I nod. "I can see that."

"I'm really glad you came," he says in a low tone that's meant just for me. "I have to go talk to them, but . . . stay? I'll find you in a bit."

The old Dani would argue with him, would be bristling at him telling me what to do, even posed slightly like a question, but this Dani . . . she's nodding. Subtly, but still.

"Okay."

This time his smile feels more real, and it surprises me how much I enjoy seeing it.

"Good." He reaches to gently brush his fingers over my elbow, and even this slight touch is enough to fill my stomach with butterflies. "I'm glad you're here."

I open my mouth to answer, but the words won't come. This is all new territory for me. So I nod again, because it's all I can think to do. I watch him weave through the crowd, my eyes lingering on his back for far too long, long enough that I don't even know how much time has passed when I jolt at a hand on my shoulder.

"Where did you find champagne?" Nate quizzes. "I got you one of those Popsicle drinks you like."

I glance at the amaretto sour in his hand, grinning. "I guess it wasn't a complete mistake bringing you."

"Arguable," Vera says, sipping her cosmo.

Nate rolls his eyes. "We all know you both love me."

"Keep telling yourself that," Vera chuckles.

Nate takes a long draw from his whiskey glass, winking at her before making a satisfied sound. "So? Are we going to liven this party up? Hit the dance floor?"

"I will not be dancing," I say immediately.

Nate hooks his arm in mine, a feat as I am now holding two drinks. "Like hell you aren't." He shoots Vera a pointed look. "You too, grouchy."

"Call me grouchy again," Vera says with narrowed eyes.

Nate grins. "It's called foreplay, babe."

I can't help the laugh that bubbles out of me. One day, the two of them are either going to make each other very happy, or I'll be representing one of them for murder. No in-between.

"Whatever," Vera huffs. "One dance."

"That's the spirit," Nate cheers.

He looks down at me expectantly, and my eyes unconsciously flick to where Ezra disappeared briefly, tearing them away immediately after and downing the rest of my champagne before setting the glass on a nearby table.

"What the hell," I say.

Nate beams. Vera barely hides her smile.

I'm still trying not to look for Ezra.

DANCING TO A string quartet in a group of three people is just as difficult as it sounds, but Nate is nothing if not determined. His good humor has always been infectious, even though I hate to admit it, and by the time the third song ends, even Vera is laughing, albeit grudgingly.

"I need a break," I tell them both at the end of the song. "My feet are killing me."

"Never understand why you ladies wear those toe stranglers," Nate says.

I point at said toes. "I have to stay in shape for my side business on FeetFinder."

Nate wrinkles his nose. "I've seen your feet. Not sure you'd be killing it over there."

"Rude," I tsk. "I'll have you know I charge *per* toe."

He waves me off with a roll of his eyes. "Go take your break, Bilbo."

"Vera?" I shoot her a look. "You coming?"

Nate grabs her arm, pouting. "Don't be a square. You wore sensible shoes for a reason."

"I didn't have dancing with you in mind when I put on my shoes," she says with a hint of amusement in her tone.

He waggles his brows. "Be that as it may . . ."

"Fine," she huffs. "One more."

"That's my girl."

"I'm not your—"

"Yeah, yeah," he laughs.

I shake my head as they move further into the crowd of geriatric fat cats shuffling in a much less ostentatious manner than my friends, casting them one last grin before I weave my way out to the edge of the ballroom floor. There are still people lingering about; murmured conversations surround me on every side, and I'm struck with the realization that almost a half hour has passed since Ezra disappeared into the throng with his father.

I can't help but let my eyes pass over the sea of people, but he's nowhere to be found. No doubt still networking with Alexander. Although, after what I've seen of their interactions of late, I can't help but wonder if it's something Ezra actually *wants* to do or it's something expected of him. I don't know what's more surprising about the idea of it—the fact that it might be true, or the fact that I'm wondering about it in the first place.

The crowd only begins to thin when I manage to wander past

the ballroom and the foyer and the other open spaces all gated off for the party, slipping into the darker rooms beyond to explore. I don't foresee Alexander leaving his guests for even a minute, not when there's palms to be greased, so I assume that I'm relatively safe to snoop around.

Beyond the party spaces there is a sitting room that houses a grand piano and an array of expensive-looking art that is as tasteful as it is boring. Everything about the room feels sterile and cold, if I'm being honest. Nothing that really has me jonesing to hang around. I pause in the center of the room to slide my heels off, slipping the straps over my finger and letting them dangle at my side as I pad over the shiny wood floors into the next room.

There's a warm light in this one that comes from a hanging lamp in the corner, and it takes me several seconds of gawking at the wall-to-wall bookshelves before I notice a person tucked away in a plush chair underneath said lamp, holding an open book.

"Oh," I startle, no doubt looking guilty. "I'm sorry, I was just—"

The woman's mouth tilts in a soft smile, one that looks genuine and amused. "Bored of the party?"

"I . . ." She's still smiling, and her brow quirks in a conciliatory way. I puff out a breath, shrugging. "To tears, honestly."

She chuckles quietly, the sound musical. I take her in then— her golden hair and her warm skin—but it isn't until I notice the viridescent glow of her eyes in the lamplight that realization dawns on me.

"Are you Ezra's mother?"

She only looks surprised for a moment, her brow knitting together and her lips pursing before she gives me a slow nod. "I am. And you are . . . ?"

"Oh, sorry, I . . ." I'm all too aware I'm standing barefoot in a room I'm not supposed to be in, talking to the mother of the guy I'm seeing. Or . . . not seeing. Whatever we're doing. "I'm Danica Pierce. I work with your son." I wrinkle my nose. "Well, not *with* him. We work closely together." Jesus Christ. "We're at different firms." I want to die a little. "We've crossed paths."

"Ah." Her grin is knowing, but what she knows, I can't begin to say. "I don't meet many of Ezra's friends, so it's a pleasure, Danica."

"Dani," I correct. "Most people call me Dani."

"Dani," she echoes kindly. "I'm Jackie."

"It's nice to meet you," I answer somewhat awkwardly. Should I go? I should, right? "So . . ." Apparently, I'm not leaving yet. Call it curiosity. I glance around her cozy hideaway; it doesn't escape me that she's practically dressed for bed, not a charity gala. "Did you also get tired of the party?"

"Not exactly." She closes her book, letting it rest in her lap. "I don't really attend these functions anymore. Not for a long time."

"Lucky," I snort. "How did you manage that?"

She's still smiling when she turns her head toward her lap, but it feels less bright now. "Well, you know. We just agreed it was better that I not participate."

We?

I want to ask for clarification—I am a lawyer, after all—but something about the way she says it gives me pause. Like it's painful, something as simple as not attending a party. It makes me realize just how little I know about Ezra outside of what we do behind closed doors. The guilt that sets off is strange.

"So, you said you've worked with my son?" She blessedly

changes the subject. "If you're from another firm, does that mean you've been opposing counsel?"

"Oh, several times."

I must not do as good a job as I think schooling my features into something other than exasperation, because Jackie chuckles. "He can be trouble, can't he?"

Trouble.

If she only knew.

"That's one word for him," I mutter. I shoot her an apologetic glance. "No offense."

"He's a good boy," she tells me with affection in her voice. "He's just got a lot on his shoulders."

My mouth practically *itches* to ask for more on that, but I know that if Ezra finds out I was pumping his mother for information about him, I'll never live it down.

"He's a good lawyer," I feel the need to tell her. "Definitely giving me a run for my money in our current case."

Her eyes widen a fraction, her lips parting in surprise. "Oh! Dani! You're his opposing counsel on Lorenzo and Bianca's divorce, aren't you?"

"Yes?" I clear my throat of the question there. "I am."

"He spoke of you," she says, her eyes glittering.

The way my voice hitches is embarrassing. "He did?"

"He did," she laughs softly. "Said you're the only person he doesn't mind losing to."

My breath catches, and I can only hope she doesn't hear it. Why does knowing Ezra spoke to his mother about me make my chest feel tight? Part of me thinks I know the answer to that, but a larger part of me doesn't want to dig too deep.

"Well . . . I don't win *too* often," I admit.

Jackie just laughs again. "I know how stubborn my son is. Winning against him at all is a feat."

"Right." My lips curl, but there's an uneasiness in my stomach. Not from talking to her, but from what her words are making me feel. I avert my gaze, pointing lamely toward the door to the library. "I'd better go and find my friends. They'll be looking for me."

"Have fun out there," she calls after me. I turn my head to catch her wrinkled nose. "If you can manage it."

I laugh out loud, nodding. "I'll do my best."

I have to pause by the huge piano to put my shoes back on; I'm assuming it wouldn't be a good look to stumble back into Alexander's swanky party barefoot, and by the time I'm reaching the well-lit areas where voices are drifting from, I'm mostly ready to reenter the fray. Mostly. I guess it depends on how much longer Ezra is occupied.

Not that I'm *waiting* for him to find me. It's just that staying here while the person who invited me is too tied up to socialize seems silly. That's all it is.

If I repeat it enough, I might start to believe it.

I can see Vera and Nate looking for me from across the ballroom when I step back inside, and I lift my hand over my head in a half wave to get their attention. The pair of them start to slip through groups of people talking to meet me, and it isn't until I see Vera skid to a halt, her mouth parting slightly with what appears to be shock, that I stop walking toward them. I watch Nate cock his head in confusion at her stunned expression before turning my way, his eyes shifting just over my shoulder to something

I can't see. I'm about to turn and see what they're looking at when I hear him.

"Dani?"

I go still, feeling every muscle of my body lock up tight. I haven't heard that voice in years. In fact, the last time I heard it, it was breaking my fucking heart.

I turn slowly, half hoping I'm mistaken even though I know I'm not, that he's *here*—however unlikely that should be. He looks the same after all these years, his hair the color of chocolate, perfectly parted to one side, his lean form still tall enough to make me look up at him, his deep brown eyes still holding a smile that never seems to go away, one that makes you want to trust him, however foolishly.

I stand there in a stupor for far too many moments as I take in his tight smile that seems awkward, as I notice the blond woman clinging to his arm and looking at me with curious eyes. I almost choke on his name the first time, feeling it stuck in my throat for several seconds before—

"Grant?"

Nineteen

DANI

MY BRAIN IS several seconds behind on the uptake, still scrambling to piece together what circumstances would bring Grant Fuller here. *Here.* To Austin. A city that five years ago, he'd been all too eager to get out of.

"Dani," he says politely, as if he didn't walk out of my life and leave it in pieces. "It's so funny seeing you here."

"Funny," I echo blankly.

Not doing so hot in the words department.

I feel a hand at my elbow and look down to see Vera's manicured nails curling around my arm. "Dani," she murmurs. "Let's go."

"Vera," Grant says with a nod. "Good to see you again."

"I can't say I feel the same," she tells him dryly.

His brows lift, but he doesn't say anything. Vera is still tugging at my elbow.

"What are you doing here, Grant?"

I have to know. For some sick reason, my brain will not let me leave this spot until I do.

"Oh . . ." He shifts nervously. "We just moved back. A few months ago, actually. I work for Kellerman and Kross now."

"You moved back," I parrot.

He smiles down at the blonde beside him, the one I'd almost forgotten about, patting her hand. "Charlotte's family is from here, and my parents are still here . . . It just made sense."

My eyes flick to the woman beside him—*Charlotte*—watching as she extends her hand, one platinum curl falling into her honey-colored eyes as she smiles brightly at me. I reach to take it dumbly, noticing the enormous diamond on her finger.

"Charlotte Fuller," she tells me. "I'm Grant's wife."

I'm Grant's wife.

It rolls around in my head, hitting the sides of my skull like a Ping-Pong ball.

"Dani," Vera says again gently. "Let's—"

"There you are, sweetheart." A new voice breaks through the chaos swirling in my head. "Sorry I'm late. I was looking every-where for you." Ezra's hand is warmer than Vera's, superseding hers to slide up the back of my arm as he steps in close to press a kiss to my cheek. "I got held up."

"I—" My mouth is probably hanging open. Did Ezra just kiss my cheek in front of all these people? "Hi."

Ezra looks a lot more collected than I currently am. He turns to regard Grant casually, extending his hand with a cool smile. "Ezra Hart."

"Oh, right." Grant takes Ezra's to shake it. "I met your father earlier. Great man."

I'm not sure if anyone else notices the slight tic in Ezra's jaw, but I do. "That's what I hear," Ezra answers blandly. He looks down at me again, effectively ending any further conversation with Grant. "You owe me a dance, baby."

Baby?

If the floor didn't feel like it was spinning, I would have a *lot* to say about that. I'm almost positive I hear Nate choking on his tongue somewhere behind me. Ezra's eyes hold mine, and the gentle pleading there, as if he's silently asking for me to let him help, is enough to keep my mouth shut on the matter.

"Right," I manage, although I'm not sure how. I force a smile. "I was looking for you."

"You know how these old men are," Ezra chuckles. "Once they start talking about work . . . well. It's hard to get them to stop." He pulls me closer into his side, casting another glance at my ex. "It was good to meet you, Greg."

"Grant," he corrects with a frown.

Ezra just keeps smiling. "Right. Sorry." He looks down at me again. "Dani?"

"Oh." I clear my throat, shaking some of my shock off as I stand a little taller. I manage to hold my tight smile long enough to look at Grant without throwing up on my shoes. "It was good to see you again, Grant."

"You too, Dani," he answers with that same casual, polite tone. As if we didn't spend almost three years planning a future together.

I hardly have time to dwell on my swirling thoughts since Ezra is already pulling me away, and I allow myself to be dragged along behind him as he leads me toward the edge of the dance floor, closer to the foyer. There are fewer people here, only a handful tucked away in quiet conversation along the entryway, and Ezra pulls me into him, grasping my waist as he starts to move me in time to the music that still lilts into the room.

"Breathe, Dani," he murmurs.

I didn't even realize I wasn't until he said it. I inhale deeply just to let it out, my breath expelling in a shaky exhale. "Why did you do that?"

"You looked like you needed saving. Was I wrong?"

I swallow, acutely aware of his fingers trailing down the length of my arm, stopping at my hand to curl it in his so that he can bring it to his shoulder to rest there. I take another deep breath, shaking my head.

"You're not . . . *not* wrong."

"Want to talk about it?"

"Am I allowed to say no?"

Ezra's gaze is soft, searching my face. "You can always say no, Dani. But do you really want to?"

"I . . ." The air in my lungs seems to expand, making my chest tight, and that feeling of the room spinning hasn't entirely subsided. "Grant is my ex."

"I gathered," he offers gently.

I arch a brow. "How?"

"You looked . . . devastated. For a moment. I have to assume the only person who could put that look on your face is someone who hurt you very badly."

How does he know that? How is it that Ezra can take one look at me and see all the things I so desperately try to keep hidden?

We continue to sway, the warmth of his palm on my hip a soothing presence, and I let my eyes drop to his chest, focusing on the silk of his tie. "We met in college. He sat next to me in Civil Procedure. He was drenched from the rain. Looked like a wet puppy." My brow furrows, remembering. "He apologized for dripping all over the floor near my desk."

"How long were you together?"

"Right up into third year. We had all these plans . . . We were going to . . ." I feel the traitorous sting of tears prickling at the corners of my eyes, and my neck heats with embarrassment over letting Ezra see me this weak. "It's stupid."

"It's not stupid," Ezra says softly, soothingly. "Not if it makes you look like you do right now."

I shut my eyes tight, getting a handle on my emotions before opening them again. "He got a job offer from a big firm in Los Angeles. Someone his father had connections with." I laugh humorlessly. "Stupidly, when he first told me that he was going to take the job, I thought he was asking me to go with him."

"Dani . . ."

"He said that he needed to focus on his career," I bite out. "That he wouldn't be able to give me the *time* I deserved. He made it sound as if he were doing me some sort of *favor*."

It isn't lost on me that I'm allowing Ezra to hold me a little closer than I probably should, just like it doesn't escape me that I don't fight it when one large palm cups the back of my head, pulling me into his chest.

"I'm sorry," he says simply, his voice soft and full of meaning.

I nod into his suit jacket, not knowing what else there is I can do. "It's over now," I mumble against the fabric of his lapel. "*I'm* over it. I just . . . Seeing him . . . it took me off guard."

"Understandably."

"You really didn't have to save me," I sigh, pulling back to look at him. "I could have handled it."

Ezra's mouth turns up at the corner in a lopsided grin, and the sight of it almost steals my breath all over again. "Dani, I have no doubts that there isn't a single thing on *earth* that you need saving from, but . . ." He shrugs one shoulder. "I'm selfish. I couldn't stand to see you looking sad for another second."

The shock and the rawness of seeing Grant again begin to ebb away, my heart thudding with a new purpose as the weight of all the changes between Ezra and me that have been happening comes flooding back.

We're still moving to the quiet music, both of us staring at each other like we don't know how to look away, and my voice is barely there when it leaves me. "Why?"

"I think you know why, Dani," he sighs.

I worry that I do, but worse than that—I worry that his reasons might match mine now. I worry about what that means for us.

I turn my face to look at some bland painting of abstract grays and blacks hanging on the wall beside us, willing my cheeks to cool. "I met your mother earlier, by the way."

Ezra goes still, his feet coming to a halt as we both stop dancing. "What?"

I frown up at him. "Your mother. I met her."

"How?"

"I got bored in there, and I started exploring the other rooms, and I . . . I found her reading in the library."

Ezra remains still for another beat, finally pulling me back against him and resuming the slow shuffling of feet to the music. "I didn't know she was down here."

I remember his mother's words then, how she had said *we'd* decided it was better she not attend these things, and I can't help but wonder if that *we* includes Ezra.

"Why is she not at the party?"

Ezra lets out a heavy breath. "That's a . . . long and complicated story."

"One you can't tell me?"

He shakes his head. "One I'm not sure you'd care to hear."

"And why wouldn't I?"

His eyes flick to mine, a flash of regret there. "Because you'd have to actually care about me to want to hear all the dirty details of my shitty family."

His words hit me like a blow, my stomach flipping so hard he might as well have landed a fist there. But it's not *him* that has me feeling so bowled over, no, it's the heavy weight of knowing that he believes I don't care about him. It's the uncertainty of not knowing when I *started* to. Even if only a little.

"I care," I say after several moments, my voice barely a whisper.

Ezra's eyes find mine, holding them. "Do you."

"Don't make me say it again," I grumble.

His mouth twitches. "But it's so nice to hear."

"Ezra," I huff.

"It really is a very long story," he tells me. He looks past me to the ballroom, which is still filled to the brim with people. "One I'm not sure I should be talking about here."

"Well . . ." I bite my lip, shrugging. "I mean . . . we could leave. Surely you've networked enough."

Ezra grins at me. "Are you asking me to get out of here, Dani?"

"I'm *telling* you that I'm bored of this stupid party, and that you owe me a story."

"Hm." His gaze sweeps down my front, heating me. "And where do you propose we run off to?"

"You're really trying your best to make me tell you to piss off and forget it, huh?"

"Can you blame me for taking advantage? This might be the nicest you've ever been to me."

I roll my eyes. "I'm . . . nice."

"Sour Patch, you're as prickly as a cactus." And when I tense, he leans in, adding, "But I love that about you."

Heat tingles over my skin, lighting me up like a live wire. I'm not thinking about Grant at all now, miraculously. I can't. Not when Ezra is so close, looking at me like he is.

"It doesn't matter," I say breathlessly. "Let's just get out of here."

The talking is further from my mind now, a steady pulse building between my legs that seems to worsen with every lingering press of Ezra's hands on my body.

"You're forgetting one thing," he says.

I pause. "What?"

"I told you"—he leans in close, his lips *barely* grazing my ear—"that the next time I had you, it would be in bed. That I would get you for the whole night. That I would do *all* the things I've been dreaming about doing to you."

A shiver creeps down my spine, and I have to bite back an embarrassing sound.

"Do you remember, Dani?"

I manage to nod, albeit shakily. "I remember."

"Good." His fingers flex against my hip, his hand covering mine against his shoulder. "So that just leaves one question, doesn't it?"

I pull back, peering up at him in confusion. "What?"

His smile is wide and brilliant, and I feel it washing over me; for a moment, all the doubts and worries of my past and my present and even my future are obliterated by the brightness of his smile. He tilts his head to let his forehead rest against mine briefly, and his voice is low, so low that I feel it in my toes when he asks—

"Yours or mine?"

Twenty

EZRA

THERE IS STILL a nagging worry in the back of my head that she's going to bolt at any given moment. She was pensive on the drive over, texting back and forth with her friends, I assume to let them know she would be leaving with me. I'm still half-worried about her changing her mind even when we're walking through my front door, letting her in first and eyeing her back as I close it behind us to lock us inside.

Purrgood comes trotting out from the other side of the couch when he hears us, and Dani smiles immediately—stooping to scratch behind his ears as she murmurs soft praise to my husky little house cat, who leans into her touch like it's the best thing in the world.

Me too, buddy.

"Do you want something to drink?"

She peeks over her shoulder, watching as I unknot my tie to let it hang on either side of my collar. "What do you have?"

"Well, you don't strike me as a whiskey drinker, but I have

some tequila and vodka behind the wet bar. I could cut it with something if you want."

"You don't think I drink whiskey?"

I cock an eyebrow. "Do you?"

"I can do whiskey," she says primly, determination in her eyes.

I have to bite back a laugh. This woman will never turn down the chance to make something simple into a challenge. I get the feeling that even if I married this woman, I'd have to drag her down the aisle kicking and screaming.

That thought gives me pause, my chest fluttering, but I brush it away as I move to the wet bar with a smirk. "Whiskey it is."

"Your cat is getting huge," she remarks as she gives said cat more scratches.

"Don't fat-shame my roommate, Dani. It's rude."

She rolls her eyes. "You won't be saying that when you have to roll him to the litter box."

"I will get him the finest kitty wagon so he can drag himself around. He's his own man."

She shakes her head, but there's a tiny smile on her face as she gives Purrgood one final stroke down the length of his back before standing again. She crosses the space to come to rest on the other side of the bar, leaning on her elbows as she watches me pour two fingers of Jameson for her and myself.

"Thanks, bartender," she says as she takes her glass.

I pause before taking a drink, watching her bring the glass warily to her lips, sniffing the contents before taking a tentative sip. Her eyes scrunch immediately, and she makes a little sound of distaste that pulls a laugh out of me.

"Shut up," she grouses.

"You don't have to drink it."

She narrows her eyes, resolutely taking another slow sip.

I shake my head as I take a drink from my own glass, sighing in content after. "So. Tell me all your woes."

"Woes?"

I nod. "That's what you're supposed to do with a bartender. Spill all your secrets."

"*You're* the one who promised me a story. Are you stalling right now?"

I frown, hiding it behind my glass as I take another drink. I let the liquid linger in my mouth for a moment before allowing it to slide down my throat, relishing the burn as I consider. "Not necessarily . . . I'm just not sure where to even start."

"The beginning is usually a good place."

I ponder again what might come from telling Dani all the sordid secrets of the Hart family. It isn't that I don't trust her; on the contrary, I have an inkling that Dani might be the only person in my life I could trust with my burdens. I think I'm more worried that she might look at me differently. That when she realizes how deep the misery goes—it might chase her away. After gaining so much ground with her . . . the idea of it makes my stomach feel leaden. I wonder for a moment how on earth I might start this conversation; the *beginning* isn't so cut-and-dried. Not with this. I finally decide on the most important detail, the one everything else branches from.

"Alexander isn't my father."

She looks shocked at my admission, as I expected her to be, her lips parting and a furrow forming between her brows as she tries to process that information. "He . . . isn't?"

"I didn't always know," I explain, looking down into my glass as I swirl the amber liquid absently. "He was . . . distant when I was a kid, but I just assumed it was because I never lived up to Eli. Eli was perfect, and I . . ." I frown, remembering. "I was never that."

She clutches her glass in both hands, her fingers flexing against it almost like she's combating an urge to reach out and touch me. I sort of wish she would. Maybe it would make me feel less unsettled. I think this might actually be the first time I've ever talked about this out loud with anyone other than my mother.

Her voice is soft when she speaks again. "When did you find out?"

My jaw tightens. This is the hardest part to talk about. It's been fifteen years, and still my stomach twists when I think about the day my life came crashing down around me. I close my eyes, breathing in through my nostrils.

"I found out the day my mother attempted to take her own life."

I can't look at her when I hear her quiet gasp; I think I want to avoid the pity that's most likely in her eyes. It's not something I want from her. I don't want Dani to soften to me out of pity. I want her to . . . Shit. I don't even know what I want her to do.

"Ezra . . ." I finally open my eyes at the sound of her voice, but miraculously, it's not *pity* in her expression, not really. It's . . . gentler. It makes my chest hurt. "What happened?"

I sigh deeply, deciding to just lay it out in one go. "My father has always been a controlling bastard, but I'm told he was better when he and my mother first got married. Apparently, after Eli was born, he started having problems at the firm he was working with. There were allegations made about . . . Well. I can't even tell you what they were about. I've never been able to dig it up. All I know is that whatever was happening in Alexander's professional life started to put strain on his and my mother's marriage. She won't talk to me about it, but from what I've been able to gather from others . . . he became cruel. I guess it was always inside him, he just needed reasons to justify letting it out."

"And she . . . ?"

"She had an affair." I'm nodding, not really looking at her as I talk. "She was going to leave Alexander. She wasn't in love with my real father; honestly, from what I understand, it was just a one-night stand with some guy who was out of the picture before she could even take a pregnancy test, but Alexander found out. Since they hadn't been intimate in some time . . . he knew that I wasn't his kid."

"But she didn't leave," Dani ventures.

I shake my head. "She couldn't. I didn't learn about any of this until years later, but Alexander threatened to have Eli taken away from her. Even with all the shit he had going on at his firm, he had powerful friends in the business. Powerful enough that my mother feared he could actually do it. That she wouldn't ever get to see my brother again. Her soft heart couldn't stand the thought of it." I puff out a breath. "Plus, for whatever reason . . . She loved Alexander. I think maybe she *still* does, although I can't fathom why."

"How old were you when she . . . ?"

"Nineteen," I tell her, knowing exactly what she's asking. "Apparently, when I was finally off to college, my mother had a moment of clarity where she realized she and Alexander were never going to be the same. She didn't have to worry about him using her children against her anymore, so she attempted to leave. Again."

I shudder at the memory of a cold waiting room and anemic

lighting. "Alexander wasn't having it. He couldn't stand the thought of losing face with his peers, of them finding out his wife was leaving him for his own shitty behavior. He—"

I suck in a breath, and I don't even realize I'm shaking until I feel Dani's hand covering mine. The warmth of it is soothing, calming me, and I exhale slowly, needing to get this out. To tell *someone*, if only just this once.

"He locked her in her room," I tell her bleakly. "For *weeks*. I . . ." I make a disgusted sound. "I didn't even know. I was so busy enjoying my newfound freedom that I didn't even bother to check in with her. She was in that room for *weeks*, and I—"

Dani squeezes my hand. "You couldn't have known, Ezra."

"Regardless," I reply woodenly. "It all became too much for her. She . . . she had sleeping pills. She—"

I close my eyes, focusing on the weight of Dani's hand still clutching mine. I don't know if I'm grateful for the bar between us or angry at it. I'm not sure at this moment if her touching me more would soothe me or have me buckling from the bad memories.

"By the time I made it to the hospital, they'd coded her twice. There was a period where they didn't think she was going to pull through. Even when they got her stabilized, they said she'd suffered oxygen deprivation to her brain. She's . . . never been the same since."

"But . . . she seemed fine when we talked."

I shrug. "She has good days and bad days. Sometimes it's just like . . . she isn't there. She calls them her 'away days.'"

"Jesus." I look up to find her shaking her head in disbelief, and I wonder if she's regretting coming back with me now. "But . . . how did that lead to you finding out you weren't Alexander's son?"

A bitter laugh escapes me, and I let go of her to slump down over the bar, resting my face in my hands as the same sound bubbles up again. "He told me," I chuckle darkly. "He fucking *told* me. By the time I found out what had really happened to my mother, he'd already managed to get a conservatorship over her. Convinced a judge it was for her own safety. When I threatened to contest it . . . he told me everything. Not only that, he assured me that if I stepped one toe out of line, he'd have my mother thrown in some out-of-state facility and toss away the key."

I rub my temples, wishing I had a hell of a lot more to drink in my system than I currently have, too afraid to look up and see if Dani is regretting all of this. If she's realizing that I'm not nearly as put together as I appear to be, that I'm nothing more than a fraud.

So it's a surprise when I feel her arms sliding around my waist. I hadn't even heard her move.

"It wasn't your fault," she says quietly, her cheek resting on my shoulder.

"Wasn't it? I wasn't there when she needed me. I couldn't do a damned thing to get her out of that hellhole, and I've been doing whatever awful thing that man has told me to do ever since. I went to law school because he liked the strong front a *family* business presented. I use his bullshit defenses to help terrible people take advantage of their spouses. I let him use me to hurt people. People just like my mother. Who's the bad guy here?"

"*He* is," she says without missing a beat. "*Alexander* is the bad guy here, Ezra. He's a fucking monster."

"But I—"

"Did the only thing you could do to protect your mom. What else could you have done? You and I both know how hard it would be to break Alexander's legal hold over your mother. Without some sort of concrete evidence of him being unfit or being hazardous to her health . . . no judge is going to lift it."

"I know," I croak, voice tight. "I've looked into it a hundred times. I always end up hitting a wall. He's too good at being fucking awful."

"I'm sorry," she offers softly. "I didn't know."

I straighten, another harsh laugh falling out of my mouth. "What would have changed if you had? You would have still hated me. I would have just been a sad asshole instead of *only* an asshole."

"I . . ." Her perfect mouth pouts, her expression pensive. "I don't . . . *hate* you, Ezra. I don't think I've ever really *hated* you."

My mouth twitches. "You haven't?"

"If anything," she grumbles, "I've hated how much I *can't* seem to hate you."

"Careful, Dani," I tease. "Next thing you know you'll be writing me love songs."

She rolls her eyes, looking annoyed, and weirdly, it makes me feel lighter. Dani finding me unbearable is the only bit of normalcy in my life. *She's* the only normal thing in my life. It's only just hitting me that this is the case.

I turn to face her fully, bringing my palm to her cheek and letting my thumb trace back and forth there. "Thank you for listening."

"It only seemed fair," she mumbles. "You listened to my sad story."

"I guess neither of us are as untouchable as we pretend to be," I muse.

Her eyes are bright as she looks up at me, her lips inviting and soft looking as the briefest flash of her pink tongue darts out to wet them. I am suddenly struck with the overwhelming realization that she's still here. That I've told her every horrible thing that haunts me, and she didn't walk away. That has to mean something . . . right?

"I want to touch you," I tell her.

She frowns. "You are touching me."

"No." I shake my head, bracing myself. "I want to touch you and know that you'll still be here when I wake up in the morning. I want to touch you and make you realize that all I ever think about is touching you, that sometimes it's the only thing that gets me through the day. I want to touch you, Dani, and know that whatever this thing is between us . . . that you're in it with me."

I hold my breath as she stares at me in disbelief; I silently count the seconds that pass as I wait for her to say something, to say anything. I notice the slim column of her throat working with a swallow, and then by some miracle, by some act of divine intervention . . . Dani pushes up on her toes and presses her mouth to mine.

Her breath is warm and sweet as it washes over my lips. "I want you to touch me too," she whispers.

I won't waste another second.

Twenty-One

EZRA

I SLIDE MY hands over her shoulders and down her sides, the silky material of her dress slipping against my palms and so thin I can feel her shiver underneath. She leans into me when I cup my hands just under her ass, tugging her up and against me as she wraps her legs around my waist. No fighting, no protest . . . just her. It's the sweetest victory of my entire life.

Her arms go around my neck as I slant my mouth against hers, and I capture the soft, breathy sound she makes with my tongue, wishing I could tuck it away for safekeeping. I push my fingers through her soft, midnight tresses, which are clipped up in a twist, pulling the plastic bit free until her hair is spilling down around her face, tickling my cheeks as she pulls me closer.

"Bed?"

I gasp the word even as her teeth nibble at my lower lip; I pray she hasn't changed her mind.

"Bed," she breathes, nodding before diving back in to lave her tongue on mine.

I move as fast as I can with her in my arms toward the hall that leads to my bedroom, still half-worried that at any second she will come up for air and decide she doesn't want this. I kick open my bedroom door and carry her inside with purpose, never slowing until my knees bump against my mattress. Her arms loosen in their grip and her legs slowly unwind, and I can feel every inch of her lithe frame as it slides down the front of me, craning my neck to keep my mouth against hers until she's sitting at the edge of my bed.

The picture she paints—her dark hair wild, her gray eyes gleaming in the moonlight, the red silk of her dress stark against my white sheets—it's like something out of a dream. Which is entirely appropriate, since I've been dreaming about having her here, right here, for months. Now that she's here . . . there's almost an uncertainty coursing through me. Like I'm not sure how I want to touch her first.

Thankfully, Dani seems to have no such reservations.

She reaches for my belt, undoing it with nimble fingers before pulling it through the loops to toss it away. She isn't looking at me while she does this, her eyes trained on my zipper as she slides it down, the sound of it loud in the quiet of my bedroom. It doesn't feel right, not having her eyes. For so much of this . . . thing we've been doing, she's been adamant about not giving them to me. I was able to deal with it before, but it's harder now. Now that I've finally gotten her to stop pretending.

I brush my fingers under her chin just as she pulls apart the fabric of my slacks, and I tilt her face up to meet her gaze. Her pupils are blown wide, her irises a thin sliver around the dark discs, and her mouth is parted to release every sharp exhale that puffs from her. She looks just like I feel.

She closes her lips around my thumb and sucks it gently, only for a second, before releasing it, and I feel pleasure rush through my veins. I gulp in a breath when she shucks my pants down my thighs, still meeting my eyes as she leans in to flick her tongue against my stiff cock, which now bobs between us. A shiver creeps down my spine when her lips envelop the tip to suck, and I can't decide what's more arousing, the sight of her pink mouth wrapped around me or the heated stare she gives me while she does it. But as good as her mouth feels, it's not even in the top five on the list of things I've thought about doing to her if I ever had her in my bed.

There's too much of *her* to see and to touch to let myself get distracted by her exploring me.

There's a quiet sound of surprise that startles out of her when my hands curl under her arms, lifting her and hauling her further up the mattress until she flounces into the center. Her hair spreads around her, looking wild and untamed, and her teeth press against her lower lip as she watches me kick off my pants and underwear before kneeling on the bed near her feet. She watches every move—my fingers undoing the buttons of my dress shirt, the roll of my shoulders as I shrug out of it—even the quick pull of my undershirt as it drags up and over my head doesn't escape her gaze. When I'm left in nothing but my skin, her hands slide down her sides as if to reach for the hem of her dress, but I quickly bat them away, crawling over her to press my hands on either side of her hips.

She cocks a brow. "You don't want me naked?"

"I want to be the one who gets you naked," I tell her, slipping a thumb under the edge of her dress, which is gathered around her thighs. I don't even know who I'm talking to when I murmur, "You look like a fucking dream."

I drop my head to press my lips to her stomach, the silky material still covering her cool and smooth against my mouth. I push my hands over the outsides of her thighs, slowly moving higher and taking her dress right along with them. I don't stop; I ease it over her hips and her belly and eventually her breasts—leaving kisses along every inch of uncovered skin I can reach before I tug it over her arms and toss it to the floor.

"Jesus, Dani," I groan.

Her black bra is sheer, teasing the dusky tips of her nipples through the thin material, and when I tilt my head down, it's clear that her underwear were made to match. I feel almost feral taking her in, reveling in the fact that she isn't telling me to go faster, that she isn't pushing me toward the end. I trail a finger between the valley of her breasts and trace a path down and down—over her navel and along the edge of her panties, drawing a slow circle just over her slit where the fabric is already damp.

"Did you think of me when you picked these out?"

She makes an indignant sound. "No."

"Liar." I feel myself grinning; even here, underneath me, she's still Dani. I love that. "I bet you did. I bet you wondered what I would think of them when I saw them."

"Maybe I never intended for you to see them," she mutters.

"You didn't?" I tease her through the fabric, rubbing the crease of her with two fingers as she squirms from my touch. "You didn't buy these thinking about how I would lose my fucking mind? Seeing how wet you are for me even though I've barely touched you yet?"

Her eyes shut tight when I start to rub little circles around her clit through her underwear, and she bites her lip as her head tilts back.

"I think it's always been for me, Dani," I croon, pulling my hand away just to hook my fingers into the elastic waistband. I want to preen when she lifts her hips to help me rid her of them. "Even when you didn't want it to be. I think every single part of you has always been for me." I brush my palms over the insides of her thighs, parting them on the journey back up as blood rushes in my ears. "Or maybe that's just wishful thinking."

I hear her breath catch when I duck my head, her fingers carding through my hair and curling tight when my tongue first parts her. I curl my hands around her thighs to hold them open, peering up over the slopes of her body as I circle the swollen bud of her clit. Her breasts heave and her belly quivers, and her harsh grip in my hair is a welcome sting, her soft cries spurring me on, making my blood sing.

"*Ezra*," she cries out when I close my lips around her to suck. "*Yes.*"

I'm distantly aware that my nails must be biting into the soft expanse of her thighs, but part of me likes the idea of marking her, proving that she was here with me just like this. As if it's somehow possible to brand her as mine.

I hum against her clit as I take it into my mouth again and again in deep pulls, twirling the tip of my tongue against the tight bundle as her hips begin to undulate against my face. I'm struck with images of yanking her thighs over my face and letting her ride my tongue. I tell myself that there will be plenty of chances for that next time. Because there *will* be a next time.

Dani is maneuvering me where she wants me as it is, and I love feeling her let go, feeling her use me for her own pleasure. Her breath leaves her in a rush and ends in a whine, her skin trembling under my hands and her pussy warm and slick under my mouth, letting me know how close she is. How she's maybe seconds from coming all over my face.

Which means her cry is downright outraged when I pull away. "The fuck?"

I lift up, licking my lips and taking in her heaving chest and her dark eyes, which are looking back at me in irritation. I can't help but grin.

"Ezra, I swear to God, if you don't—"

I'm already crawling up her body before she opens her mouth, cutting off her words with mine as her garbled sentence ends on my tongue. It takes her a moment to melt into it, her indignation turning to pliancy as I let her taste herself in my kiss. I leave a soft peck before I pull back, catching the dreamy look on her face.

"I want to feel it," I rasp. "When you come." I kiss her cheek, feeling her shudder when I slide my length between her legs. "I want you to come all over my cock and my sheets so I'll still smell you there tomorrow."

She tilts her hips up to push me deeper against her, her warm breath puffing against my temple as she turns her face to graze her lips along my skin. My eyes roll back as the slick slide of her coats my shaft, my muscles tensing as I lose myself in the feel of her.

"Wait," I groan, her movements becoming so frantic that the crown of my cock almost notches against her entrance. "Condom."

I'm trying to move away from her toward my bedside table when she drags me back, wrapping her arms under my shoulders and holding me tight against her. "I—" Her throat works with a swallow. "I have an IUD," she whispers. "And I'm negative. If you . . ."

"So am I." The words tumble out of my mouth in a rush. "Are you sure?"

She narrows her eyes at me. "When am I ever not sure?"

"Right." My lips curl. "Yes, ma'am."

Her long legs hook around my thighs, urging me, and if I weren't also so damned impatient to get inside her, I might even tease her about her eagerness. As it is, I take her mouth again, petting her tongue with mine as I roll my hips against the wet warmth of her.

"I like you greedy for me," I tell her huskily.

A breathy sigh escapes her as I press against her, not pushing inside but teasing her. "Who said I'm greedy for you?"

"You aren't?" My lips trace her jaw, breathing in the warm scent of her skin. "You don't want my cock?"

"Ezra," she says through gritted teeth. "I swear—*fuck.*"

I slip inside her, giving her every inch slowly, making her feel each one. "Because I'm greedy for you, Dani," I manage tightly, the slick grip of her making my vision blur with how good it feels. "I'm so goddamned greedy for you that I'd keep you here like this for days if I could." I only linger for a minute when she's full of me, a low moan tearing out of me from the sensation of pulling back out. "*Fuck.* I'd keep you so full of me that you'd feel me every time you took a step."

"What makes you think"—she whimpers—"I'd let you do that?"

"Tell me you wouldn't," I huff, a stuttered chuckle escaping me as I kiss her throat. "Tell me you don't want to be full of my come." I snap my hips a little harder, enjoying the mewl it draws out of her. "Tell me you wouldn't let me fuck you like this for days."

A sharp laugh rushes from her, and I have about three seconds to recognize what's happening when she hoists all her weight to slam into my side, catching me off guard and rolling me to my back. I stare up at her in shock as she swings her leg over my hips, smirking at me from above as she slowly slides back down onto my cock.

"Who says I wouldn't be the one to fuck *you*?"

My palms graze her thighs, coming to rest at her waist so I can grip her there. "By all means," I say with a lazy grin. "I'm an equal opportunist sort of guy."

"Mm-hmm." Her lashes flutter as she pulls up and off my cock just to sink back down. "It should be a crime how good this feels."

I tilt my hips to meet her as she starts to ride me. "Can you say that again?"

"In your dreams," she sighs.

My smile falters as she moves faster, my lips parting as air rushes from my lungs. I roll my hips to meet every thrust, every wet glide of her pussy as she takes me inside again and again. Her nails bite into my abdomen as she braces herself, bouncing on my cock and taking what she needs from me while somehow giving me everything I need from her in return. It's everything I imagined it would be, having her here like this, it's *more*—and I have to fight to keep my eyes open at the onslaught of raw pleasure from her body, not wanting to miss a single second of this.

"That's it," I hum, curling my palms over her hips to grip her ass. "Take what you need, baby." There's a familiar pressure buzzing at the base of my spine, blooming outward and tingling down the length of my cock. "You feel so good."

She throws her head back, slipping her fingers between her legs and rubbing her clit frantically as she moves faster, *harder*—

and I grit my teeth, trying to keep the urge to come at bay. It seems fucking impossible with how good she feels, but I want to see her lose control first. I want to feel her coming on me, in my *bed*. I want to imprint that image on the back of my eyelids so I can revisit it whenever I want. I'm moving with her as well as I can, straining every muscle in my body to meet her thrust for thrust as wild, untethered sounds fill my bedroom, so many that I can't be sure which ones come from her and which come from me.

"Ezra," she gasps, digging her nails into my skin. "*Ezra*."

"Come for me, baby," I urge her breathily. "Come all over me."

"*Ah*."

She's trembling everywhere; her thighs are shaking and her body is drawn tight, and there is a gush that makes everything hotter, *wetter*—her pussy cinching around me so tight that it's involuntary, the way I follow her. I come with a shout, my hips bowing from the bed and lifting her with me as I grind against her hard, trying to get as deep as possible as I empty myself inside her still-quivering heat.

There are stars in my eyes when I settle back into the sheets, feeling boneless and spent. Dani must feel something similar; she drapes herself over me, allowing me to wrap my arms around her and hold her close even while I'm still half-inside her. I leave lazy kisses all over the side of her face; even being this close to her, it's like I can't get enough of touching her. Like I need to be connected to her even more than I already am.

I hum against her skin. "Did you pass out?"

"You wish you were that good," she snorts.

"Me? I was only worried about how . . . enthusiastic you were." I'm fully aware she can feel my grin against her cheek. "You must really like me."

"I will bite you," she grumbles into my shoulder.

"Mm. Promises, promises." She moves to shift off me, but I tug her back, keeping her close. "Oh, no," I chide. "You're staying right here."

"You cannot expect us to stay like this all night."

"Wow, all night? Presumptuous of you."

"I hate you."

I chuckle, nibbling at her throat. "No you don't."

"I might," she says with no bite.

"Nope. Besides, I fully intend to keep you here all night." I run my hand up and down the length of her spine idly. "You're not nearly as full of me as I'd like you to be."

"God," she groans. "You're going to be insufferable now, aren't you."

"Oh, the absolute worst."

"And here I thought you couldn't *get* any worse."

"Oh, I'm full of untapped potential, Ms. Pierce. Speaking of untapped potential . . ."

I reach to give a light smack to the soft swell of her backside, and she huffs out an amused sound.

"I think most would say that's been thoroughly tapped," she scoffs.

I push my fingers through her now-tangled hair, cradling her head and forcing it up so that she has to look at me. Her features are lax and sated, and to my surprise, there is a soft smile on her face despite all her grousing. She's so fucking stunning. All of her. I wonder how I ever thought I would be able to be just casual with someone like Dani. She's the kind of person who leaves a mark, an impression that never really fades, and she's marked me up good.

Not that I'm complaining.

I lift my head, brushing my lips against hers briefly before leaning back to rest against the bed once more. "Tell me you'll stay the night."

I don't miss the flicker of indecision in her eyes, but I imagine it will take more than one good night to chase away all of Dani's fight-or-flight instincts. I'm happy to wait as long as it takes.

"I'll stay," she says finally, quietly.

"Good." I beam up at her. "I told you, Dani. I have a whole list of things I've wanted to do to you." I slide my thumb across her lower lip, meeting her gaze. "And I'm nowhere near done with you."

I have a swelling feeling that I never will be.

But I definitely don't tell her that.

Twenty-Two

DANI

IT TAKES ME a moment to realize that I'm not in my own bed. I nuzzle my face against sheets that feel like they have a higher thread count than my functioning brain cells at this hour, reaching beside myself blindly to grab a pillow. I roughly tug it over my face to block out the sun, thinking a few more minutes of sleep won't hurt.

Then I smell the bacon.

I shoot up in bed, the events of last night coming back to me in a rush. The sudden movement jostles a very fat ball of gray fur, Purrgood blinking at me with a look of disdain that only a cat can give, his back arching for a moment before he settles back into the sheets, looking miffed that I dared to disturb him.

"Excuse me, Your Highness," I mutter, reaching to scratch behind his ears as I take in the room.

In the light of day, Ezra's room seems much bigger than it did last night. Granted, I didn't see beyond the bed, but still. The walls are painted a warm sienna, the mahogany furniture staged neatly. It's masculine and very bachelor-playboy-esque—all the things I thought Ezra to be before last night. Or maybe I've been realizing for a while that he was more than I first thought him to be, and last night just put a period on the thought.

I pull the sheets up to cover myself as I rub the sleep from my eyes, Ezra's confession about his fucked-up family flooding back into my thoughts. *Nothing* about any of what he'd told me had even been in the realm of what I'd considered possible when I happened to spare thoughts about Ezra's family, and knowing what I know now, it almost makes me feel . . . guilty. For all the times I've spit venom at him for his less-than-savory methods. Had he ever even had a choice in them?

And then there was after.

A shiver passes through me as I remember everything *else* that happened last night, things that happened more than once, truth be told. God, I'm sore. My thighs ache and my core feels tight, but when I press my hand over my navel, all I can focus on is the fluttering that comes with the memories of all the things we did in this bed the night prior. And what's more . . . I'm acutely aware of how I can't dredge up even a single regret, not even the slightest urge to stomp into the other room and convince Ezra that it was a mistake, that it won't be happening again.

There's a sweet smell wafting in now to mingle with the easily recognizable one of sizzling bacon, and my stomach rumbles as if on instinct. I'm sure Ezra would be thrilled to comment on the appetite we worked up together. I'm already rolling my eyes at the thought.

I steal his dress shirt from the floor, throwing it on and buttoning several of the buttons before slipping back into my underwear. I won't be invited to Fashion Week anytime soon, but it

beats cramming myself into last night's dress. I check my appearance in the mirror in the attached bathroom, grimacing at the
black streaks under my eyes, a clear sign of someone who has
been thoroughly debauched. I clean them as best as I can with
Ezra's soap, deciding that it's the best I can do given the circumstances. I swipe some of his toothpaste afterward and brush my
teeth with my finger, not quite satisfied with this either, but Ezra
is just going to have to take it or leave it.

Purrgood has migrated to the edge of the bed when I step out
of the bathroom, plopping down from the mattress with a soft
thud that speaks of his heft. Seriously, this cat has a primordial
pouch that drags on the ground. He rubs my legs in the doorway,
and seeing as I can't seem to say no to *either* of the men in this
apartment, I stoop to pick him up and cradle him to my chest,
petting his back. I leave Ezra's bedroom and wander back down
the hall toward the open space of the living room, immediately
spotting Ezra's broad back behind the island. He's bent over the
stove, working quietly on what I have to assume is our breakfast.

No one has made me breakfast since Grant. I don't know how
to feel about that.

He hears me coming by the time I'm passing the back of the
couch, turning to flash me an easy smile. "Morning." He gestures
to the pan he's holding by the handle. "I didn't know how you
liked your eggs, but I figured scrambled is pretty standard."

"Did you make pancakes?"

"From scratch," he tells me proudly.

He abandons the pan for a moment, circling the kitchen island and reaching to cup my face in his hands so that he can steal
a slow kiss. Which leads to more fluttering in my stomach.

"I like you in my clothes," he murmurs against my mouth.

"Well, it was this or nothing."

"Mm. That's a real Sophie's choice." He notices his roommate in my arms. "Should I be jealous?"

I shrug one shoulder. "Well, Purrgood would never leave a lady alone in his bed, I'm sure."

"Someone had to cook the lady breakfast to try to entice her to stay longer."

"Oh, is that your ploy?"

"I don't know, is it working?"

My eyes dart to the stove, where the delicious smells are originating from, my lips pursing. Ezra laughs, knowing he's won. He pecks another swift kiss against my mouth, abandoning me on admittedly swaying feet as he goes back to the stove. I let Purrgood down on the floor, and he trots off lazily as I slip into one of the seats at the island, leaning on my elbow to watch him.

It seems wholly unfair that I woke up looking like a drowned rat, and yet Ezra seems to simply . . . *own* that "just out of bed" look. His golden hair looks tantalizingly mussed, which makes me think about the number of times I tugged on it with my fingers. His worn, thin T-shirt clings to the sculpted lines of his shoulders perfectly, which makes me think about how I traced some of those lines with my tongue. Even the way his flannel pajama bottoms hug his ass sends me on a downward spiral of dirty memories. It could become a real problem if I don't get a handle on it quickly.

"Smells good," I comment.

He shoots me another grin over his shoulder. "I figured you'd need the fuel after last night."

"Oh, did you," I answer dryly.

"Definitely." He nods down at the stove before peeking at me again with a smirk. "Especially with all the snoring you did."

"I do *not* snore," I scoff.

"Oh, you snore, Dani. Like a hibernating bear." Another smile for my trouble. "But a very cute bear."

"I hate you," I grumble.

He blows me a kiss. "Gonna be a tougher sell on that after last night."

"Whatever."

"How many pancakes?"

"Just one." He shoots me a look, and I roll my eyes. "Fine, *fine.* Two."

He slides two pancakes onto a plate, adding eggs and bacon to the side before pushing it in front of me and dropping the bottle of syrup just beside a glass of orange juice. I slather on a lot more syrup than necessary; my usual breakfast consists of protein bars or egg-white omelets whenever I have the time, and I have to admit, after all the . . . activity last night, the more indulgent breakfast is exactly what I didn't know I needed. I pop a bite of pancake into my mouth, chewing for a moment before a satisfied moan slips out.

"Oh my God."

Ezra looks smug as he takes the seat beside me at the island. "Wow, I don't think you made noises like that last night."

"Maybe you need to up your game," I tell him through a mouthful of pancake.

He drapes his hand over the back of my neck, his thumb rubbing there and leaving goose bumps in its wake. "I think we both know my game was just fine."

"I refuse to feed your ego," I mutter after far too many seconds recovering from his touch.

"Of course not," he chuckles before digging into his own food.

We eat in silence for a few minutes, each one making me feel increasingly more nervous about this whole thing. It hadn't hit me yet what last night really means, and now I'm sitting here wondering what in the hell we are, what we're doing, what will happen next.

"I can practically hear you thinking," Ezra says.

I peek at him from the side. "No you can't."

"You're second-guessing everything."

I pause. Am I? I consider this, deciding that's not entirely true. "Not . . . second-guessing. No. Just assessing."

"Evaluating the evidence?"

"What evidence?"

"Hm." He pushes his plate away, turning in his seat to lean on the counter with one arm. He uses his other hand to hold up one finger. "Item one: You stayed the night." He holds up another finger. "Item two: You're eating breakfast with me without threatening me with bodily harm—"

"There's still time," I snort.

"And item three . . ." His lips curl in a blinding smile, one that makes my stomach twist. "You totally like me, Dani."

I stare at him, stunned, torn between wanting to lash out at his arrogance and kiss the stupid smile off his face. Maybe both. Has it always been both? "That evidence seems circumstantial."

"Oh, I have several cited sources."

"I'm afraid I'm going to have to object."

"Oh?" His fingers find my hip, teasing me where his shirt has rucked up from the way I'm sitting. "On what grounds?"

"It's speculative."

"Hmm."

He leans in, and I don't fight it, don't even attempt to pull away from his mouth on mine. My lashes flutter as his lips move languidly, his mouth tasting of syrup and appropriately giving me a rush that goes straight to my head. I'm a little dazed when he pulls away, and it's clear that I'm fighting a losing battle here.

"Overruled, I'd say," he says softly, his green eyes shining with amusement.

I blow out a breath, running my fingers through my slightly tangled hair. "This is crazy, Ezra."

"Is it?"

"We're opposing counsel."

"Yeah, but fighting is sort of foreplay for us. I don't foresee that being a problem."

I narrow my eyes, but I can't exactly disagree. "I'm still going to do everything I can to win."

"I would expect nothing less, Dani." He takes a sip from his glass of juice, shrugging. "It's just a job. It doesn't have to have any bearing on what we do outside of the courtroom."

"And your fa—" I frown, correcting myself. "What about Alexander?"

Ezra's jaw tenses. "Probably best to keep it from him. At least for now."

There's a crackle of tension as we're both most likely remembering what he told me last night, and the instinct to soothe him is powerful. I give in to it, sliding my hand over his knee. "I'm . . . sorry, Ezra. About your mother. About all of it."

"It's just . . . how things are," he says with a sigh. "My mother has to *want* to leave him for there to be any real change. Half the time, she's still convinced that she deserves this. Not to mention that she's still clinging to the way things used to be. He practically has her constantly begging for scraps of his affection."

"That's . . . tough."

"Right," he huffs. "Be grateful your parents are so well adjusted postdivorce. I'm jealous of how well they get along."

I bristle, feeling irritated by his casual assessment but then guilty for even feeling that way. Sure, I have hang-ups about my parents, but my experience is *nothing* compared to Ezra's. Honestly, the entire thing with his mother is casting a new perspective on my situation.

"You know," I tell him, wanting to give him something after everything he's shared with me. "I was so mad at them for so long."

"Because of the divorce?"

I shake my head. "No, I . . ." I breathe out a sigh. "They lied to me. For *years*, they let me believe they were the happiest couple that ever existed. It was all a fucking lie."

"People fall out of love all the time. It's not uncommon for couples to try to make it work for the child."

I laugh derisively. "There was no 'falling out of love,'" I tell him. "My parents were best friends growing up. Both of their dads were alcoholics, and they lived near each other. They spent most of their lives taking care of each other. Then in college . . ." I feel his hand cover mine where it's still resting on his knee, squeezing gently. It makes it easier to keep talking. "They thought maybe they were supposed to be more. They realized after one night that the love they had for each other was nothing more than friendship, that it never would be, and that *should* have been that, but . . ."

"They had you," he offers gently.

I nod. "They thought it would be easy to raise me together.

Neither of them had ever dated seriously, so to them, marrying their best friend and giving their child a two-parent household—something neither of them ever had—seemed like a good idea at the time."

"When did you find out?"

"I found the divorce paperwork the day of my high school graduation. They didn't mean for me to find out that way, but after . . . they sat me down and basically told me that my entire life was a lie. That they'd spent all those years together because of *me*." I cast him a forlorn glance. "I stole half their life from them."

"Hey." His fingers tighten around my hand, and he leans in closer. "No, you didn't. They're adults, and they made a choice because they loved you. None of that falls on you."

"Maybe you're right. I've just . . . I've been so angry for so long."

"Well . . . I can promise you this, Dani," he says gently. "There are worse things than having parents who love you *too* much."

I wince. "God, I'm sorry. I'm babbling about this stupid shit when you're—"

"No. None of that. My experience doesn't trump yours. Everyone's allowed to process their pain. Understand?"

I let out a watery laugh, reaching to wipe my eye. "You are sounding dangerously wise."

"Don't worry, I'll go back to being an intolerable asshole by tomorrow, I'm sure."

"Unfortunately, you keep getting more tolerable by the minute."

"Wow." He barks out a laugh. "Did you read that off of a Hallmark card?"

"Yeah, well, you're not the only one well versed in being an intolerable asshole, I guess."

"But I like you prickly, Sour Patch," he says with a kiss on my cheek.

I shrug him off. "I don't like that the nickname is becoming a thing."

"Well, obviously I will take your request into consideration."

"I'm sure you will," I deadpan.

"Enough trauma bonding," he tells me pointedly, gesturing at my plate. "Finish your food before it gets cold."

"Yes, sir," I huff.

He winks at me. "I could get used to that."

I shake my head, stabbing my fork into my pancake and biting back the urge to laugh.

"I wouldn't."

There is another stretch of comfortable silence between us, and it isn't until I hear the clatter of Ezra's fork against his plate that he speaks again. "But we're . . ." His brow furrows, his teeth worrying at his lip as if he's truly bothered by whatever he's thinking. "I'm not crazy, right? There is something here. Between you and me."

I regard him carefully, quickly passing over his emerald eyes, which are all too easy to get lost in, and his full mouth, which I never really stop thinking about, and all the wild things that come out of it that never fail to make me fume or flush, and—

"No," I answer honestly. "You're not crazy."

He beams. "Practically a marriage proposal, coming from you."

"Don't get ahead of yourself."

"Oh, I'm already picking out china patterns."

"Of course you are."

"Mm. I'm thinking a June wedding. It'll be a lavish affair."

I wrinkle my nose. "Yuck. All those people? No thank you."

"Not a fan of big weddings?"

"Absolutely not," I scoff. "I'd rather get married at the court-house on a random Tuesday."

"How romantic."

"That is what they say about me."

"Mm. You're as romantic as they come, baby."

"Is that another endearment we are set on?"

He gives me a mock pout. "You don't want to be my baby?"

"You're being purposefully infuriating."

"There's no one I want to purposefully infuriate more than you, Dani."

It's a ridiculous statement, but I feel my cheeks heat all the same. I shove another forkful of eggs into my mouth to save me from answering, pointedly looking away from him.

"Do you have to go in today?"

I shake my head. "No. Although I'm sure Nate and Vera will be tracking me down at some point."

"Sounds like we have plenty of time to shower then."

"We?"

"Oh, yeah. It's another tick off my top-ten list." He gestures to my plate. "If you hurry, I'll let you wash my back."

I wrinkle my nose. "I am not washing your back."

He grabs his plate from the counter, slipping from his seat and moving around me as if to take it to the sink. He pauses on the other side of me, leaning in close to let his lips hover against my jaw.

"Mm, but I'd be happy to wash yours," he murmurs. His mouth presses a chaste kiss to my skin. "And something tells me it won't take much convincing for you to return the favor."

I say nothing as he saunters off with his plate, not trusting myself to answer.

Especially since he's probably right.

Twenty-Three

DANI

I'VE HAD MORE than twenty-four hours to prepare myself for what will surely be a full-on onslaught when I arrive at the firm on Monday, but I should have known it wouldn't be enough. Something that is made evident to me within five seconds of stepping down the hall.

"Danica Joan Pierce!"

I wince at the use of my middle name. My mother has been and always will be a die-hard fan of the Runaways. I suppose there are worse things to be named after than the queen of rock and roll.

"Lots of work to do," I call over my shoulder as I start an awkward maneuver toward my office that is somewhere between skipping and trotting.

I can hear twin sets of footprints hot on my tail. "Dani!"

I actually try to slam the door on the pair of them, but Nate shoves his foot in the space to stop me. "Ow! Really? What are we, seven?"

"Seven would be a step up for you," Vera snarks.

Nate's hand grips the edge of the door. "You've been ignoring our texts. Do you have no respect for our group chat?"

"I haven't been *ignoring* you," I lie weakly.

Vera shoves her shoulder against Nate's hand and peeks around the door. "We haven't heard from you since you abandoned us in the less-fun version of the Boddy Estate."

"Are you implying that murder makes a place more fun?" I ask with an arched brow, finally easing the door open wider.

"Well," Vera huffs, following Nate into my office. "A murder investigation would have been a hell of a lot more fun than the string quartet."

Nate scowls, pointing a finger at Vera. "Stop making references I don't understand." He turns to aim that finger at me. "Tell us what happened between you and Ezra or else."

"Or else?" I cross my arms. "Really?"

"I'll make Vera rough you up," he warns.

Vera rounds on him. "I'm not your muscle."

"She listens to you!" he huffs, throwing up his arms.

"Guys," I sigh, sinking down to the edge of my desk, resting my hands on the edge. "Shut up."

"Come *on*," Nate practically whines, like he isn't a thirty-five-year-old man. "You know how I get when nobody will let me in on the gossip. Do you want that for us? Do you want to subject all of us to that?"

"Because it would be my fault," I muse.

Nate throws up his hands. "Well, obviously."

"He's not wrong," Vera chimes in.

I tilt my head back, puffing out a long breath between my lips. "You two are the worst gossips I have ever met."

"Don't lump me in with him," Vera tuts.

"Oh shut up," Nate says with a cluck of his tongue. "You've been champing at the bit just as much as I have."

"*Fine*," I sigh. "I went home with him."

"Obviously," Nate snorts. "Did you . . . ?"

"I think that much is also obvious," I respond dryly.

"You're being infuriatingly vague," he quips.

I roll my eyes. "How dare I be vague with my own business."

"Oh, for fuck's sake, you tease," Vera scoffs. "Are you guys a thing or not?"

My eyes go round at her cross tone, and I realize she is definitely just as invested in this as Nate is. They really are more alike than they give themselves credit for.

"We're not . . . *not* a thing," I offer. "Maybe." I tilt forward, slipping off my desk just to start pacing. "I don't know. I don't know what the fuck we are."

"Oh God," Nate groans. "She's going to marry him. We're all going to end up working for Ezra Hart. They'll call her the Heartbreak Princess. Or will it be queen? What happens when you marry a prince?"

"Shut up, Nate," Vera and I both say in unison.

Vera tilts her head at me. "Seriously, are you okay?"

"Of course I'm okay," I say too quickly.

Vera's look is imperious, and I cave.

"Okay," I try again. "I'm freaking out a little."

Vera nods. "There it is."

"I just . . ." I stop pacing, running my fingers through my hair. "I hated him, you know? Or at least, I thought I did. I mean, the sex was always good, but spending time with him was never at the top of my to-do list."

Nate leans in like I'm telling his favorite bedtime story. "But . . . ?"

"*But*, I . . . I don't know. He's . . . I just . . ." I shake my head. "I've realized I haven't been fair to him."

"A duchess," Vera says.

I cock an eyebrow. "What?"

"That's what happens when you marry a prince," she clarifies. "You become a duchess."

"Duchess Dani," Nate croons.

"I hate both of you," I grumble.

"You hated Ezra too," Nate teases. "Does that mean we'll all be a . . . would it be a quadruple?"

"Okay." I nod heavily. "Out. Both of you. I have work to do."

"You have court this afternoon," Vera points out.

"I'm well aware."

"What are you going to do?"

"I'm going to do what I always do."

Nate makes a face. "But . . . you're up against your boyfriend now."

"He's not my—" I close my eyes, taking a breath. "Listen, when I know something, you guys will be the first to know."

"Somehow I doubt that," Nate tuts, turning on his heel and muttering the whole way out of my office. "No respect for the group chat, I swear."

"Go on now," I urge.

"Just be careful," Vera says before she steps out. "I don't want to see this blow up in your face."

"I'm always careful," I assure her.

Her lips curl in a grin. "I know."

Her words stay with me even as she shuts the door behind her;

the truth is, my head is *full* of worry. There are a thousand things that could go wrong, a million ways that pursuing anything deeper with Ezra could blow up in my face. But after last night . . . I'm just not sure I have it in me to pretend anymore that I don't want him anyway.

I WOULD LIKE to say that I did exactly as I told Vera I would, that I was perfectly normal and on my game during court today. But I hadn't expected to be so much more . . . *aware* of Ezra than I already was. Before, his authoritative confidence in the courtroom was a point of annoyance for me, and maybe it still is, to a degree, but also . . . now it also sort of turns me on. Something I *definitely* didn't expect. More than once today, there were moments when I didn't respond as succinctly as I should have, that I caught myself watching him work with an intensity that had me forgetting myself.

Definitely not good for business.

Now, I'm browsing my notes on my couch hours after court ended—my faded University of Texas T-shirt and a very large glass of wine providing comfort after a long day. We're still waiting on a subpoena for Lorenzo's mistress to be approved, Ezra's team blocking it at every turn, but I'm confident that it will happen. I feel it in my gut that none of Ezra's silly defenses will work this time.

That gives me pause, remembering that they are more than likely not *Ezra's* silly defenses. That there is a good chance that every lowball tactic he's used has come straight from his father— or, well, Alexander. It's all so much to wrap my head around. I catch myself thinking about his mother, something I have been doing a lot since that night at his place when he confessed every-thing, and there is a panging sense of regret that rings through me when I think of the quiet, lonely-looking woman I spoke with in Alexander's library. When I think about how much she's been through, how much *Ezra* has been through. I know that the chances of helping her when Ezra has most likely exhausted all possible avenues already are slim, but it doesn't stop me from wishing I could anyway.

My phone buzzes on the coffee table by my couch, pulling me out of my thoughts, and I lean to snatch it up, my pulse quicken-ing when I read the recently changed name.

Ezra: Are you busy right now?

I glance at my notes and my glass of wine, knowing it's prob-ably better that I say yes. That I should probably put a little space between Ezra and me while we're still figuring this out. Except . . . I don't *want* to.

Me: Not overwhelmingly. Just going over some notes.

His reply comes through immediately.

Ezra: Can I come over?

I bite my lip. It's strange, the way my entire body perks up at the idea of seeing him, and if I analyze it for too long, I know that I will have to face the fact that it's *always* reacted this way to Ezra. That it's just the rest of me that's finally catching up.

Me: Sure.

Ezra: Good. I'm outside your door.

I sit up straight to eye my closed apartment door, gaping at it for only a second before scrambling off my couch and rushing across the room to wrench it open. And he's there, just like he said, dressed in jeans and a heathered Yankees T-shirt and leaning on my doorframe with his phone still in his hand.

"What if I'd said I was busy?"

He shrugs one shoulder, his mouth quirking. "Then I would have left."

"This is all very Joe from *You*."

"I don't need to stalk you," he teases, his eyes glinting. "You like having me around too much."

I roll my eyes, but I can't help the flicker of a grin that forms. "Whatever. Come in then."

He steps past me as I close and lock the door behind him; he moves in my space as if it belongs to him. He plops down on my couch with a sigh, turning his head to look at me from over the back and patting the cushion beside him. "Come on. I won't bite."

I move to join him slowly, sinking down into the couch cushion a good distance away from where he gestured, only for him to reach and pull me into his side.

"Nope," he says. "None of that. We're cuddling tonight."

I frown even as I surreptitiously breathe in the scent of his cologne, which clings to his shirt. "Are we?"

"Yep." His arm curls around my shoulders. "You're going to tell me about your day."

"You know about my day. I saw you five hours ago."

"Well, tell me everything else."

Seems like a silly exercise to me, but his thumb that has begun to trace the soft skin of my upper arm is distracting, and I find myself leaning further into him, getting comfortable.

"Nate and Vera cornered me in my office this morning," I tell him.

"And how did that go?"

"About as well as I expected," I snort. "Nate is already planning the wedding."

"Wow, your friends must really want the best for you then."

I poke him in the side, and he chuckles as he squirms away. "Vera thinks it's a bad idea, I can tell."

"Do *you* think it's a bad idea?"

I hesitate, thinking. His thumb pauses in its slow back-and-forth on my skin, only resuming its path when I speak again.

"I think that I *should* think it's a bad idea," I admit.

He releases a breath. "But you don't?"

"No." My brow furrows. "Or maybe I do, but I'm just too tired to keep pretending I don't want it anyway."

"'It' being me, yeah?"

I can hear the smile in his voice without even looking at him. "I'm not feeding your ego. It's already as huge as your cat."

"Big as other things too," he says slyly.

"That was awful," I groan.

"I think we did okay today," Ezra muses. "You didn't ogle me very often, so that's something."

"I never *ogled* you."

"Sure you didn't."

I purse my lips. "You're imagining things."

"Keep telling yourself that, Sour Patch."

I can't help the dry chuckle that escapes me, but when its echo fades, there is nothing left but that slow stroking of his thumb and our quiet breathing. It's . . . almost comforting. It's been so long since I've allowed myself to be close to anyone like this that I'd almost forgotten how good it can be. I've spent so many years post-Grant locking every vulnerable part of myself up tight, ensuring that no one could ever hurt me like that again, that I had truly come to believe that I was incapable of feeling this kind of easy comfort with another person.

"Tell me what you're thinking about," Ezra says eventually, breaking the silence.

"I just . . ." I feel my cheeks heat, my voice lowering in embarrassment. "I can't believe that I'm here with *you*."

Ezra barks out a laugh. "Wow, thanks."

"You know what I mean. Can you honestly say that you ever saw this becoming anything more?"

Ezra thinks about it for a moment, and then: "No, I didn't." Ridiculously, that almost makes me deflate, but then he continues, "But I hoped."

I turn my face up to look at him, finding he has already turned my way so that I can meet his eyes. "You did?"

"I just always assumed you were too good for me," he admits.

I snort at that. "Hardly. I'm a mess and a half."

"Then I'd say we're perfect for each other, don't you think?"

My teeth worry at my lower lip, sensations bubbling up inside me that make me want to squirm. I can't bring myself to answer that, so I take the coward's way out.

"So what did you want to be before you changed your degree to law?"

He looks surprised by the question, his mouth opening and

closing as if he's never been asked it before, like he's trying to remember the answer. "I'm not even sure I had a real plan," he admits. "I was just happy to be out of Alexander's house for the first time, if I'm being honest."

"You never had a pipe dream as a kid?"

"Oh, I had plenty," he laughs. "When I was eight I watched *Patch Adams*. Went through a doctor phase for a while. My mom even got me this kit, and I was constantly making her let me listen to her heartbeat."

"You know," I chuckle. "I think you might have actually made a good doctor."

"You think?"

"Yeah, you're too fucking stubborn not to be."

"Pot calling the kettle black, don't you think?" He nudges his shoulder against mine. "What about you? Did you always want to be a lawyer?"

"For as long as I can remember," I tell him. "My mom used to say I would argue with a fence post."

"Now *that* I can see," he chuffs.

I poke him in the side again. "It wasn't until law school that I decided on divorce law though."

"Because of your parents?"

I blow out a breath. "I mean, that's the obvious answer. They had both gotten remarried at this point, and don't get me wrong, I was happy that they were happy. I still am. But I just . . ." I look down at my lap, wringing my hands together. "I just never understood it, I guess. Even after coming to terms with everything, a part of me never understood how two people who worked so perfectly as a unit couldn't love each other the way I thought they did."

"And you thought going into divorce law would help you understand?"

"I guess I thought if I experienced enough couples meeting the end of their marriage, that maybe I could finally make peace with why my parents had to."

"And did you?"

"I . . . think so. I know it's ridiculous to be so hung up over it after so long. Especially when they're both so happy."

"Your entire world got turned upside down," he says soothingly. "It's not unreasonable that it would affect you."

"I haven't talked to anyone about this," I confess. "Not since Grant. I think maybe . . . I think that's why it fucked me up so badly when he left. He knew *everything*. He knew all my hang-ups and all the secret parts of myself I tried to keep hidden, and when he left, it felt like maybe it was because I wasn't enough. Then I spent a long time wondering if I stole a part of *his* life too."

"Fuck that," Ezra balks. "He was a prick who chose his job over you. He didn't deserve you."

"I don't know if that's true."

"*I* do," he stresses, his fingers pressing under my chin to force me to look at him. "Look at me." And I am looking at him, getting lost in his green eyes, just like I've always been afraid of doing. "If he couldn't stay for you, then he didn't fucking deserve you. Understand? Because you're worth staying for, Dani."

There's a lump in my throat that makes it hard to speak, so I just nod slowly, not even sure what I would say to that anyway. He saves me from the need to when he leans in to cover my mouth with his in a gentle but firm kiss. He takes his time with it, like he's not in any hurry to make it become something more, and miraculously, I *like* this slow change of pace. If I'm being honest with myself, I've liked everything about this evening that is so different from any other one we've shared.

"You want to watch a movie?" he murmurs when he pulls away.

I quirk a brow. "Really?"

"Why not? It's called decompressing. I hear it's a thing people do."

"Oh, you mean bringing your work home and stressing about it until you pass out isn't the normal way of things?"

"It's an option, but there are always other avenues to explore."

"Are you an expert on the subject?"

"No, but I'd like to be an expert on you, eventually."

My lips part in shock, his casual line actually leaving me speechless for a breath until I collect myself. "You really think you're smooth, don't you."

"Mm." He drops another kiss to the tip of my nose. "I know I'm smooth, baby."

He untangles himself to go after my remote, taking my wineglass from the coffee table and offering to refill it before he tells me to pick out a movie for his *decompression session,* as he is now referring to it.

Scrolling through titles, it hits me how *domestic* this all feels. Months ago, the thought of spending an evening like this with Ezra fucking Hart would have made me laugh. Now I'm afraid of how much I might begin to crave it, how simply I could slip into a familiarity of this easy time with him.

And that might be the most terrifying thing about any of this.

Twenty-Four

DANI

THE NEXT FEW weeks *do* go remarkably well.

We have had several sessions in court since that night at my apartment, and while I kept expecting them to feel strange, separating work from home came surprisingly easy.

We spent one session arguing with each other about a particular piece of shared property that neither Lorenzo or Bianca had wanted to concede on, and then later that night, Ezra came over to my place with Chinese food to watch *Patch Adams*. He'd said it was imperative that I watch after admitting that I'd never seen it.

Another session saw us getting heated over Ezra's jabs at Bianca's spending habits over the years; he made several implications about her lifestyle, implying some sort of greed factor there, and by the end of it, Judge Harding was threatening to separate us. But then later at his apartment, we were laughing over Ezra's brief obsession with a foreign brand of vitamin water that he'd had delivered to his place by the case until he was so sick of the taste of coconut that he almost hurled at his mother's birthday party because they'd served a German chocolate cake.

It's been strange but exhilarating getting to know Ezra, and the more I learn about him, the more I wonder how I ever thought I stood a chance of keeping my distance (outside of the physical, that is). Sure, he's still an intolerable asshole most of the time, but beyond that, he's charming, funny, and surprisingly loyal.

Maybe that's why I'm so messed up today.

Today's session had started like any other, but for some reason, when Ezra began grilling his witness—a petite woman who had been a longtime friend of Bianca's—about any potential motive Bianca might have to ruin her husband, I'd been unable to keep things separate.

I think that it wounded me a little, watching Ezra defend Lorenzo's character like that. Maybe it's because deep down, I'm fairly certain that Ezra *knows* what a piece of shit Lorenzo is, and still he's trying to rob Bianca of well-deserved retribution on his behalf.

Which, I'm aware, is a grossly unfair line of thinking. That at the end of the day, Ezra is doing his *job*, and what's more, there's a good chance that he *hates* having to defend Lorenzo. He hasn't said as much directly; it would be highly unethical if he did, but still, I can sense it, I think.

So why am I sulking about it in my office after hours?

Ezra has texted me a few times after court let out, and normally we would have been at one of each other's places by now, but I haven't been able to bring myself to answer him tonight. Not when I have all these conflicting feelings.

I thumb through financial documents, making notes that seem relevant; Ezra will finally be calling Bianca to the stand the next time we are in court, and I want to be prepared for the inevitable question about the first time she filed for divorce. I've already worked out a relatively solid redirect, but as I'm all too aware when it comes to Ezra, you can never be too prepared.

Something that is made overly evident when the person in question knocks on my office door.

I startle when he pokes his head through the unlocked door after opening it; I want to be surprised, but honestly, knowing Ezra's tenacity the way I do, I'm really not.

"How did you get in?"

"Bribed the security guard," he says with a grin. "You really should pay that guy more."

"I have it on good authority that Larry is excellent at his job."

"Oh, he really is," Ezra admits. "Actually, I told him that you were expecting me, and that I had some documents to drop off. I guess I'm just too charming to question."

"You're too *something*," I scoff.

Ezra steps inside, closing the door behind him. I hear the soft *snick* of the lock, peeking up at him in question as he moves deeper into the room.

"I figured we needed to talk," he explains as he settles into the chair on the other side of my desk. "I can tell you were ruffled after we let out today."

"I'm not . . . ruffled," I protest.

Ezra just laughs. "You forget that for the first few months that I knew you, all I ever saw was ruffled Dani. I'm definitely an expert on what she looks like."

"It's nothing," I try, not deigning to look at him in favor of the document in front of me. "I just had a lot to go over and forgot to text you back."

"No, you didn't," he pushes calmly. "None of this is going to work if you aren't honest with me, Dani."

"It's stupid," I sigh, leaning back in my chair to pinch the bridge of my nose. "Seriously, it sounds ridiculous even in my head."

"I doubt that. Just talk to me."

"I just . . . it's so hard watching you defend him."

Ezra arches a brow. "Lorenzo?"

"I know, I know. It's your job. You have to. I know that you have to play the cards you're dealt, just like the rest of us, but . . ." I shake my head. "He's such a bastard."

Ezra frowns, looking down at his laced fingers resting in his lap. "We knew this wasn't going to be easy," he starts. "But it's just a job, Dani. You know that."

"I know that, I do," I assure him. "I just . . . I've gotten to know Bianca. She's . . . she's been through so much. I feel like I'm failing her sometimes."

This is a dangerous conversation, one that we've carefully avoided the last few weeks. Both of us know that discussing our clients is tricky territory. I don't even know why I've admitted any of this to begin with.

"Listen," he says finally. "Things will be better when this is over. We do this job to the best of both of our abilities, and then after . . . maybe we disclose. We can avoid being on opposite sides going forward."

I suck in a breath. "Disclose?"

"You don't want to?"

"I . . ." I swallow. "I didn't know *you* would. Alexander . . ."

"Alexander has done a great job of ruining my life for the last thirty-four years," Ezra says, his voice hard. "I won't be letting him do that with you."

I frown. "And your mother? What if he disapproves? Will she suffer?"

"I . . ." There's a flash of pain in his eyes, and I know he's considered it. "I don't know."

"Maybe . . . maybe we could work together on her case," I offer. "Maybe we can find something you overlooked."

His eyes search mine for several seconds, softening. "You'd do that?"

"Of course I would. I hate that he uses her against you."

Another long moment passes with him studying me, and I'm half-desperate to know what he's thinking. After a long while, a small smile forms on his face, and he gives me a slow nod. "I'd like that."

"I'm sorry I was weird today," I tell him.

He shakes his head. "We're going to have weird days. It's a weird situation we're in."

"It is," I agree.

He pushes up out of his seat, circling my desk in a predatory way until he's turning my chair toward him, resting his hands on the arms on either side of me. "Worth it though," he murmurs.

"Yeah?"

"Mm-hmm."

He dips his head, and I push up to meet him, closing my eyes at the feel of his mouth against mine. It's crazy that in a matter of weeks, I seem to have lost all will to resist this. Truthfully, after the strange melancholy I've been in for the last few hours, Ezra's easy kisses and warm touch are a welcome distraction.

"Stand up," he bids softly. "I want to try something."

I let him coax me out of my chair with strong hands at my waist, not even pretending to protest when he turns me and pushes me back against my desk. His palms shove at the hem of my skirt, pushing it higher until they can cup the back of my thighs as he urges me to sit on top of the desk.

"I have been thinking about you on this desk since the last time I had you here," he admits.

"You were entirely too cocky," I snort.

I feel his smile against my throat, where he's buried his face, his hands teasing the lace-covered edges of my thigh-highs. "I just knew what I wanted."

"You . . ." I bite my lip, my lashes fluttering when I feel his fingertips teasing the silky material of my underwear at my hips. "You said I was yours."

His lips trail kisses up my neck, lingering below my jaw. "Aren't you?"

"I . . ."

"Because I want you to be," he confesses, his warm breath puffing against my ear before his mouth traces along my jaw. "I think I did even then."

"Ezra," I manage shakily.

"Do you remember what I said about these skirts you wear?" He's inching the fabric of said skirt up higher now, cool air licking at my thighs with every revealed bit of skin. "Do you remember what I said they made me want to do to you?"

"I remember," I whimper, actually *whimper*.

"Do you want that?" He kisses the corner of my mouth gently, speaking directly against my lips. "Tell me what you want."

There's still that *tiny* sliver of resistance, a small streak of stubborn defiance toward giving in to him, but I tamp it down. I've realized in the last few weeks that giving in to Ezra is not a concession. It's a revelation.

"I want you," I tell him, because it's the truth, and I'm long past tired of pretending it isn't. "Just like you said."

He grins against my mouth. "Here? Right here?"

"Shut up and touch me, asshole."

He rumbles out a laugh. "Since you asked so nicely."

I close my eyes when he kisses me, not because I can't look at him, not anymore, but because sometimes kissing Ezra feels like too much. The weight of his mouth is heavier than just a physical presence, it's a consuming thing that I feel everywhere; it's too *much*, kissing Ezra. Part of me thinks it always has been. Maybe that's why I've always been so afraid of it.

But I'm not now.

His tongue slides against mine in a slow caress, his hands rucking up my skirt until it's gathered at my waist with decidedly more urgency. He groans when his palms slide across the lace on my thighs, hovering there only for a moment before moving higher to hook his fingers into the elastic of my underwear.

"Sometimes I pretend you're not wearing these under your skirt," he says huskily, still nipping at my lower lip as he begins to inch them down. "I pretend that you're always ready for me. That at any moment I could have you just like this. Fill your soft, wet cunt anytime I like." My thighs clench when his fingers caress me there, proving that I'm just as wet as he's describing. "Would you let me, Dani?"

"Fucking touch me and find out," I practically growl.

Ezra just chuckles, still slipping his fingers between my legs in a lazy exploration. "But I am touching you."

"You're being purposely infuriating again."

"It's one of my favorite pastimes."

I huff as I reach for the zipper of his slacks, deciding to take matters into my own hands. This is the twenty-first century, after all. If Ezra wants to be intolerable, that's his prerogative. I'll just take what I want myself.

"Someone's eager," he croons as I shove his fly apart.

I curl my other hand around his nape, pulling him close and smashing his lips to mine just after uttering a quiet "Shut up."

His low moan tumbles into my mouth when I get my hands around his cock, giving him a slow stroke from root to tip, going at the same infuriatingly slow pace that he teased me with. My lips curl when he begins to try to fuck into my fist, pulling back as I squeeze him tight enough to make him hiss.

"Not so fun when you're on the receiving end, is it?"

He chuffs out a strained laugh. "Fine. You win. Have your way with me."

"God, I hate you," I say with absolutely no bite.

He's already leaning in to kiss me again. "Sure you do."

I wrap my arms around his neck when he *finally* sinks two fingers inside me, pumping them deep and curling them to stroke at my inner wall until I shudder with it. I'm dripping for him, and I know that there will be a mess at the edge of my desk that is going to deeply embarrass me later, but right now I can't find it in me to care. Not when I can feel the slick crown of him rubbing against my inner thigh. And he's right. I *would* let him bend me over my own desk. At this moment, I would let Ezra do whatever the fuck he wanted to me.

I press my knees to his hips, trying to draw him closer. "Enough with your fingers. Want the real thing."

"Fuck, Dani. I really like you greedy."

I don't argue. It's pointless. I *am* greedy for him.

His fingers are still wet from me when his hands hold my

hips, his mouth open on mine as he notches against me. His harsh breath matches mine as he starts to push inside, and the delicious way he fills me, leaving no part of me untouched, is a sensation I've become wholly addicted to.

"Move," I beg breathlessly. "Fuck me."

I feel his palm between my breasts, pushing against my torso and urging me down to my back. He spreads me out over my notes and files, and there's something about the idea of it that has my stomach twisting with desire. The picture we paint, both dressed and neat from the waist up but completely undone where our bodies are joined, has me clenching around him where he's still buried inside.

"Look at you," he murmurs, eyes raking down the length of me and settling between my legs. "You're fucking edible, Dani."

His hands curl under my thighs, pressing at the backs of them to push them higher toward my stomach, leaving me splayed out for him. He leans to press his lips to the lace of my thigh-highs, his eyes shuttering as he draws his hips back just to glide back inside. I bite my lip when he does it again, and I try to hold back my sounds for fear of Larry wandering too close to my office outside.

Ezra's head lolls as he watches the way he's begun to steadily thrust in and out of me, seeming enraptured at how we're connected. If he didn't look so in awe of it, I might be mortified by the way he's gazing at me. As it is, it only makes me burn hotter.

"Tell me this pussy is mine," he rasps, snapping his hips forward so hard that a sharp cry escapes me despite my efforts. "I want to hear it."

"Ezra, fuck, I—"

"*Say*"—his cock slides home roughly as I sizzle with delicious friction—"*it*."

"It's yours," I moan. "*Fuck*. Harder."

"Touch yourself." His nails bite into the soft flesh of my thighs, and he picks up his pace until I have to reach behind me and grip the other edge of my desk to keep myself from scooting higher. "Please, Dani? I want to see you play with yourself. I want to feel you come *hard*."

I watch him through heavy-lidded eyes as I obey, slipping my fingers between my legs and circling the already-swollen bud of my clit as sparks of pleasure prickle inside. My mouth parts in a silent gasp, the onslaught of his cock and my hand pushing me so close to the edge that I can practically taste my orgasm.

"That's it," he coos. "So perfect." He bends his body, releasing my legs so I'm forced to wrap them around his waist. His hands brace on either side of me, leaning in close so that he can brush his lips against mine. "Now say that you're mine."

My back bows as I tense up around him, shutting my eyes for only a second as that sweet pressure starts to crest. "I'm—"

"That's it," he whispers, kissing me so gently that it feels impossible to reconcile with the still-furious pounding of his hips. "Tell me. Please."

"*Ah*." My legs start to shake, my pussy trembling as my vision blurs. Ezra is still moving, prolonging the almost-too-intense sensation that sparks inside, but his rhythm is stuttered now, his cock swelling so thick that I feel fit to bursting. "*I'm yours*," I shout hoarsely.

Ezra groans long and loud, and I know that if *anyone* is outside of my office, it will be obvious what's happening here. I just . . . don't care. Not when he looks utterly blissed-out. Not when I can feel him twitching inside. Not when his body is so close that it almost feels like a part of me. His face is buried against my neck, and I make no move to shove him away, running my fingers through his slightly damp hair as we both try to collect our breath. I don't know how much time passes before he finally lifts himself to hover over me, studying my expression with a sated look and a dreamy smile.

"Now that's what I call a successful mediation," he says.

I shake my head, but I can feel myself grinning. "Idiot."

"But I'm *your* idiot."

I pause at that, feeling suddenly unsure. I know what I said in the heat of the moment, but . . .

"Are you?"

His brow furrows. "What?"

"You said . . . you said I'm yours," I manage, my voice too thick to even remotely pass as casual. "But are you mine?"

His smile is brilliant, and that increasingly familiar feeling of it lighting up all the dark corners hiding inside me is overwhelming.

"I've been yours for ages, Dani," he says, his voice a low, sweet murmur. "I've just been waiting for you to catch up."

I have to tug him down to my mouth, hiding my emotions with a kiss. Hiding the way I practically melt at his words. Like the last little bit of ice surrounding my heart dripping away. He really is purposefully infuriating, Ezra.

I'm starting to love that about him.

Twenty-Five

EZRA

"EZRA, ARE YOU even listening?"

I look up from my phone to find Alexander glaring at me from across his desk. I want to tell him that *no*, I wasn't listening, that I could go my entire life without ever listening to him again, but I don't do that. I keep my expression neutral.

"I'm listening."

"I hope that whatever is on your phone is more important than work," he chides.

I have to physically restrain myself from grinning. Alexander would absolutely become apoplectic if he knew I was sitting across from him and just beside his sleazy client flirting with the opposing counsel, and the image of that is enough to make me gleeful.

"Just checking an email," I answer blandly. "I'm waiting on some news."

"News that will help with the case, I hope," Lorenzo snorts.

I resist the urge to roll my eyes. The truth is, every day in court is tipping the scales in Bianca and Dani's favor. The more Dani's team discovers about Lorenzo, the more slimy it makes him appear. Even more truthfully, I am secretly all too glad to witness it happening. Alexander may be forcing my hand to participate in this farce of a trial to save his friend's ass, but that doesn't mean I have to root for the bastard.

"It certainly didn't look good when your mistress forgot her own 'diagnosis' that you've been helping her pay the bills for when they called her to the stand," I remark dryly.

Lorenzo's face turns blotchy and red. "If you had done a proper job, she would not have been on the stand at all."

"It's hard to continue to quash subpoenas on the grounds of confidential information when we can't provide anything more than vague references and a fucking plastic surgeon instead of an actual primary care physician."

"I told you that you should have scheduled more prepping," Alexander grouses. "LeeAnn isn't exactly what one would call quick on the uptake."

"Do not speak of her that way," Lorenzo snarls.

Alexander lifts his hands in apology. "I'm on your side, Lorenzo. But we need to get on top of this or you're going to be shelling out millions to your wife."

"Bianca thinks she can just take what's mine," Lorenzo huffs. "Her and that bitch of a little lawyer she employs. They make quite a pair."

My fingers grip the arms of the chair I'm sitting in, and I'm struck with the strong desire to reach over and cave in Lorenzo's teeth. The way his lip curls when he mentions Dani, calling her that . . . it's enough to have my blood boiling.

"Bianca will take the stand this week," I remind them both through clenched teeth.

"Where you will remind the court that she has pulled this move before," Alexander says. "No one trusts a boy who cries wolf."

"We have to assume that Da—" I cover my slip by clearing my throat. "That Ms. Pierce will have come up with a solid reasoning for why Bianca filed and then withdrew."

Lorenzo crosses his arms. "We paint her as money hungry, yes?" He glances at Alexander. "Her trust took quite the hit that year."

"Which Ms. Pierce will say is circumstantial," I counter.

"He's not wrong," Alexander admits begrudgingly, resting his steepled fingers against his mouth. "Perhaps we should take a more unorthodox approach."

My brow quirks. "Such as?"

"We tell the truth," he tells me with a sly grin.

My confusion is evident by my frown. "What do you mean?"

"We cannot tell the *truth*," Lorenzo stutters. "I will not be the only one who suffers from the truth," he goes on, voice rising. "You will also—"

"That isn't what I meant," Alexander says quickly, cutting him off.

Curiosity prickles in my brain at whatever Lorenzo was about to say. Is he implying Alexander has some connection to him? To Bianca? Alexander keeps going, not allowing me very much time to ponder the possibility.

"We tell the court that Bianca filed for divorce because she accused you of infidelity," Alexander says simply.

Lorenzo reels. "Excuse me?"

"That seems . . . a little more than unorthodox," I tell Alexander, secretly disgusted by the roundabout casual admission that he *is* a fucking cheater, even if I've known it all along.

"It's perfect," Alexander says confidently. "Because just like now . . . Bianca had no way to prove her allegations."

Lorenzo still looks unconvinced. "So?"

"*So*," Alexander stresses. "We convince the judge that Bianca has a tendency to . . . cry wolf when it suits her. This establishes a pattern. Not many women would change their mind if they *actually* believed their husband was cheating. The fact that she stayed only strengthens our point that this is all a ploy. Just a way to ruin Lorenzo for her own purposes."

I can't help but snort. "And you really think that anyone is going to buy that?"

"Why not?" Alexander leans back in his chair, looking smug. "They cannot prove otherwise, so does it really matter?"

Lorenzo looks thoughtful now, stroking his chin. "It *would* be very satisfying to see Bianca's face when she hears this. If you truly think it will work."

"Ezra will *make* it work," Alexander tells him confidently. He shoots me a cold look. "Won't you."

Pure rage is coursing through me, and I'm feeling helpless and trapped between these two disgusting men and their equally horrible whims. Every part of me wants to end this right now, to get up and walk out and tell Alexander that he can go fuck himself, but my mother's face flashes in my eyes. What would Alexander do if I were to tell him no? Would he actually send her away? Would he make it that much harder to see her?

Not knowing keeps me from doing any of the things I really want to, so I nod numbly instead.

"I will," I answer hollowly, knowing I have few other options.

"Excellent," Alexander says with a smug grin. "You and Lorenzo can prep tomorrow." He looks expectantly at my client. "Let's grab lunch, Lorenzo. We have things to discuss."

There's a hardness to his gaze, and my mind wanders back to Lorenzo's outburst. I wonder for the first time if there is more between them than I was originally led to believe. Could there be a deeper reason for Alexander's insistence upon the importance of this case other than his and Lorenzo's "friendship"?

Alexander dismisses me, leaving me to my musings.

I'm back in my office before I remember Dani's text that I was forced to stow away, leaning back in my chair and pushing thoughts of Alexander and Lorenzo's bullshit far away as I give her my undivided attention.

> **Sour Patch:** Who says it was YOU I wanted to see? Maybe I just want to check on Purrgood. I miss him.

I grin, knowing full well that it wasn't Purrgood on her mind when she asked what I was doing tonight, but I'm happy to let her pretend. It's more fun that way.

> **Me:** He misses you too. You should probably come over and make sure I'm not overfeeding him.

> **Sour Patch:** I have no doubts that you're overfeeding him, but I guess if you really want me to . . .

> **Me:** Just assume I always
> want you to.

Sour Patch: Fine. So needy.

> **Me:** No arguments there.
> See you tonight. 😘

I let out a sigh as I drop my phone on the desk, running my fingers through my hair. Seeing Dani is exactly what I need to forget this hellish day. I wonder what she would think if she knew how incredibly gone I am for her. The thought makes me smile. My prickly little lawyer would most likely fight the idea of feeling something more for me tooth and nail.

But a guy can dream.

"GOD," DANI GROANS. "No wonder Purrgood is so huge. If you feed him like you just fed me."

"No one made you get a second helping," I point out, eyeing her from the kitchen island, where I'm washing the dishes. She offered, but the sight of her stretched out on my couch was too tempting to pass up. "I'm starting to think you only like me for my cooking."

She cracks one eye open to glare at me. "You've only cooked for me like, three times."

"And you raved and raved about each one," I preen.

She rolls her eyes before closing them again, resuming her slow stroking of Purrgood's belly as he lounges in her lap. "Whatever. You had to be good at something."

"I'd argue I'm good at several things where you're concerned," I say slyly, drying my hands on a dish towel.

Dani blows a raspberry in lieu of answering, and I bark out a laugh as I pad out of the kitchen to settle on the opposite end of the couch. She eyes me suspiciously when I grab for one of her feet, which are draped over the side, pulling it into my lap and working it with my fingers as she relaxes with a satisfied sound.

"Now you're just trying to butter me up," she mumbles.

I press the pad of my thumb into the arch of her foot, rubbing a hard line down the length. "I do what I have to."

"Well, keep doing it," she hums.

It's been a relatively uneventful evening; we ate chicken carbonara that I made and drank the wine that she likes (she still won't admit how pleased it made her when she found out I started keeping a bottle of it here), talking about everything and nothing. I find that I like this time with her almost as much as touching her intimately. Maybe even more so. I can't be sure. It really is a toss-up, if I'm being honest. I'm greedy for any time I get to spend with her.

"So how is the Preston case going?" I ask casually. "Did Nate get the receipts for the wife's sex addiction therapy?"

Dani snorts. "He hasn't shut up about it. Didn't know it was a thing, apparently. I swear to God, if I have to hear him muse about potential treatments for it one more time, I'm going to throw myself out the window."

"I'm sure Vera is enjoying that immensely," I chuckle, rolling my thumb into the ball of her foot as she gives a satisfied hum.

"I wish they'd just fuck and get it over with," she grumbles. "I swear they fight like it's foreplay."

"Sounds familiar," I tease.

She opens one eye again to peek at me. "I guess Nate just hasn't been intolerable enough to convince Vera to fall into bed with him yet."

"It is a gift," I answer matter-of-factly.

I don't miss the slight smile that curves her mouth before her eyes close again. For a moment I just watch her fingers stroke back and forth through Purrgood's fur, glancing at him and catching him blinking at me lazily. He's completely abandoned me at this point, considering Dani as a more desirable object of his affections, and I can't even say I blame the guy.

"Mm. Keep doing that," she murmurs.

"Bossy," I tut.

"How was your meeting today? Was Alexander insufferable?"

I pause for a moment, knowing I can't actually tell her the fine details, not that she expects me to, but there is a brief urge to do so anyway. For a moment, I *really* want to unburden myself to her. I resume the slow stroking of her foot, deciding against it. We don't need to complicate things between us any more than they already are by breaking any more rules.

"As much as usual," I tell her. "Sometimes when he talks, I like to fantasize about something very large and heavy falling out of the sky and crushing him."

"Like a piano," Dani laughs.

My lips curl. "Or a small meteor."

"It's a nice dream," she muses.

She continues to watch me as I relinquish her foot just to give my attention to the other, her brow furrowing in thought.

"What?"

She bites her lip. "I don't want you to think I overstepped, but . . ."

"What is it?"

"I was looking into some old case examples on broken conservatorships today."

I go still, my breath catching. "You were?"

"There was a case in California where the family was able to transfer the conservatorship from a father to an aunt when they found out he'd changed the parameters to her will without her consent."

"Alexander would raise all sorts of hell if I were to go digging through my mom's legal profile."

"Would he have to know? Where do you think he keeps those records?"

"In his office at home, most likely. He keeps it locked up tight when he's not using it."

She frowns, thinking. "There was another case where a sister was able to establish via medical records that their condition had gotten better. That they no longer needed the conservatorship."

"I've looked into it," I tell her, "but my mother really hasn't gotten any better. There's no doubt that she needs care . . . just not Alexander's."

"Could you convince her to testify that you would be a better conservator for her?"

"We've talked about it," I admit. "She always stresses that she doesn't want to be a burden on me. Without her cooperation, it would be almost impossible."

Dani looks frustrated, the corners of her mouth turning down and her eyes far away in thought. I can see her brain working ninety miles an hour, and I know without a doubt that it's not something she's likely to give up on. Dani is nothing if not tenacious.

"We'll think of something," she says determinedly. "I'll keep looking."

My chest feels too tight at the resolution in her eyes, and I have a swelling feeling inside that makes it just a little harder to breathe. Dani keeps talking, looking at Purrgood with concentration as she draws patterns into his belly, but her words are harder to make out with the sudden thumping of my pulse, which sounds deafening in my ears.

If you had asked me all those months ago if I ever thought I would be here with her like this, that she would be casually enjoying my touch and my space while doing her best to help me, to *reassure* me, I would have told you that you were crazy. I can't even pinpoint a direct path to how we got here, but I'm suddenly struck with the realization that there is absolutely nowhere I would rather be. That this prickly woman with her hidden smile and her fierce demeanor has somehow become the reason I get out of bed in the morning, the person I think about just before I go to sleep. She's become *everything*.

And I'm completely, irrevocably in love with her.

She keeps rambling about old court cases, talking to herself like it's a problem she can work around and arrive at a solution all on her own, completely oblivious to the revelation I'm having only a few feet away. What *would* Dani do if she knew? Would she run away? Would she hide? Could she ever feel the same about me?

I know it's too soon to tell her. That Dani's walls are more fragile now but by no means broken down, and I urge my racing heart to calm, begging my heavy tongue to stay silent. Because I can wait, I tell myself. Until she's ready to hear it. I'll wait as long as it takes for her.

Because I meant it, what I told her all those weeks ago. That she's absolutely worth staying for.

And that's exactly what I intend to do.

Twenty-Six

DANI

"NOW, WHEN HE calls you to the stand, don't give them any emotion," I remind Bianca as we settle into our seats at the front of the courtroom.

Bianca gives me an imperious look. "When have I struck you as emotional, Danica?"

"Fair," I sigh. "I just know they're going to throw everything they have at you today."

"I am prepared for what this man wants to say about me," she says with a cluck of her tongue. "I do not fear a man just because he wears a suit."

I grin, shaking my head as I jot something down. "Just remember what we talked about," I encourage. "Stick to what we rehearsed. No more surprises."

"You must let things go, Danica," Bianca huffs. "Your long memory will give you wrinkles if you are not careful."

"Yeah, yeah," I chuckle. I really do sort of love this woman.

I hear the chair opposite our table scraping across the floor, turning my head as Ezra settles into his seat. I've gotten very good at keeping my expression neutral when we're in court; the last thing I need is for someone to catch me *ogling* him, as he puts it, but I have to admit that he looks . . . utterly delicious in his three-piece navy suit. He flashes me a smile from his seat, and I have to bite my lip not to return it, allowing myself only a few seconds to appreciate the way his suit jacket hugs his broad shoulders perfectly before giving my attention back to my notepad in front of me.

Still my mind wanders to the night before—a quiet, easy night of Thai food in my living room while Ezra told me stories about his first disastrous mock trial in second year. I almost smile at the memory; his animated recounting of forgetting all the precedents he'd memorized the moment he approached the stand had me laughing at an embarrassing decibel. He'd slept over, and I have to admit, waking up with his warm body wrapped around me hadn't been the worst thing in the world.

Not that I'll ever admit that to him.

"I see Lorenzo's *puttana* is now attending," Bianca mutters.

I turn to see Lorenzo's mistress sitting in the seats on their side of the courtroom, my eyes widening. That's a bold fucking move. Especially since it's barely been a week since she fucked up on the stand and forgot her imaginary diagnosis. What the hell are they playing at?

"You can't say 'whore' in court," I hiss back.

"It is fine if no one knows I say it," she says, waving me off.

"All rise," the bailiff announces, quieting the ripple of low conversation throughout the room. The bailiff introduces the session, then the judge. "The Honorable Judge Harding is presiding."

We all remain standing while Judge Harding enters the room and gets settled in her chair, only taking our seats when she gives us permission to do so.

"Good morning, ladies and gentlemen," Harding drones. "Let's all try to stay civil today, shall we?"

Bianca's spine stiffens beside me, and I try not to flinch. There have been a few heated sessions in the last couple of weeks, I suppose. I had to physically clap a hand over Bianca's mouth several times when Lorenzo's mistress was on the stand last week.

Harding peers over her glasses at her notes in front of her. "I believe Mrs. Casiraghi is set to take the stand today, correct?"

"That's correct, Your Honor," Ezra answers, standing.

Harding nods at Bianca. "Mrs. Casiraghi." She tilts her head toward the stand. "If you will."

Bianca leaves her chair with her usual fluid grace, her head high and her nose in the air as she glides to the stand and settles into the seat behind it. She never glances in Lorenzo's direction while the bailiff swears her in, but when I look over, I find him glaring at the side of her face with open disdain. Prick.

Ezra carries a folder casually as he strolls toward where Bianca is seated, flashing her his best smile. It's dangerous, that smile. "Good morning, Mrs. Casiraghi. It's good to see you again."

"Save your pleasantries," she tuts. "Ask your questions."

"Right," Ezra chuckles, unruffled. "Straight to business then."

Now that I'm allowing myself to appreciate it, it really is amazing, the way he can remain calm under almost any circumstances. I once thought his general aloofness to be an insult to the craft, but I realize now that it's a carefully constructed persona meant to unsettle someone with a weaker composure than Bianca's. As it is, I'm not worried for her.

"Now, Mrs. Casiraghi," he starts, keeping his attention on the page in front of him as if he's trying to remember what he was going to ask. I know that's a tactic as well. I fight to roll my eyes.

"We spoke briefly while you were being deposed on the events of 1994, do you remember?"

"I remember," Bianca answers primly.

"Now, just to clarify for the rest of the court, those events included you filing for divorce from your husband, Mr. Casiraghi, correct?"

"Correct."

"But you didn't follow through, is that right?"

"You continue to be right, yes," she says, a heavily veiled irritation laced into her tone that others might not catch, but I do. I have to bite back a laugh.

"Can you tell me why you withdrew your petition of divorce only a month after filing?"

Bianca laces her fingers in her lap, and I find myself nodding almost imperceptibly, waiting for her to give the carefully practiced reasoning we went over during prep.

"I was very young," she says. "Lorenzo worked many hours in that time. I barely saw him. I grew lonely. We had a whirlwind romance in Italy before we moved here, and when that changed, I did not handle it well."

"I see," Ezra replies thoughtfully. He glances down at his notes again. "So you just decided to work it out?"

"Yes," she says. "I loved my husband, and we talked. We agreed to make it work." Her eyes narrow slightly. "Not prudent on my part, it seems."

"Mrs. Casiraghi," Harding sighs. "If you could keep your answers relevant to the question at hand, please."

Bianca nods stiffly.

I know what's coming, and we've prepared for that too, but still I tense in my chair, watching Ezra closely as I wait for him to deliver the inevitable blow.

"So you withdrawing your petition had nothing to do with your trust fund seeing major losses only weeks after you filed for divorce?"

My eyes flick to Bianca, silently encouraging her. *You've got this.*

"It did not," she tells him coolly. "My trust fund is handled by lawyers like yourself, Mr. Hart. I am only privy to significant changes when it is made clear that my trust is in real danger. My advisor foresaw loss, and explained to me later that it was not of concern, that he expected it to reconcile within a few short months. And it did. I was not made aware of such losses until many months after they occurred. By then, the problem had solved itself. The two events have nothing to do with one another."

"I see," Ezra muses calmly. Too calmly, I think. His uncanny ability to remain unperturbed might be impressive, but it can also be frustrating as hell. "Perhaps they don't."

I suck in a quiet breath. There's no way it could be that easy. I expected arguments, a full-on fight, counters—*anything* besides a quiet acquiescence. But Ezra is turning away from the stand, still looking at his notes with a frown as if at any moment he might pass the witness.

Wow, I think with astonishment. *I am so going to tease him later about being too eager to make me dinner again.*

But Ezra isn't done, as it turns out.

"Ah, wait," he says with a puzzled expression, as if he'd almost just forgotten whatever he is about to say. "Actually, I had another question about your divorce petition."

"Ask as many as you like," Bianca tells him. "My answer will stay the same."

"Of course," he says with a sly grin that makes my stomach flutter with both arousal and anticipation at whatever bogus thing

Alexander has no doubt fed him to counter with. "I just wanted to clarify . . ." He takes one last look at his notes, and I realize I'm leaning in just a little. "Did you not accuse your husband of being unfaithful then as well?"

My entire body goes rigid.

I can feel my mouth slowly parting in a shocked expression without my consent, and I stare at the side of Ezra's face as the sensation of having the wind knocked out of me nearly bowls me over. How did he . . . ? I turn to look at Lorenzo, who looks at me with a smirk. He couldn't have—there's no *way* they would have—

"Excuse me?"

Bianca's slightly stricken tone brings me back to the moment. Her eyes meet mine from across the room, and there is a flicker of hurt and, what's worse, betrayal in them. Does she think that this is *my* doing? She has to know that I would never tell Ezra anything said to me in confidence. Even *if* we're seeing each other. Something that she's not even aware of.

So how does he know?

"Mrs. Casiraghi," Ezra urges calmly. "Is it correct that you accused your husband of infidelity in 1994 before filing for divorce and then withdrew that same petition hardly a month later?"

"I—" Bianca's eyes dart to me again, looking unsure for the first time since I've known her. Looking almost *ashamed*. "That is—it is because—he *was* unfaithful."

"Objection," Ezra replies softly. "Hearsay."

"Sustained," Judge Harding says.

"Mrs. Casiraghi," Ezra grills. "Does it not seem strange to you that *both* times you have filed for divorce from your husband, you have claimed that he was unfaithful without having any kind of concrete evidence?"

Bianca's cheeks are flushed now. "I—"

"Is it not a fair assessment to say that twice in the course of your marriage you have made bold accusations against my client that at their core are unfounded?"

I need to say something, I need to say *anything*. Why am I still frozen?

"No, that is not—"

"It appears to me," Ezra says with more edge to his tone, clearly going in for the kill, "that your accusations of infidelity are nothing more than a convenient ploy to exact a public vendetta against your husband for your purposes. Does that not seem more feasible than him being unfaithful without any consequences?"

It is Bianca's helpless expression when her eyes find mine again that finally rouses me to act. "Objection," I grind out, my heart thumping in my ears as I shoot up from my chair. "Speculation. My client has never been on record making such claims about her petition in 1994."

"But she just admitted it here for everyone to hear," Ezra says calmly. "Didn't she."

I gape at him for a long moment that feels like hours rather than seconds, the worst possible scenario flickering through my thoughts and leaving me feeling cold and hollow. Because deep down it seems there is only one way that Ezra might have come across a defense like this.

And that possibility is breaking my fucking heart.

Knowing my chances are slim, I have to ask: "Your Honor," I say with only a slight shake to my tone. "I would like to request a continuance."

Ezra looks at me with surprise, and I have to force myself to turn my eyes away from him and focus on the judge. I might do something drastic if I keep looking at him, like yell at him right here in open court. Or worse, start crying.

Judge Harding looks skeptical. "Ms. Pierce, this case has already seen several continuances."

"Yes, Your Honor," I answer tightly. "I'm aware of that, but these new allegations threaten my client's credibility. I would like the opportunity to gather refuting evidence."

Judge Harding studies me for a long moment, her thin lips pursing as she peers at me from over her glasses. For a moment, I think she is going to refuse, and I don't know what I will do if she does. I don't think I can continue, not when it feels like I'm falling to pieces.

Thankfully, something decides to go my way today. "All right," she concedes. "I will grant your continuance. I want everyone back here one week from today with their closing arguments, understand?"

"Yes, Your Honor," I manage quietly.

Bianca still looks as stunned as I feel as the bailiff helps her down from the stand. She steps across the tiles and stops just beside me with accusation in her eyes. "You promised," she whispers. "You promised I would not be made a fool."

"Bianca," I plead. "I didn't—I *promise*—"

"Your promises are empty," she cuts me off coldly. "Clearly." Her fists tighten at her sides. "We will speak tomorrow at your office. I need time today."

I nod dumbly, because what else can I do?

She's not even out the door when I start snatching up my things, needing to get out of this room as fast as humanly possible. As if putting distance between myself and Ezra will make the likelihood of his betrayal less possible.

But I don't even make it into the foyer.

"Dani," he calls, but I keep walking briskly, avoiding the elevator and getting all the way to the stairwell with every intention of fleeing that way, before his hand catches my elbow. "*Dani.*"

I tug at my arm, pushing through the heavy door leading to the stairs, but he follows me there too.

"Just wait a minute," he huffs. "I don't know what you're—"

I drop my notes onto the floor, wheeling around to shove at his chest. "How fucking *dare* you."

"What?" His eyes round. "What are you talking about?"

"You know exactly what you did," I seethe. "Bringing up her accusations from back then."

"Dani," he says incredulously. "We talked about this. This is a job. I have to—"

My eyes have begun to water, and I willfully beg them to stay dry. "When did you go through my notes, Ezra?"

To his credit, he looks properly taken aback.

"What?"

"Don't play dumb. Was it at my house? When we fucked in my office? When was it, Ezra? Were you always planning to fuck me over? Or are you going to tell me it was an accident? That you were just doing your *job?*"

"Go through your . . . Dani." He reaches for me, but I jerk away. I ignore his hurt expression. "Dani, I didn't go through your notes. I would *never* betray your trust like that. How could you even think that?"

"Tell me how you knew then," I practically spit, anger and hurt coursing through me and robbing me of my good sense. "How the fuck did you know why she left? She told me that in confidence."

Ezra looks slightly desperate now, and there's an errant urge to comfort him, but I fight it vehemently.

"Dani, I—" He shakes his head, still looking dazed. "You know I can't tell you about my private conversations with my client. You *know* that. But I am looking you in the eye right now and telling you I would *never* go through your notes or do anything like you're accusing me of doing. You have to know I would never do that."

"So you just want me to believe that, what? He told you? You *happened* to come across it? Both of those scenarios seem very fucking unlikely."

"Dani, you're being unreasonable," he huffs. "You can't—"

"I'm being *unreasonable?*" I feel myself gaping, hot fury licking over my entire body. "Let me tell you about *unreasonable*, Ezra. *Unreasonable* is you acting like a fucking snake so that you can save that slimeball of a human from paying what he fucking owes Bianca. You sit there and call me unreasonable while inhaling every lie Alexander gives you like a good little lapdog just to save an asshole a few bucks."

Ezra breathes in sharply at the same time that I do. I regret it immediately.

"I mean . . ." I swallow hard, trying to catch my breath and gather my thoughts, which are a scattered mess right now. "That's not what I—"

Ezra holds up a hand to stop me. "Yes, it is." His face is suddenly devastatingly blank. "It's exactly what you meant."

His jaw twitches, and the urge to apologize is there; I know what I just said was a low blow, but so is rifling through my notes. Which *has* to be what he did. Right?

Ezra huffs out a laugh, but there's no humor in it. Like a caricature of the act. It's scornful and laced with pain. "It's what you believe deep down. Isn't it, Dani? That I'm just as much of a piece of shit as Alexander is? It's what you always thought."

"That's not what I—"

"I just thought the last few weeks had changed that," he says woodenly. "I thought maybe you'd realized that I . . ." He shakes his head again. "But deep down, part of you will always think that, won't you."

"Ezra, don't try to make me the villain here. You're the one who—"

"You know," he says with another joyless laugh. "If you weren't so determined to get in your own way, one of these days you might realize that people really do care about you. That these walls you've built up in your head are doing nothing but keeping you from seeing just how much."

Confusion bleeds into the rage, leaving me unsure. "Ezra, you—"

"I'm sorry," he cuts me off. "I need some time. If you decide you want to talk about this like an actual adult, you know where to find me."

In a daze, I watch him turn and leave the stairwell, combing over every moment of that interaction, trying to piece together at what part of it *I* became the bad guy. I draw in a shaky breath as I kneel to gather my notes, steeling my resolve.

It's just another tactic, I tell myself even as painful uncertainty roils in my gut. *I'm not the one who fucked up here.*

But even when I've walked down three flights of stairs, even when I'm out of the building, even *hours* later while I sit lonely and miserable in my apartment . . . that uncertainty clings to me, filling me with doubt.

And I can't help but wonder if I *did* fuck up somewhere.

Twenty-Seven

DANI

"I TRUSTED YOU, Danica!" Bianca glares at me from her seat next to mine on the other side of Manuel's desk. "You betrayed me. You promised what I told you would not come up in court."

"I didn't betray you!" I shout back. "I don't know how Ezra got that information, but it did *not* come from me."

I have to stave off the compulsion to wince, knowing that this is not entirely true, most likely. I haven't spoken to Ezra since our blowup in the stairwell yesterday, and I won't pretend that the silence hasn't been hard. His despondent expression hasn't left my mind, and the doubt that plagues me over my quick assumptions kept me up for most of the night. But it's not something I can afford to dwell on right now.

Manuel watches the interaction between Bianca and me with steepled fingers resting against his chin, his expression unreadable. I know that Bianca's anger is enough to warrant her requesting a change of counsel, and not only would that wound me personally, given how I've come to care for her, but it would ruin my chances of being promoted. There's only so much Manny can do.

"Bianca," I try again, calming myself. I turn in my chair, taking her hand. Thankfully, she doesn't snatch it away. "I need you to look at me." Her eyes find mine, still wary. "I swear to you, I did not say a word about what you told me. Not one word. I can't say for sure what led to Lorenzo's team using that tactic"—not a lie, technically—"but I promise you, I did not betray your trust."

Not purposely, at least.

Bianca's red lips are still pressed into a tight line, her calculating gaze studying my expression as if searching for a lie. I force myself not to blink, not to break eye contact, needing her to see the sincerity there. Because no matter what Ezra may or may not have done, I did *not* betray Bianca willingly. I need her to know that.

"Bianca, I know you're my client, but I need you to know that I respect you deeply," I urge. "I would *never* do anything to hurt you. Not willfully."

Bianca's jaw works as she considers, several long moments passing before she finally breathes out a sigh. "I believe you," she tells me dolefully. "You are not the type to make this kind of mistake."

Except I might be, I think guiltily. *Just because I didn't do it on purpose doesn't mean it isn't my fault.*

"Thank you, Bianca." I exhale in relief all the same. "Really. I will fix this."

Manuel chooses this moment to speak up. "Is it possible that Lorenzo might have *told* his team about this?"

"Why would he do that?" My brow furrows. "The chances of it backfiring are too high. He'd have to be crazy to go that route."

"Unless he was that confident that we couldn't dispute it," Manuel points out. "It's not something we ever expected from them, and clearly, it took us off guard. Maybe that was the plan all along."

The idea of it gives me pause; it's more or less a scenario that I'd mockingly thrown at Ezra yesterday, but at the time, it had been too ridiculous to consider. Impossible, even. Now my mind's first instinct is to reject it, because if it's true, then I . . .

I shake my head. "There's no way Lorenzo would risk that. First he's inviting his mistress to sit in during sessions, and now he's openly admitting this isn't the first time he's been accused of infidelity? What does he have to gain from that?"

"It could be about power," Bianca muses. "It seems like something Lorenzo would do."

"I . . ." Panic simmers in my chest; that cannot be the answer. It *can't*. My brain physically cannot consider the idea that I hurt Ezra for no reason. I'm already so on edge that this new revelation would break me to pieces. "It doesn't matter where it came from."

Liar, my brain whispers. *It absolutely matters.*

"All we need to be concerned with is how to get on top of it. We have one week left before Judge Harding expects closing arguments. I'm *going* to make sure ours leaves no room for doubt that Lorenzo is a cheating piece of shit."

"We still haven't found anything that we can use as irrefutable proof of his infidelity," Manuel reminds me.

"I know," I sigh. "I know that. But . . . I know it's there. I can feel how close we are. And I'm going to find it. No distractions." I shoot Bianca a determined look. "I promise."

It takes her a second to tilt her head in a nod, but she looks less angry than she did before; she looks almost like she might give me another chance. "I hope so, Danica."

Bitterly, I can't help but think about the fact that there won't be anything to distract me this week, that there is nothing waiting for me at home but the freedom to throw myself into work.

I tell myself that I'm fine with that.

IT TAKES TWO days after the disastrous day in court for Vera and Nate to show up to my apartment and drag me outside of it, telling me that forty-eight hours without leaving is serial killer behavior. I didn't exactly come willingly to my mother's house for dinner, where we've all been invited; I fought them both through getting dressed and brushing my hair and even when they were shoving me out the door—but I'm here now, sulking in a corner and nursing a glass of wine while my parents and their spouses and my friends all laugh and work themselves into a good buzz.

"Dani!" my dad calls from his place on the couch. "Stop hiding and come talk to us."

"Vera was just going to tell us about how big of a crush she has on me," Nate laughs before taking a swig of his beer.

Vera lets out a snort that is much louder than normal; I assume the glass of wine she's holding isn't her first. "In your dreams."

"Only the *best* dreams," Nate coos.

"I think the two of you would make the sweetest couple," my mom sighs, her eyes noticeably bleary even from my place across the room. I *know* the glass in *her* hand is at least her third. "Bill, don't you think they would make the sweetest couple?"

My stepfather glances away from the television screen, where he's been scrolling to find the soccer game he's been going on and on about, giving my friends a confused expression. "I thought they were already together?"

"Nate *wishes*," Vera snorts.

Nate gives her a dreamy sort of smile that only comes from him being very tipsy. "With all three from the genie, babe."

My stepmother, Patty, touches my arm, making me jolt. "You need a refill, honey?"

Normally I would say no; two glasses is my limit on a typical weeknight—but I've been throwing myself at Bianca's case so hard that I won't think about Ezra and all the uncertainty surrounding our fight. The idea of thinking about absolutely nothing tonight is incredibly appealing.

"Sure," I tell her, holding out my glass so she can pour more wine into it. "Why not?"

"You look tired, dear," Patty tuts. "Are you getting enough sleep?"

"Knowing her," Nate calls, "she isn't getting *any* sleep. She's probably too busy with—"

"*Nate*," Vera hisses.

He has the good grace to look sheepish. "Work," he says. "I was going to say work."

We both know it's a lie, and I do my best to keep my expression neutral. I haven't told either of them about what happened with Ezra. Yes, they've heard about what went down in court, and yes, they've made their own assumptions, but I haven't been able to bring myself to tell them about the things I said to him after. I'm not even sure why. Am I embarrassed? That seems ridiculous, since all the things I'd said felt justified at the time, but the more time that passes . . . the more my doubt grows.

"We should play charades," my mother suggests loudly.

My dad groans. "You're terrible at charades. Especially when you're drunk."

"I am not drunk!" she protests, even though the flush of her cheeks says otherwise. "Dani!" She looks at me expectantly. "Do you want to play?"

I've already gulped down a third of my new glass, my head swimming a little. "I actually think I need some air," I say. "You guys start without me."

Vera perks up. "Want me to come with?"

"No, no." I shake my head. "I'll just be a minute."

It's warmer outside on the deck, the summer air stifling and making my already warm cheeks even more heated. Still, goose bumps break out over my skin, but I suspect that's more to do with my inner turmoil than the weather. I sink into one of the deck chairs morosely, blinking out over the backyard and trying not to think about the last time I was out here. What that Fourth of July party set in motion.

What's worse than the doubt is the overwhelming feeling of something being *missing*. I'd gotten so used to seeing Ezra every day, to talking to him throughout, that now that he's gone, it feels like there is a hole in my life. A big, stupid, blond-haired hole.

I *miss* him, and that's the most agonizing part of all this. That the asshole I never should have come to care for could make me miss him this badly.

It's not a good idea, I'm well aware of that fact as I place my glass on a side table and pull my phone out of my pocket; I'm three drinks in and feeling sorry for myself, and that's a recipe for disaster. But it doesn't stop me from finding our message thread. From hovering over his last text while something squeezes tightly in my chest.

Ezra: Don't miss me too badly today. 😉

My eyes well up, and I swipe away the tears forming quickly, telling myself I'm being stupid. For what, I can't even say at this point. Am I stupid for still missing him? Am I stupid for accusing him of something that deep down doesn't *feel* like Ezra? Or am I just stupid for continuing with this radio silence without even trying to talk to him, cutting him off with no attempt to meet him halfway?

I tap out a text before I can overthink it.

Me: Hi.

I stare at my phone until my vision blurs, and it takes several agonizing minutes for the little dots to appear, several more before he finally sends a reply.

Ezra: Hi.

I exhale shakily, relief flooding me.

Me: How are you?

His answer comes quicker this time.

Ezra: Really? Three days of silence
and that's what you want to
ask me?

                              Me: Yes?

Ezra: Do you still think I went
through your things?

                    Me: I don't know.

It's the truth, and right now, with my inhibitions low, I can't
give him anything but.

Ezra: How could you think
that I would do that to you,
Dani? After everything?
I thought you knew me better
than that.

                    Me: I thought I did too.

Ezra: Apparently not well enough.

              Me: Ezra . . . You've used some
              pretty shady tactics in the past.
              You have to admit that.

The dots dance for a long time, and I bite my lip as I wait.

> **Ezra:** You and I both know how
> unfair it is of you to throw that at me.

I wince. Deep down I *do* know it's unfair. I know how much he loathes having to follow Alexander's every whim. But I also know that there is a part of me, buried even deeper, that can't just accept it. Maybe I didn't even realize it was there before our fight.

> **Me:** But you still do it, Ezra. I know
> you have a good reason, but can
> you really say that you wouldn't
> purposefully hurt me if Alexander
> told you to? How am I to know if
> he found out about us? How do I
> know he didn't TELL you to
> go through my things?

> **Ezra:** That's bullshit, Dani. you
> KNOW that's bullshit.

> **Me:** But I don't. Maybe that's
> why I'm so scared.

I realize it's true as I say it. Maybe I ignored it before. Maybe I was too wrapped up in the glow of the thing blossoming between us to even realize how terrified I was of being left behind again. Because he would, I think. Leave me behind. If Alexander told him to. And what's more, knowing what I know about his family, about his mother . . . could I even blame him?

Ezra: Dani . . . I would never hurt
you. Not on purpose.

Ezra: I care about you too much to
even consider it.

A tear slips down my cheek, and I don't bother wiping it away.
My chest hurts, because I *want* to believe that. I want to tell him
to come find me. I want to tell him that we can work this out. That
I know he would never hurt me on purpose.

But I've been proven wrong too many times before, and in my
wine-addled brain . . . the idea of ending it before it can happen
seems better for both of us.

Me: It's probably better this way.

Me: It would have been a mess
between us, you know?

Me: There's almost no chance it
would have ever worked out.

I hold my breath as I watch him typing, tears readily falling
down my face now. I want to take the words back even as I type
them. Why don't I do that?

Ezra: Are you saying that because
you believe it? Or because you're
scared of even trying?

I consider the question. I don't think it's one I can give him an answer to, but if I'm being honest . . . it isn't because I don't *know* the answer.

> **Me:** I'm sorry about the
> things I said.

> **Me:** I really am. I overstepped.

> **Me:** But maybe it's better this way.

The dots appear, then disappear—the pattern repeating over and over for what feels like forever before:

> **Ezra:** If that's what you really
> want. I can't chase you if you don't
> want to be caught, Dani.

I choke back a sob.

> **Me:** I'm sorry.

His answer comes immediately.

> **Ezra:** So am I.

I swipe out of the thread and toss my phone on the table near my wineglass, dropping my face in my hands. I've spent the last few days burying every emotion I had in regard to Ezra, and now it seems like the dam has finally burst, leaving me a sobbing mess.

I want to believe him, I realize. I want to believe that he didn't do the things I accused him of. Deep down, I think I might already.

But a part of me also believes what I said. That the chances of us working out with so many things weighed against us are slim to none. How could we ever make things work when his mother will always come first? When I couldn't love him if she didn't?

I choke on a shaky inhale.

Love?

I can't—there's no way that I—

But you do, a more sensible part of my brain whispers. *You know you do.*

I snatch my wineglass and down what's left, pushing up from the deck chair with every intention of calling an Uber and getting back to my apartment before anyone can catch me wallowing. I can't be around people right now. I shove my phone back in my pocket after calling a ride, wiping my eyes as best I can and hoping I can blame the redness that's surely there on the copious amounts of wine that I've had.

My parents and stepparents are still laughing on the couch when I reenter the living room, but my friends are missing.

"Honey?" my mother calls, her brows furrowing as if she's trying to suss out my emotions from just my expression. Thank God she's already hammered. "Are you okay?"

"I'm fine," I croak. "Where are Nate and Vera?"

"Oh, I think they said something about grabbing a game from the closet. Do you want to play?"

I shake my head. "I actually think I'm going to head out. I have a lot of work to do tomorrow."

"Well, okay," my mother says with a slight frown. "Don't work too hard, all right?"

I give her my best impression of a smile, but it feels wrong. "I'll try."

I head through the kitchen toward the hall so that I can tell Nate and Vera that I'm leaving. The hallway closet where we keep the board games is open, but my friends are missing. Frowning, I move around the open door just to notice the guest bedroom door beside it is ajar, sounds coming from inside. Are they fighting again?

My hand is shoving the door open as I move to break up whatever it is they're fussing about, barely getting two words out before I stop dead in my tracks.

"Hey, I'm gonna— What the fuck?"

Nate and Vera break apart, Nate's hair a wild mess and Vera's no better, her braids, which she'd had clipped back from her face, now falling loosely around her shoulders. They're both wide eyed and swollen mouthed, and even in the dimness of the room, it's obvious that I just caught the tail end of the tipping point of their will-they-won't-they.

"Are you fucking kidding me?" I groan. "You chose to cave to this *now*?"

Vera gapes at me. "I—"

Nate looks much the same. "We—"

"Fucking hell." I close my eyes, breathing deeply just to let it out. Of course they're finally realizing they're perfect for each other on the same night my love life is falling apart. "Congratulations. Don't stop on my account. God knows you waited long enough."

"It isn't—" Vera clears her throat. "It's not what you—"

"Oh, shut up," I sigh. "If my life wasn't a fucking mess right now, I'd be planning your wedding."

Nate immediately looks concerned. "Wait, what?"

"Nothing." I shake my head. "Not something I want to get into at this moment. I just came to tell you guys I called an Uber. I'm heading out."

Vera frowns. "Do we need to talk about something?"

"No," I tell her wearily. "I honestly can't right now." I gesture between them. "I expect a full report on *this* tomorrow when I'm more sober."

"I mean," Nate says with a grin. "We all knew she couldn't resist me."

He yelps when Vera pinches his side. "If you ever want to kiss me again, you'll shut up right now."

"Yes, ma'am," he laughs.

My heart aches watching them. It's strange, being happy for someone when you're so miserable yourself. My phone pings, signaling my Uber has arrived.

"My ride's here," I manage tightly. "I'll talk to you guys tomorrow."

I close the door behind me, taking another deep, steadying breath as I will myself to look normal so that my parents won't realize anything is amiss when I leave. I don't text Ezra again, not even when the urge to do so becomes unbearable. He doesn't text me either.

And what's worse . . . I have a feeling that he might never do so again.

Twenty-Eight

EZRA

FOUR DAYS AFTER walking away from Dani, and mostly, I'm just numb. There isn't a moment that passes that I don't want to go to her, to beg her to see reason, to *shake* some sense into her if I have to—but I know it won't do any good. I know that someone like Dani can't be forced into making a decision. She has to come to the conclusion on her own.

I just hope that conclusion involves me, somehow.

I meant it when I said that she was worth staying for, but I never anticipated that she would actively push me away. In hindsight, maybe I should have seen it coming. She's so convinced that anyone she gets close to will hurt her, will lie to her or leave her behind, that she runs from any opportunity that might give them the chance.

But I don't have time to dwell on that right now.

Lorenzo's office is the last place I want to be, but given that he's apparently "too busy" today to stop by mine and sign the documents I need from him, he left me with no other choice. I ride the sleek elevator up to his floor in doleful silence, trying to ignore the heavy weight of my silent phone in my pocket. There is so much more I wanted to say to her last night, but it was the truth when I said I can't chase her if she doesn't want to be chased. That bullshit platitude about setting something free if you love it flits through my mind, and I snort out a laugh.

Dani's more likely to run for the hills without looking back.

The elevator doors open to spill out onto Lorenzo's floor, and I steel myself for what will surely be an unpleasant visit as I traipse through the hall toward his office. It rests at the corner of the building, and I take a deep breath when I reach it, knocking on his door and readying myself to play nice.

When he doesn't answer, I knock again, pressing my ear to the door and catching two raised male voices on the other side.

"—said that no one would find out," one of them says.

Lorenzo, I recognize. Not surprising. The other one, however, is.

"And they won't," the voice of Alexander answers tersely. "Not if you keep your mouth shut. There's no proof that anyone would be able to piece together. I've buried the records so deep in Bianca's financials that not even the world's greatest accountant could piece it together."

I press closer to the door. What are they talking about?

"If Bianca finds out what we did," Lorenzo stresses, "she will ruin us both."

"She *won't*," Alexander hisses. "Not if you—"

They both go quiet, and I manage to pull away and compose myself as if I hadn't just been listening at the door when it swings open.

Alexander's icy blue eyes meet mine. "What are you doing out here?"

"My job?" I keep my tone casual as I hold up the packet of documents. "I need Lorenzo's signature on these. Apparently, he was too busy to come to me."

Alexander lingers in the doorway for a moment, studying my features as if trying to determine whether it's possible I heard anything. I school them to remain completely neutral.

"You wanna let him sign them so I can get back to work?"

"Fine," Alexander concedes. "Hurry up."

Lorenzo looks out of sorts when I step into the room, his already-lined face wearier, a flush creeping up his neck. "You said you would be later," he accuses.

"Didn't realize I'd be interrupting," I answer coolly.

Lorenzo sneers as he snatches the documents from me, leaning over his desk as he begins to sign each one. I turn to Alexander, eyeing him. "What are you doing here, anyway?"

"None of your business," he says flatly.

"A lot of things about *my* case seem to be none of my business," I chuckle. "But that's nothing new, I guess."

"You are such an unruly child," Lorenzo snorts, straightening and handing the documents back to me. "I would never let a son of mine speak to me this way."

"It's a good thing I'm not Alexander's son then, isn't it."

Lorenzo scoffs. "It is good for him, I think. Nothing but a disappointment, your whole life. So ungrateful when he raised you as his own. And your whore mother—"

I crowd him, fisting his tie roughly in the blink of an eye. "Don't you say another fucking word about my mother."

"He isn't saying anything that isn't true." Alexander laughs cruelly from behind me.

I turn on him, curling my lip. "You're just pissed that she finally found the good sense to try to get away from you. She realized what a piece of shit you are."

"Careful, boy." Alexander's expression darkens. "You don't want to say anything that you might regret."

I hear his warning, and I know exactly what it means. I know that it's not *me* who will regret my outburst, and the thought turns my stomach. I can't say why today is different, why I can't brush off the casual threat, but my heart is hammering now. But my skin feels too tight and my blood feels too hot, and my vision blurs until I can hardly see anymore.

It's Lorenzo's callous insults. It's Alexander's blasé tone in regard to holding me under his thumb. It's Dani's voice in my head, telling me that even if I had good reasons to follow him, I still *do* it. Even knowing how evil he is. It's *all* of it.

And I realize all at once that I've had enough.

"And what are you going to do, Alexander?" I release Lorenzo's tie, stepping closer to the other man. "Are you going to threaten me? My mother? Are you going to push her so hard she wants to die again?"

Alexander looks unruffled, and that only makes me angrier. But not nearly as much as what he says next.

"It would have probably been easier on everyone if she had," he says coldly, his face devoid of emotion. "At least then I wouldn't still be putting up with the pair of you."

I hear a roaring in my head, my body moving before I even recognize what's happening. One second I'm standing a foot away from the man who has made my life a living hell, made my *mother's* life a living hell, and the next, he's crumpling to the floor, blood streaming from his nose. That same blood covering my knuckles.

"You worthless piece of shit," Alexander snarls, clutching his bloody nose. "I'll fucking end you. I'll lock your mother up in a hole and make sure she *never* sees—"

I crouch, grabbing him by the lapel of his jacket and forcing his head up. "Try it," I warn. "I think you'll find that when you push someone to the point where they have nothing to lose, you won't like what they're capable of. Do you want to see what I'm capable of, Alexander?"

For the first time in my entire life, there is a flash of fear in the old man's eyes. For the first time ever—I *don't* feel fear when I look into them. He's just a man, I realize. Just an evil old man with more power than he deserves.

"I'm going to make sure you never touch her again," I tell him resolutely. "I don't care what it takes. And if you do, if you put one hand on her, if you so much as mess up her fucking hair—I will kill you. Do you understand me?"

"You can't threaten me—"

"I just did," I seethe. "Nothing to lose, remember? But go ahead, call the police. I'll have plenty to say about you if they want to talk. *Plenty* to say."

Again there is that flicker of alarm in the depths of his blue eyes, his pupils dilating and his throat bobbing with a swallow. I swipe my bloody knuckles on his suit jacket, standing to my full height and turning to point a finger at Lorenzo.

"If I ever hear you insult my mother again, I'll extend you the same warning."

Lorenzo grits his teeth. "You cannot—"

"Again," I tell him calmly. "I just did."

I straighten my suit, taking a deep breath and blowing it out, feeling lighter than I have in years. I step over Alexander's crumpled figure, moving toward the door. I pause just before I open it, turning back to him one last time.

"Oh, and one more thing," I call, my mouth splitting into a grin. "I quit."

Alexander starts yelling again as I shut the door, but I'm over it. Closing the door on his bloody, irate form feels like closing the door on a part of my life that I've long yearned to escape from.

I feel . . . free. For maybe the first time.

I'm still smiling as I start moving back through the halls, only slowing when I catch sight of Lorenzo's mistress in the foyer talking to his assistant. I frown as I watch them embrace, thinking that it's weird that they would be so close.

But that's not my problem anymore, I suppose.

I ride back down the elevators in a completely different mood than I rode up in. But I have another stop to make.

IF I NEVER have to come back to this house again, it will be too soon. I stare up at the massive structure where I spent my childhood, the elegant details and expensive features a point of envy to anyone who wouldn't know any better. No one could know just looking at it what sort of hell lurks inside.

I push open the heavy French doors without knocking, stepping into the foyer and calling my mother's name. Rita appears from the kitchen to give me a puzzled look, but I ignore her, calling for my mother again. I hear her voice faintly from the direction of her library, and I stomp toward it in a rush, only letting out the breath I'm holding when I find her sitting in her favorite chair, looking at me quizzically.

"Ezra?"

I cross the space in just a few short steps, falling to my knees and wrapping my arms around her waist to hug her tight.

"Ezra?" Her hand falls to my hair, stroking her fingers through it. "What's wrong?"

"I want you to leave with me, Mom," I whisper.

"Darling, what are you talking about? You know I can't—"

"I hit him."

"Him? Who?"

"Alexander," I tell her. "I hit him. I think I might have broken his nose." I pull back, tilting my head up to meet her eyes. "I told him if he ever touched you again, I would kill him. I don't regret it either."

My mother's mouth parts in surprise, a myriad of emotions flickering across her face one after the other. "Ezra . . . you shouldn't have done that."

I shut my eyes tight, feeling stung by her soft admonition. "Mom, he's horrible. I can't just sit here and let him use you anymore. Because that's what he's doing, don't you see that? He's *using* you. Using us both. That's all we are to him. Pawns. That's all *anyone* is to him."

My mother is quiet for several seconds, her eyes becoming glassy and her lips quivering. "I know you must think I'm weak," she admits. "For being so placid for so long."

"No, Mom, I don't—"

She holds up a hand to stop me. "You'd be right, Ezra." And when I try to protest again, "No, you would be. Because I am. I know that."

Despite her words, she smiles at me.

"I think . . . for a long time now, I've felt like I deserve this. Every choice I've ever made has only hurt you or your brother."

"That's bullshit, you've—"

"Let me get this out," she says with more force than I've ever heard her use. "Every choice I've made has caused you pain. Has pushed your brother away from me. Those are my burdens to bear. But I can't let you take on any more for yourself. Not because of me."

"It's too late," I tell her. "I quit. I quit, and I'm not going back. You and I both know that it's *you* he's going to take it out on. That *you* will be the one who suffers, just so that he can make me suffer."

"Ezra . . ."

"Come with me," I beg. "Just leave. I'll keep you safe. We can fight this together. I won't ever let him hurt either of us again if you'll just *let* me."

She considers this, her eyes thoughtful and sad. "He won't allow it. You know that. He'll come after us both. He knows too many people, Ezra. There's nothing we can do to him."

"We won't know unless we try," I urge. "I'm just asking you to give me the chance to *try*."

"And what happens when he starts making your life worse? It won't be just you he'll come after, Ezra. It will be your friends. Anyone you care about."

I wince at the thought of Dani, grateful at least that it seems like there will be no chance now that Alexander will ever know what she means to me.

I huff out a humorless laugh. "I don't think that will be an issue. Not anymore. There's no one in my life close enough to me for him to use."

"What about the woman you were seeing?"

I shake my head. "That was nothing, Mom. It's done."

"That was her, wasn't it? The woman I met the night of the party?"

I consider lying to her, but I'm so fucking raw that I just don't have it in me to do so. "It was," I admit hoarsely.

"She seemed nice," my mother offers.

"She is," I agree. "But it doesn't matter. It didn't work out. It's better that way, honestly. It means that there's nothing Alexander can do to me. There's no reason for you not to say yes."

Her thumb traces lightly back and forth across my jaw, her eyes as lucid as I've ever seen them. I can see the moment she comes to a decision; her spine goes a little straighter, and her shoulders square, and for one brief moment, she reminds me of the woman she used to be. The one who I believed could do anything.

"All right, Ezra," she says softly. "I will come with you."

"Good." I kiss her hand, rising to my feet. "I want you to go to your room and pack some clothes. Just the essentials. I want to be gone in ten minutes."

"Okay," she answers just as quietly, nodding as she starts to push up out of her chair.

I don't wait for her, moving back through the house as I hear her heading toward the stairs, deciding to wait by the door so I can watch and make sure I don't miss it if Alexander decides to come home early.

"This is stupid," a voice sounds from behind me, making me jump.

Eli is leaning against the entrance to the sitting room just off the entryway, his arms crossed and his eyes hard. "You know that Dad will never let you get away with this."

"I would like to see either of you try to stop me," I say in warning. "She's not going to suffer for one more second in this fucking house. Do you understand?"

"Suffer," Eli scoffs. "Because being pampered around the clock by nurses while having every comfort at her beck and call is *suffering*."

"She's a *prisoner*, Eli," I spit. "Your own mother has been locked up in this house with no say about any part of her life, and you've never lifted a finger to help her. You've never said a *word*."

"I'm not the one who—"

"Shut the fuck up," I growl. "I'm talking now. That man you worship so much is a monster. A fucking *monster*. He locked our mother in her room. He made her hate herself so much that she wanted to *die*. Do you get that? Or are you so deluded by Alexander's lies that you've actually convinced yourself that *she's* the villain in that story? For what? For trying to find any semblance of happiness in this hellhole she was trapped in with that man who treated her like she wasn't worth his time?"

Eli's brow knits, his mouth turning down in a frown. I watch as he averts his eyes to the floor, no doubt mulling over my words. "That's easy for you to say," he says quietly. "It was always about you, after she had you. You were all that she cared about."

"That's not true."

We both turn at the sound of my mother's voice, and I watch as she drops her bag on the floor, closing the distance between Eli and her until she stands directly in front of him. She reaches up to press her palm against his cheek, a tear slipping down hers as she gives him a sad smile.

"I have loved you since before you were born, Eli," she tells him. "I have loved you every day since. I'm sorry that I didn't fight harder to show you. I'm sorry that I couldn't bring myself to speak out against your father's lies. But don't you think for one second that I loved you any less than your brother. Not for one second."

To my utter shock, I watch as my brother's lip trembles, his hand twitching as if he might place it over Mom's for the briefest of moments. When he swallows, getting himself under control and saying nothing, I decide we can't wait any longer.

"Mom," I remind her gently. "We need to go."

Mom lingers where she's at for another second, brushing her thumb across Eli's cheek. "I love you. I'm sorry if you ever thought that I didn't." She pushes up on her toes, pressing a kiss to the place her thumb just was, and Eli's eyes shut, his mouth a tight line. "Be happy, Eli," she whispers. Then she turns on her heel, grabs her bag, and follows me out.

I send up a silent promise then and there that she'll never come back here again.

Twenty-Nine

DANI

FIVE DAYS AFTER Ezra walked away from me, and mostly, I'm just lost. I've gone over that day in the stairwell more times than I can count, picking apart the conversation we had via text an equal number of times. There is a deep, needy part of me that wishes he would come after me—even though I know it's irrational to feel that way. Ezra made it clear that he won't be chasing after me anymore.

And deep down, I know that's my fault.

I think I knew even when I accused him of betraying me that it wasn't something he would do. I've had hours and hours to agonize over the possibility, and the conclusion I keep coming to is that I acted irrationally, that I should have given him a chance to explain himself. But the truth is . . . I *am* afraid of this thing that's been brewing between us. Maybe I didn't fully realize before that day in court, maybe my subconscious had been just looking for something to attach to so that it could protect my heart from another potential break; I can't be sure. All I know is that regardless of how I feel or what I know . . . I miss him.

But how can I go to him after all the horrible things I said? I wouldn't even know where to begin. "I'm sorry" feels trite in the face of throwing the most painful parts of his life back at him. No matter how I look at it, I'm the asshole now. I've spent so long pushing people away . . . I don't even know how to begin to pull them closer.

There are only two days left before we're expected to reconvene in court to deliver our closing arguments, and outside of the knowledge that I will have to face Ezra again, that I will have to *see* him again and pretend that I don't miss him terribly—I still have practically nothing concrete to bring home Bianca's case. I've been over her financials again and again. I've combed through record after record of bland business dealings from Lorenzo's office; there is a mountain of paperwork sitting on my kitchen table that I've read twice over and come up with nothing.

Which means that not only have I failed in my personal life, I'm going to fall flat on my face at work too.

I'm currently sifting through a massive loan contract on the second mortgage in Lorenzo's mistress's name; in my heart I know there's something there, but I just can't seem to put the pieces together. Is it where they meet up? Did he buy it for her? She has it listed as a "rental property," which, by all accounts, makes absolutely no sense given that there's no paper trail of any tenants.

I'm drowning in a sea of my own making when a knock sounds at my door, and I have to physically shove piles of paperwork away just so I can swim my way out of the mess. I assume it's Nate reporting back after his self-appointed stakeout; he insisted last night that he should go sit outside the "rental property" today and see if he could see anything fishy going on. Like he's some sort of PI now. It got him out of my hair, which means I haven't had to answer any questions about Ezra, so I allowed it.

All of this to say it comes as a complete surprise when I wrench my door open to reveal a very haggard-looking Ezra Hart leaning against my doorframe. His normally bright green eyes seem duller, and there is a few days' worth of stubble at his jaw that he normally keeps shaved. It's darker than his hair, and the ruggedness it adds to his already unfairly attractive appearance is downright sinful. Even knowing it's not the time to notice these things, I can't help but do it anyway.

Every molecule in my body seems to ready itself in a position that would force me to leap into his arms, and it's an *actual* physical toll, resisting the urge. "Ezra," I say in slight shock. "What are you doing here?"

The dark circles under his eyes conflict with the thin smile he gives me, and he shrugs one shoulder, crossing his arms over his chest. "That's a good question."

"Do you—" My tongue feels tangled, like it's forgotten how to make words. "Do you want to come in?"

My heart sinks when he shakes his head. "I won't be long."

"Oh."

I don't know what else to say. I thought him showing up here meant . . . But no. He said he wasn't going to chase me, didn't he? So why is he here?

"I just had some things to say," he tells me carefully, "and then I'm going to get out of your hair."

Don't go, I want to beg. *Stay in my hair. Nest there, for all I care.*

I say none of that. "What did you want to say?"

"I needed you to know that I didn't do what you thought I did," he says evenly, holding my gaze with sincerity in his eyes. "I'm not here to plead my case, but I need you to know that I would *never* betray your trust like that."

"I . . ." A pressure builds in my chest, one that feels too big, too much. It makes the words harder. "I know," I say honestly. "I know you wouldn't."

I don't know what I expected him to do with my admission, but a solemn nod was the last thing on my mind. Though that's all I get.

"Good." Another slow nod.

His jaw works as if he's rolling his next words over his tongue, unsure if he wants to let them out or not. I know that I should say something, that I should tell him I'm sorry, that I didn't mean what I said, that I know he would never hurt me on purpose—but fear keeps my mouth shut. Because I don't know what will happen if he's forced to choose between being with me or keeping his mother safe. I know I could never *ask* him to choose.

And maybe that means I was right, as much as it kills me. Maybe this was never going to work out.

"I shouldn't have said what I said," I tell him, knowing I can't let him walk away without saying it. "In the stairwell. I went too far."

His head ducks as he watches his feet, shifting his weight from one foot to the other as he nods. "You weren't exactly wrong."

"No, Ezra, I—"

"I was a coward," he admits quietly. "I *did* do everything he wanted, because I was too afraid to refuse him. I was acting like I was still just a kid hiding in my room from this scary man that lived in my house. Thinking that if I kept my head down, he wouldn't notice me, that I could get by."

"Ezra, that isn't—"

"But you made me realize that getting by isn't going to solve anything," he says determinedly, turning up his face to meet my gaze. "And I think I needed that."

It feels harder to breathe. "You did?"

"I did," he answers gently. "And for that I wanted to say thank you."

I can't help it, I bark out a laugh. "You're *thanking* me?"

"Yeah," he chuckles. "I guess I am."

"Jesus Christ," I scoff, scrubbing a hand down my face.

It's the lightest moment I've had in days, and everything about it makes me want to pull him close, to wrap my arms around him, but at this point, I don't even know if he'd want me to. It keeps me rooted in place.

"There was one more thing I wanted to tell you," he says, straightening.

My breath catches when he takes a step closer, his hand lifting to cup my cheek. My voice comes out on an exhale. "Yeah?"

"I meant everything I said to you." His eyes search my face, and I have to force myself to keep still, to not lean into him. "You *are* worth staying for," he murmurs. "I still believe that." My lashes flutter when his lips press to mine, too soft to even be called a kiss, but I feel it in my toes all the same. He lets out a stuttered breath after. "But *you* have to believe that too."

He pulls back, and I sway on my feet before catching myself.

"And when you realize that," he says slowly, "I want to be the first one to know."

I blink at him in a daze, a million things running through my mind but not one of them making its way out of my mouth. I just . . . stand there.

"That's all I wanted to say."

"I . . ." My mouth hangs open, and the words are right there, right *there*—but so is that fear. "You will be."

I expect him to be angry, or disappointed, but instead, Ezra smiles at me. That same one that feels too bright, the one that lights me up.

"Good," he answers softly.

We both continue to stare at each other, but I can see the moment that Ezra is gearing up to leave. He shifts, just a little, and he gives me a short nod, and all I can seem to do is the same.

"I'll let you get back to it," he says.

"Okay."

He turns on his heel, and I'm three seconds from calling out to him when he turns back, looking strangely lighter. "Oh, and also . . . Anton Andrews."

My nose wrinkles as I'm caught off guard. "What?"

He doesn't answer, just flashes me one last sweet smile, before he leaves me standing in my open door, more lost than I've ever been.

But what's more, I feel surprisingly hopeful for the first time in days.

Even if I have no idea why.

IT TAKES ME barely twenty minutes to find everything I need to know about Anton Andrews. Twenty-nine years old, no outstanding debt . . . So far, I haven't come across anything that would lead Ezra to believe it's a name I should be looking into. It has to be important, Ezra wouldn't have mentioned him otherwise, but at first glance, I just can't seem to determine why. The name sounds familiar, nagging at the back of my brain, but I can't seem to grasp it.

I haven't allowed myself to think about everything else he said, because I know if I start down that road, I'll get lost on it. I tell myself that it's something I will face after this trial. After that there is nothing else between us either way. After that . . . no matter what happens, I won't have any more excuses not to face the things I'm actively avoiding.

Things like how much it hurts to think about never seeing Ezra again. How devastating a possibility it is that he might never smile at me like he did today ever again. I know that the answer is there, staring me in the face, but I stubbornly push it aside, just like I do everything else.

I push a stack of Bianca's financial statements for her trust away so I can reach a folder I'm hunting for; it's the last bit we were able to find in Bianca's storage, mostly concerning the transfer of the funds from Italy to the United States—and while I'm sure it will yield as little as all the ones I've already looked at, I want to be able to say I've exhausted every option. I jolt when my phone rings, causing me to knock the entire stack onto the floor, and papers scatter everywhere.

"Fuck," I mutter.

Ignoring the mess, I snatch up my phone and bring it to my ear. "Yeah?"

"So I'm still on my stakeout," Nate tells me. "And you'll never guess what I've found."

I breathe out a sigh. "You know you're not a detective, right? Only you would waste your time on this."

"Hey! Vera is here too."

"I refuse to believe that."

There's a moment of silence before: "Um, I didn't have anything else to do today."

"Damn it, Vera," I groan. "You're supposed to be the smart one."

"Are you saying I'm not smart?" Nate huffs.

"I'm assuming you called for a reason," I venture, kneeling on my living room floor so that I can start gathering the strewn documents. "Or did you need coffee and doughnuts?"

"I'm starting to think I shouldn't even tell you my amazing news," Nate practically *hmph*s. "You're being awfully testy."

"We're due back in court in *two* days, I have nothing concrete yet, and now Ez—" I press my lips together. "I'm just a little stressed, okay?"

I should have known Nate wasn't going to let it slide. "Did you say Ezra? What's wrong with Ezra?"

"Nothing is wrong with Ezra," I mumble. "Forget I said anything."

Vera's voice nears the phone, like she's pulling it away from Nate. "Do I need to kick someone's ass?"

Yeah, I think bitterly. *Mine.*

"Never mind that." I sweep papers into a pile. "Tell me why you called."

"So we're outside the mistress's rental property, right? And at first, I thought it was vacant. It's so . . . tidy. There's no lawn furniture, or signs, or outdoor rugs . . . nothing."

"So is it vacant?"

"No," Vera starts. "Actually—"

"No, no, no," Nate tuts. "I want to tell her. This was my idea."

Vera snorts. "What does it matter?"

"Because you said this was a dumb idea," he counters.

"At the time," she deadpans, "I thought it was."

"I would like a written apology from you both," Nate says smugly.

"Yeah," Vera replies. "That's not going to happen."

"Well, maybe I won't—"

"*Guys.*" I snatch up the haphazard pile I've made, pushing to my feet and throwing the entire thing onto the table. "Can you just tell me why you called?"

"Right," Nate answers contritely. "So, it's not empty. Actually, you'll never guess who's living there."

He pauses for effect, and I roll my eyes as I stoop to grab one last document I left on the floor. I'm just about to add it to the pile on my table as Nate starts talking again, but a signature at the bottom catches my eye. Nate's voice fades a bit as I stare at it in disbelief, scanning the rest of the page and feeling my heart rate quicken with every new line. I start sifting through the other pages, and even though there isn't another occurrence of the signature—not that there needs to be, the one is damning enough—there *is* an obvious pattern. One that has my blood rushing in my ears.

"Hello?" Nate sounds impatient. "Did you hear me? Are you even listening?"

"No," I tell him honestly. "Sorry. I wasn't."

"Oh my God, stop spacing out. This is important! I think we really have something here."

I swallow thickly, glancing at the signature on the first page again before setting it gently back on the table.

"Yeah . . ." I say breathlessly. "Yeah, I think I do too."

Thirty

DANI

"YOU ARE SQUIRMING, Danica."

I will my knee to stop bouncing, glancing at Bianca, who is smirking at me from her seat. "They're late."

"Perhaps Lorenzo needs time to fix his hair," Bianca muses. "It is looking very thin lately."

My mouth quirks. "Not everyone ages gracefully, I guess."

"It is a gift, this is true."

"At least we'll be the ones doing the surprising today," I tell her. "We can make fools of *them* for a change."

Bianca makes a disgusted sound. "I never knew Lorenzo would be so sure of himself that he would stoop so low. I should have known better."

"Lorenzo?"

"I spoke with him," she says.

"What?" I turn in my seat. "When?"

"He called me a few days ago." Her expression is resigned, not sad, just . . . final. "He wanted to try to bully me into going away.

I told him if he thinks I would, he is much more of an idiot than I thought. But he told me as much that day. That it was his idea to use the truth against me."

My pulse quickens; it's a truth I've already arrived at on my own, that Ezra didn't betray me like I accused him of doing, but hearing it plainly . . . it's a strange emotion. Like guilt and relief all wrapped into one.

"And you're . . . okay? To proceed as planned?"

She nods heavily. "I am ready to put it behind me."

"I just want to make sure that it's not too much for you, what we found."

She shakes her head. "I have made peace with Lorenzo's mistakes. I will not mourn what I cannot change."

"Listen," I tell her, placing my hand over hers. "Today, *he's* going to be mourning his mistakes." I haven't told her everything; there are people who need to hear the things I've uncovered first, as selfish as that makes me, but knowing that she'll have more justice than what she will surely gain today steels my resolve. "I promise you that, Bianca. And this time, I won't break it."

Bianca pats the back of my hand, covering it with her free one, smiling at me warmly. "You never did, dear," she assures me. "You are a powerful woman. I knew this from our first meeting. I am glad I chose you."

I have to swallow around the thick lump that forms in my throat; I don't trust my voice. I nod at her instead, her approval meaning more to me than she'll ever know. Bianca Casiraghi is a culmination of hardship and tribulation being overcome and recycled into power. I can only hope that one day I can be half the woman she is.

"I'm glad you chose me too," I finally manage tightly.

The courtroom doors burst open before she can reply, and we turn in our seats to watch Lorenzo following an unexpected face. I frown at Eli Hart leading him to his seat, turning back to the door to search for Ezra and wondering why Eli would be joining him so late in the game. When he never shows, my confusion only intensifies.

"Sorry we're late, Your Honor," Eli says, addressing the judge. "There have been some changes to Mr. Casiraghi's counsel."

Judge Harding arches one brow. "I can see that. The other Mr. Hart won't be joining us?"

"Unfortunately," Eli answers. "Ezra Hart is no longer employed at our firm."

My mouth parts in surprise, my eyes widening. The fuck? Ezra doesn't work for Alexander anymore? Did he quit? Was he fired? What about his mom? Did he not work there when he came to see me? The questions bounce around my brain like a dropped rubber ball. I do my best to clear the shock from my face.

"Are you still prepared to continue?" Judge Harding asks.

Eli nods. "I have been familiar with the case, and I'm confident that I'm still good to proceed."

"Very well then," Judge Harding says with a nod. "We can continue." She adjusts her glasses, looking at her notes. "Now, Ms. Pierce, you may proceed with your witness."

"We are, Your Honor," I say, standing and trying to calm my racing heart. "Before we give closing arguments, I would like to call Anton Andrews to the stand."

"Objection," Eli says. "Mr. Andrews wasn't listed as a witness."

"Your Honor," I counter calmly. "Mr. Andrews has been previously deposed. He is on the witness list, and he has already been cross-examined once during the course of this trial."

Judge Harding looks thoughtful, glancing back at my potential witness with a glimmer of interest in her eyes. I hold my
breath for a few precious seconds as I wait for her to decide, only
exhaling in relief when she dips her head in a brief nod. "Mr.
Hart, Ms. Pierce is allowed to call any witness that has already
been listed." She eyes him over her glasses. "Perhaps you aren't as
prepared for this case as you thought."

"Thank you, Your Honor," I say. I straighten, turning back to
Anton, and gesturing between him and the stand. "Mr. Andrews,
if you please."

The man looks like a baby deer as he wobbles from his seat,
his eyes darting between me and the stand and Lorenzo, who
won't so much as look at him. I keep my expression neutral as the
bailiff swears Anton in, trying not to let my excitement show.

"Mr. Andrews," I greet him as I take a few steps closer. "Sorry
to take you by surprise, I know you've already answered my questions once before."

His eyes glance toward Lorenzo's table, but I don't look to see
if Lorenzo acknowledges him. I wouldn't, if I were him. "T-that's
all right," Anton responds shakily.

"Can you tell us again how long you've worked for Mr. Casiraghi?"

"Nine years, ma'am."

"And what did you do for work before being hired by his
company?"

"I was in college before I was hired by Mr. Casiraghi," he says.
"I was hired by his company after graduation."

"And what college did you attend?"

"Northwestern, ma'am."

"Impressive," I note. "What was your degree?"

"Business, ma'am."

"And you always intended to become a personal assistant?"

"Objection," Eli calls. "Relevance."

I give my attention to Judge Harding. "Your Honor, it couldn't be *more* relevant."

"Overruled," she answers, giving me a flat look. "But if you have a point, let's get there, Ms. Pierce."

"Yes, Your Honor." I look back to Anton. "Mr. Andrews?"

"I . . . I'm not sure," he says nervously. "My father wanted me to earn a business degree."

"Interesting." I turn away from him, my hands behind my back as if I'm thinking. I look at Lorenzo's table, noticing his knuckles are white from the way he's clenching his fist. "It's interesting, Mr. Andrews," I continue, still looking out at the court instead of back at him. "Because we were unable to find anyone by your name that was enrolled at Northwestern University during the years you supposedly attended."

I turn back to see his shocked expression, not missing the way his eyes dart yet again to Lorenzo's table. "I—"

"I thought that was strange," I go on, "but only until I found that you legally changed your name in 2014, isn't that right?"

"Objection!" Eli shouts, his chair scraping as he stands.

I step over to my table, pulling out a folder of documents and walking it back to the bench. "You'll notice this is marked item number forty-seven, a document disclosed to both parties in pretrial that overviews the employment records of Mr. Andrews. If you turn to page seven, under the section 'Other Names,' Mr. Andrews has listed his former legal name. This already-admitted evidence means it's completely admissible for our team to follow up on the matter."

Judge Harding skims the document, nodding before handing it back. "She's right, Mr. Hart. It's previously disclosed."

"This is outrageous!" Lorenzo slams his fists on the table. "You cannot—"

"Order," Judge Harding says harshly, slamming her gavel before pointing it at Eli. "Get your client under control, Mr. Hart."

I have to bite back my smile. Lorenzo must realize that he's dug his own grave, and I'm happy to be holding the shovel. I take the documents back from the judge, calmly extending them to Anton so that he can see page seven.

"Mr. Andrews," I say sweetly. "Can you please read to me the name you listed on your employment application for Casiraghi Development in 2015?"

Anton looks as white as a sheet. Clearly, his nervous disposition wasn't an inherited one.

When he doesn't immediately answer, I urge, "Mr. Andrews?"

"A-Anton Kinsley," he stutters.

Satisfaction washes over me. "Which would mean you share the same last name as the woman we believe to have been in a long-standing romantic relationship with Mr. Casiraghi, would it not?"

His eyes are wide, and I notice he doesn't dare to glance at Lorenzo now. "Yes."

"Very interesting." I pull out another document from my folder. "Can you tell me what this document is?"

Anton sucks in a breath. "It's my registration paperwork for Northwestern."

"That's right." I flip the page. "And can you tell me what this document is that you submitted with that paperwork for proof of age?"

"My birth certificate," he practically whispers.

"What was that?"

"My birth certificate," he says louder.

"And can you please read for the court who are listed as your parents on this document?"

Anton is starting to look a little green, and he *does* glance back to Lorenzo for a brief moment, looking even worse after doing so. I almost feel bad for the guy. When he gives his attention back to the document in front of him, I wonder if he will need a bucket soon.

"LeeAnn Kinsley and . . . Lorenzo Casiraghi."

There's an outburst behind me, Lorenzo starting to shout in Italian as a collective murmur sets off through the room, but I give none of it my attention, already thanking Mr. Andrews for his time and calmly passing the witness even as Judge Harding starts banging her gavel to try to get control of the room.

Bianca's eyes are bright and wet when they meet mine as I join her back at our table, and she reaches to pat my cheek silently even as chaos ensues around us. It's one of the most gratifying moments of my life, and my entire being radiates with pride and fulfillment as Bianca mouths a quiet *Thank you.*

I shake my head to let her know no thanks is needed; this moment is all I need.

And *in* this moment . . . all I can think about is the one person I wish were here to see it.

LORENZO IS LONG gone when we exit the courtroom; once we adjourned, I caught him shouting at a blank-faced Eli in a mix of English and Italian before he stormed out of the room in a rage, and honestly, who can blame him? I imagine losing half your fortune because you can't keep your dick in your pants has to be a heavy blow. I almost feel sorry for him, knowing that his woes are far from over. Almost.

Bianca and I promise to meet in the following week to finalize things, and as much as I would like to tell her about the rest of the revelations I stumbled across this week, it feels wrong not to tell Ezra first. I can only hope that she won't be too angry when she learns I wasn't immediately forthcoming about them.

But the last thing I expect after winning the biggest case of my career against all odds, I think, is for Eli Hart to find me after, his fingers touching my elbow gently to get my attention. I expect him to have some sort of cutting words for me, to leave me with one last barb to assuage his ego, so what he *actually* says nearly floors me.

"You did a good job in there."

I rear back, thinking I've misheard him. "Excuse me?"

"Don't get a big head," he chuckles. "But it was impressive."

"Did you sustain some sort of brain injury before you got here?"

"I can see why he likes you," Eli muses, leaving me gaping.

"What?"

"I am a lot of things," he says with a smile that looks unpracticed. "But stupid is not one of them. My brother isn't exactly subtle."

"You have no idea what you're—"

"It's fine, Danica," he placates me, holding up a hand to stop me. "I'm not going to say anything. Actually, I . . ." He frowns, his expression weary, and I notice for the first time today how tired he looks. So unlike his normal confident aloofness. "I wanted to give you something."

I rack my brain for anything that Eli Hart could possibly want to give me, coming up with nothing. Which means I say nothing as he reaches into the breast pocket of his suit, handing me a flash drive.

"I want you to give this to my brother," he tells me.

"To Ezra?" I take the flash drive gingerly. "Why can't you?"

"I doubt he wants to hear from me," he says, a sad smile forming on his mouth. "And honestly, I don't blame him. I have some work to do before I can see either of them."

"Either of them?"

Eli cocks his head. "He didn't tell you?"

"Um . . . no. We haven't . . . spoken in a while."

"Ah." He looks at his feet, frowning. "He quit the firm last week. Then he went straight to our parents' house and took my mother away. My dad is furious, of course, but so far, he hasn't done anything." He looks back up at me, nodding toward the flash drive I'm still holding in my hand. "That will ensure that he never can."

"What's on it?"

"Everything I was able to copy from my father's laptop," he tells me. "Hopefully, it will be enough."

I feel shock coursing through me. "You're really going to help them? Why?"

"Because . . . she's my mother," he says quietly. "And I . . . haven't been the best son. I want to try to make up for that."

I look down at the tiny drive between my fingers, feeling floored and oddly touched on Ezra's and Jackie's behalf. I swallow, nodding. "You know, I've found things too," I inform him.

"That doesn't surprise me," he chuffs with a laugh.

"Things that will mean some rough times for your father," I go on. "He isn't innocent, Eli. I intend to make sure everyone knows that. Are you okay with that?"

Eli looks away from me, shoving his hands in his pockets and pursing his lips. "You know, I've learned a lot about family in the last few days. I've learned that the loyalty we give because of blood isn't always deserved. It's something I wish I'd learned a lot sooner, but all I can do is try to make up for it now." He nods solemnly, turning back to me. "So yes, I'm okay with it. I can't sit idly by anymore while people suffer. And if you can . . . tell my mother . . ." His eyes shine, and the emotion there makes him look more human. Maybe more than he's ever looked. "Tell her I'm sorry that I ever did."

I tuck the drive into my pocket. "I think she'd rather hear it from you."

"Right," he says thickly. "Hopefully she will someday. When I deserve to tell her."

I nod, not knowing what else to say. Everything about today has been an emotional roller coaster. Eli returns my nod, clearing his throat and holding out his hand. I eye it for a second before tentatively reaching to clasp it in a slow shake.

"Congratulations on your win, Ms. Pierce," he says.

I grin, feeling the full weight of my victory. "Thank you, Mr. Hart."

He lets go of my hand to leave me standing there, and it takes several seconds for me to remember how to use my feet, still slightly stunned by the conversation we just had. I don't believe I will actually *need* the drive in my pocket to take down Alexander— but the fact that Eli would give it . . . I know it will mean the world to their mother. I intend to make sure she hears all about it, if I can.

Which reminds me . . . I have somewhere to be.

Thirty-One

EZRA

"MOM, I CAN take you," I try for the third time.

She waves me off. "I miss Rita. She's fine to take me to the doctor, Ezra. Don't hover."

"Of course I'm going to hover," I grumble.

"Don't I know it," she laughs. "You've been doing it for days."

I narrow my eyes, but she just laughs again, closing the distance between us and patting my cheek. "I love you, darling, but you need to get out of this apartment. I'll be fine."

I believe it, to a degree. It's only been a few days that my mother has been staying with me, but in just that short time she's been . . . lighter. Lighter than I've ever seen her. Like she's finally free, and maybe even feels like she deserves to be. It makes me feel lighter too.

Mostly.

I'm still trying not to think about the Dani-shaped hole in my life.

"I just worry about you."

My mother smiles softly. "I know, darling. You've been playing the role of a parent for so many years now . . . and I'm so grateful. But I have to figure out how to be that for you now, okay? Let me try to do things on my own. Even if just a little. Have to start somewhere, right?"

"Fine," I concede. "But call me when you're done. Let me know if you go anywhere else."

"Yes, yes," she huffs. "I will. Try to do something fun, okay? You're starting to stress *me* out with all your moping, and I'm supposed to be the basket case."

"Don't joke like that," I chide. "You are not."

Still, I have to admit that hearing her make a joke is exhilarating, even if I hate that it's at her expense.

"I'll see you in a few hours, okay?"

I nod, biting my tongue at the urge to ask to take her again. "All right."

I try not to let worry overcome me as I watch her sling her purse over her shoulder, telling me that Rita is waiting on her in the lobby and, once again, that she doesn't need me to see her down. I know she wants to feel this independence; it's not something she's been able to have in years, and I want to give that to her, even if just a little.

I have no idea what I'm supposed to do when she's gone since the last few days have revolved around her completely, trying to get her settled into my guest room. I've been plagued with worry that any moment could be the one that Alexander came after us, and each one that he doesn't only worsens my anxiety. Like waiting for the other shoe to drop.

I try to do what my mother asks, doing my best to make myself busy in her absence. She's been such a staple feature in my apartment the last few days, and I've loved having her here. It feels more like the us we were when I was a kid. I can only hope that with each day away from Alexander's hold, it will get even better.

I'm sick of TV after the first hour, and by the second, I'm going a little stir crazy. I feed Purrgood; he's been angry at me for days, I suspect because he misses Dani, which, join the club, my guy. I've been doing my best not to think about her, because I'm afraid if I do, I might just break down completely. I told her more or less that I would wait for her, hoping beyond hope that she would eventually decide to give us a real shot, but deep down . . . I'm afraid she might never be there.

Purrgood yowls at me, and I glance down to find him giving me a reproachful look, if that's even possible for a cat. "Don't look at me like that," I tut. "Traitor."

I leave him to his judging, padding into the kitchen to try to find something bad for me to distract from the stress that is my life right now. Something covered with cheese, I think. I'm still digging through a cabinet when I hear a knock at my door. I peer over my shoulder and frown, wondering if Mom forgot her key.

I jog through the living room to grab the handle, turning it. "Hey, did you forget your—?"

It's not my mother.

My mouth hangs open, my question lost to the air as I stare at the woman in front of me, wondering if she's a figment of my imagination. God knows I've thought about her enough this week to physically manifest her.

"Dani?"

"Hi." She shifts in her heels, still in court clothes. It hits me then what day it is. "Can I come in?"

"I . . . yeah," I manage, remembering myself. "Come in."

She steps past me, making a happy sound when she spots my traitor cat trotting up to greet her. She bends to scratch behind his ears, and the sight is so reminiscent of easier days between us that it makes my chest hurt.

"Hey, big guy," she coos. "Miss me?"

"He's not the only one," I tell her truthfully, causing her to peek back at me from over her shoulder with wide eyes.

She straightens, smoothing the fabric of her slacks and looking up at me through her lashes, and I notice for the first time the manila envelope in her hand. "I . . . missed you too."

"Did you?"

It's not a facetious question, I'm actually desperate to confirm it.

She chews on the inside of her lip, watching me. I feel like I'm standing on the edge of a high ledge as I wait for her to keep speaking. My heart thumps against my ribs; I still can't be sure what it is she's come to tell me. Whether or not she's putting me out of my misery or ensuring it's going to continue for a very long time.

But surprisingly, she doesn't do either of those things.

"I won today," she tells me.

"I . . . congratulations."

"Did you know Anton was Lorenzo's son?"

"I had suspicions," I tell her with a shrug. "I didn't have any proof."

"So how did you know that telling me to look into him would work out?"

"I didn't know for sure," I say honestly. My mouth quirks. "But I knew if anyone could find the dirt to take that sleazeball down, it would be you."

Still, her expression gives me nothing, her jaw working in thought. "Why didn't you tell me that you quit?"

I breathe out a sigh. "Because . . . I didn't want to put any more pressure on you."

"Pressure."

"Yes, pressure. I know that everything that happened between us was a lot for you to process, and with that and the trial . . . I figured you had enough on your plate without adding any more confusing elements."

"How is you quitting and taking your mother out of that house confusing?"

"I just— Wait. How did you know about my mother?"

"Eli told me."

My face scrunches up. "Eli? You talked to Eli?"

"He caught me after court today," she says. "We talked."

"You . . . talked."

"Trust me," she snorts. "I found it just as bizarre of an experience."

"I don't understand." I shake my head. "Did he . . . he didn't threaten her, did he? Because I swear to God, I will—"

"No, no, no!" She waves her hands back and forth. "He didn't. I promise. He just— Well, you see—" She exhales sharply, thrusting the folder out to give to me. "Here. This is for you."

"What?" I take it from her, frowning down at it. "What is it?"

"Documents detailing the transfer of Bianca's trust from Italy to America the year she came of age."

I look at her and then back at the envelope, furrowing my brow. "I don't understand."

"Look at the signature of the lawyer who handled the transfer," she says.

I'm still frowning as I pull documents from the folder, shuffling through them until I see the signature she's referencing. A cold sort of shock passes over me, and I gape up at her. "Is this really . . . ?"

"Alexander's signature? Yes. And if you go through the rest of the documents, and hell, the financial records for the next several years, you can trace a clear pattern of withdrawals made by Lorenzo that were possible because *Alexander* falsified documents naming him as a co-beneficiary. I compared the signature on those documents to Bianca's. They don't match."

"You mean . . . ?"

She nods. "Alexander must have forged it. Or Lorenzo. Regardless, they're both complicit in stealing from her for years while Lorenzo built his business."

"But what did Alexander gain from this?"

"As far as I can tell, a giant payout. I checked bank records we had copies of for the trial. Lorenzo deposited a huge sum of money into Alexander's account a month after all this went down."

"Jesus."

I stare down at the documents in my hands, still in slight disbelief that I'm really holding evidence that can prove Alexander is as much a snake as I've always believed him to be. That I might be holding what I need to make sure that my mother never suffers at the hands of Alexander Hart ever again.

"Wow, I . . . wow."

She reaches into her pocket, pulling out a flash drive and handing that over too. "Oh, and this is from Eli. Apparently, he broke into Alexander's office and copied whatever he could get his hands on off his laptop. I guess it's his way of extending an olive branch."

"I feel like I'm in the twilight zone."

"Yeah, I know it's a lot. He actually told me to tell your mother he was sorry."

"I think he should tell her that himself," I scoff.

She gives me a small smile. "I agree."

"Dani, I . . . thank you." My voice sounds too thick, and I have to breathe deep through my nostrils. "Seriously. I can't believe you did this."

"You can't?"

Her eyes are softer now, her smile just a little more sad. "No, I can. I really can."

There's so much more I want to say to her; fuck, the way I want to *touch* her. My body is practically vibrating with the need to. But I told her I would wait until she was ready, and I meant that. Even if it kills me.

"Is that . . ." My throat bobs with a swallow. "Is that all you came to say?"

"I . . . well. I guess it is."

"Oh." I nod, looking at my feet to try to hide my disappointment. "Right. Well. I really appreciate this."

"Ezra, it was nothing. Really."

All I can do is nod again. "Right."

"Fuck." I look up as she runs her fingers through her hair, blowing out a breath. "That's a lie."

"What?"

"That's not all I came to say."

"I'm confused."

"I know." She nods, looking miserable. "And that's my fault."

"No, Dani, that's not what I—"

She holds up a hand. "No, I need to get this out."

She takes a deep breath, the determination on her perfect face so like her that I might laugh if this were any other time. She looks at me like she's about to deliver an opening address to a judge and jury. Her eyes hold that same ferocity that she gives to everything else in her life.

Maybe that's why what she says nearly knocks me over.

"I'm in love with you."

I don't think I have ever *actually* been in a position where I have nothing to say. Retorts normally come so easily to me, but Dani has managed to render me speechless with only five short words. She takes advantage of my silence, barreling onward like she won't be able to get it out if she stops.

"I know that I fucked up with you," she says hoarsely. "I have spent so long telling myself that people are a foregone conclusion, that anything good I might find will eventually end, so what's the point of even trying? Maybe that's why I took the first chance I got to push you away." She shakes her head. "Not that it makes it right." Her brow wrinkles. "You were right to stop chasing me. You shouldn't be chasing me."

"Dani—"

"I'm going to chase *you* this time," she says resolutely, nodding as if asserting her decision. "So however long it takes for you to forgive me, I'm going to wait. Because you're worth staying for too, Ezra. And I'm sorry if I made you feel like you weren't. I promise if you give me another chance, I'll—"

She makes a surprised sound when I cross the distance in the blink of an eye, pulling her to me and crushing her mouth to mine. She's still for only a moment before she melts into it, her hands wrapping around my biceps and squeezing before she slips her arms around my neck. I feel every doubt, every worry, *all* of it—seeping out of me in droves as her mouth moves against mine. Like everything that comes after this will be easy, because now I know she'll be here for it.

"I mean it," she gasps between kisses. "I'll wait for you—"

"Shut up, Dani." I press my lips to hers, lingering. "Don't be stupid."

She pushes at my chest, only staying close to me because I have my arms wrapped firmly around her waist. "*Stupid?*"

Her indignant expression makes me smile; it probably means *I'm* a basket case, how elated her looking at me like that makes me.

"Very stupid," I tease, holding her tight so she can't squirm away. "If you think I'm letting you out of my sight for another second . . ."

She stops fighting my grip, her eyes softening. "What?"

"Don't you know?" I lean in, brushing my lips across hers, smiling. "I've loved you for ages, Dani. I've just been waiting for you to catch up."

She blinks back at me like she's trying to process what I've said, and the moment she does, her eyes crinkle in pleasure, her smile wide and open, and the effect it has on my heart is something very similar. She lunges herself at me, zippering her body to mine and shoving her fingers in my hair. She pulls at the strands hard enough to sting, but I'm just so happy to have her hands on me again that I welcome it.

"Wow," I hum against her mouth. "You must have *really* missed me."

"Barely at all."

I grin, kissing her jaw. "Didn't even spare me a thought."

"Almost forgot your name at one point," she laughs breathily.

"Really?" I nip at her bottom lip. "Maybe I should make you scream it. So you don't forget."

"Does that *actually* work for you?"

My hand curves along her jaw. "You tell me."

"I can't stand you," she says with no bite.

"Oh, no," I chuckle. "You *love* me. No take backs. I'm going to be driving you crazy for the rest of your life."

"Promise?"

Her humor dims just for a second, and I can see it there in her eyes, that lingering uncertainty. I kiss the tip of her nose. "Baby, you're never getting rid of me."

God, I love when she smiles. I silently promise to make sure she does it for the rest of our lives.

I'm pulling her closer with every intention of taking her to my room and showing her exactly how much I missed her, but my well-intentioned plans come to a screeching halt when keys rattle at my front door, my mother clamoring inside, her arms laden with shopping bags.

"Hey, honey! I got you a new shower curtain for the guest room. That gray one is just so— Oh." My mother's face lights up, a mischievous glint in her eye, as she takes in Dani untangling herself from my arms. "Well, hello."

"Mrs. Hart," Dani croaks, pushing me away. "Hi. Sorry. We were just—"

"Oh, don't apologize, dear," Mom says. "I remember what kissing is. Dani, are you staying for dinner?" Mom sets her bags down, stepping over and looping her arm through Dani's. "I was just saying to Ezra this morning that I was in the mood for chicken Alfredo. Ezra makes the best homemade sauce."

"I . . ." Dani looks at me expectantly, and I shrug, shooting her a grin that she hesitantly returns before turning it toward my mom. "I'd love to stay for dinner."

"Good." Mom pats her hand. "Now you come and tell me all about yourself."

"Oh . . . sure."

Seeing them together causes a swelling sensation in my chest, a peace settling over me that I hadn't even realized I'd craved until this very second. Like everything I'll ever need is right here in this room. Knowing that Dani is the reason that my mother will never suffer again only makes it all the more sweet.

Mom steps away to start hunting for something to drink, and I move closer to press a kiss to Dani's cheek, whispering, "To be continued."

"If you're lucky," she mumbles back.

I bite my lip to keep from laughing. She'd just roll her eyes if I told her that I think I already am.

"SHUT UP," SHE hisses, covering my mouth. "Your mother is right down the hall."

I smile against her neck, sucking at her pulse point after. "You made the noise, Sour Patch."

"Because you—*fuck*," she gasps.

I tilt my hips again, letting my length tease through her slippery heat. "Because I did that?"

"God, you're infuriating," she groans as quietly as she can manage.

I capture her mouth, letting my tongue slip inside just as I start to fill her.

"You love me."

Her arms wind around my neck. "Stop reminding me."

"Fuck." I bury my face in her throat, grinding deeper. "I missed you."

"Miss me faster."

"Has anyone ever told you that you top from the bottom?"

"Ezra," she huffs.

I kiss under her jaw, snapping my hips against her. "Like that?"

"*Yes.* Just like that."

"I think you missed me too," I rasp.

"Yeah?"

"I know you missed at least one part of me," I croon.

Her nails dig into my shoulders as I start to move faster, my eyes shutting as her perfect, wet cunt grips me tight.

"I can't believe I love you," she says with a laugh that ends with a deep sigh. "You're an idiot."

"But I'm *your* idiot."

I pull my head back to look at her, and her flushed face is beautiful in the warm glow of my bedside lamp, her smile filling me up. She lifts her head to meet my mouth, pulling me down to her and slipping her tongue between my lips. I groan into her kiss as I thrust deeper, her legs wrapping around my waist.

I lose myself in her body, reveling in the fact that I can touch her like this, that I'll be able to tomorrow and every day after that. It's so different, having her kiss me sweetly while I fill her again and again, so much different from the days where she wouldn't even look at me when we were like this. I think I knew then that it was inevitable that I would come to need her this desperately, that there would never be anyone else who could compare after having her.

And now I'm completely sure.

"Harder," she says on an inhale, tilting her head back.

I brace my elbows beside her on the bed, leaning on my forearms as I drive my hips until I'm pounding between her legs, watching every facet of her expression as she loses herself in it. Her eyes drift open to meet mine, and I hold myself up so that I can trail one hand down between us, dipping between her legs to roll her clit under the pads of my fingers. I'm too close, too greedy for her—and I want her with me when I fall over the edge.

"Can you come for me, Dani?"

"Just like that," she breathes.

I work the slick bundle a little faster, never slowing the deep slide of my cock as she envelops me.

"Want your eyes when you come," I murmur. "Want you with me."

She nods dazedly, biting her lip. "Okay."

"You love me?"

Another nod, her eyes heavy lidded. "I love you."

"Forever?"

Her lips curl. "We'll see."

"Now who's the asshole," I choke out, a stuttered groan following it as pressure starts to swell, so close I can practically feel it in my teeth. "*Fuck*, Dani. You feel good."

"Don't stop."

"Never."

I work my wrist faster, I sling my hips *harder*—moving inside her like nothing else matters, because at this moment, I'm not sure that it does. Right now, nothing could be more important than the way she looks beneath me, the way she feels around me, the way she's woven herself into every part of my head and my heart. Right now . . . she's everything. I think she always will be.

She lets out a quiet sound when she comes, and I feel every tremor of it pass through her, her tight heat cinching around me, practically forcing me to follow. Every pulse inside only prolongs the pleasure, and by the time we're both still, I feel boneless, hardly able to keep from collapsing on top of her.

I give in to the urge eventually, and Dani lets out a soft *oomph*.

"You're smothering me," she says breathlessly.

"Mm. It's way too soon in our relationship for you to start making those sorts of accusations."

"Are you always going to be this impossible?"

I roll, stretching out beside her and flashing her a grin as I pull her into my side. "Absolutely."

"That checks out."

"You love it."

I feel her lips curving against my skin. "I guess I do."

"Fuck, I love you too. I'm going to say that a million times before I'm done. You realize that, right?"

"It's better than 'baby.'"

"You love it when I call you that. Admit it, Sour Patch."

"God," she groans. "That one's even worse."

I kiss her hair, feeling lighter and happier than I've ever been. Like every moment in my life has been leading to this exact one.

"I'm going to have to confront Alexander," I tell her after a stretch of contented silence.

She nods against my side. "I know."

"Will you come with me?"

She tilts her face up, wriggling higher until she can brush her lips against my cheek. "Of course I will."

And strangely, knowing that means I don't feel any uncertainty about whatever the outcome may be. I know that as long as she's with me, everything will work out. I bring my fingers to her chin, tilting it up higher so I can claim her mouth. It's soft and sweet and unlike anything about the wild ride we took to get here, but I wouldn't change a single minute of it. I wouldn't trade this prickly, obstinate woman whose hard-earned smiles light up my life for anything.

And the best part is . . . I'll never have to.

Thirty-Two

EZRA

I REALLY HAD hoped I would never have to come back here again, but strangely, this is the first time that walking through the front doors of Alexander's house—because it's his, I realize, it's never been a home to me—doesn't fill me with dread. No, this time, that same peace that I've felt since Dani came back to me and handed me all the missing pieces sticks to my bones, leaving me feeling calmer than I've ever been inside these walls.

I know he's here; I never thought that I would ever in my life be calling Eli for help, but our conversation this morning about Alexander's whereabouts, while stilted, left me feeling oddly . . . hopeful. Like maybe one day we might actually be something to each other.

I catalog the sparkling interior and the fine furniture as I move through the house, adamant that this will be the last time I ever have to look at any of it. That if today goes as planned—which I have full faith it will—I can walk back out those front doors and never think about this place ever again. The thought is freeing.

There's a light shining under Alexander's office door, telling me he's inside, and I hesitate outside it for a few seconds, collecting my thoughts and preparing myself for the inevitable onslaught that I'll be facing when I step inside. I remind myself that I have the power now. That he's just a man. That he can never hurt me or anyone I love ever again.

I don't bother knocking, partly because I know that annoys him, turning the handle and pushing the door open without any warning and stepping inside the massive room to find Alexander sitting behind his desk, shooting me a glare when I enter. His nose is bandaged, his eyes black with bruises from the punch I landed, and it takes all I have not to smile at the sight, feeling an immense satisfaction at seeing him look so weakened.

"You've got a lot of nerve showing up here," he says darkly.

I do smile then, closing the door behind me. I clasp my hands behind my back casually, strolling over to the massive built-ins and studying the rows upon rows of law books and ledgers lining the shelves as if I can't even be bothered to give him my full attention. I pluck a random volume from the shelf, eyeing it, turning it over in my hands just to fill him with even more anger by not immediately responding.

"You know," I say finally. "I used to sneak in here as a kid when you weren't home." I slide the book back into place, still not looking at him. "I used to think that if I could learn more about what you did, maybe you'd start to care about me." I clench my teeth. "I was so damned desperate for your approval back then."

"You never did anything to deserve it," Alexander sneers.

Remarkably, his disdain only makes me smile harder, and I finally turn back to him to let him see, which only makes him look angrier. "I never stood a chance though, did I? You hated me from the day I was born."

"You can blame your tramp mother for that."

I tamp down the desire to hit him again, willing myself to remain calm.

Don't let him gain the upper hand. This will all be worth it soon.

"Can you really blame her for seeking out some scrap of affection? God knows you weren't giving it to her. Did you ever even love her?"

His narrowed eyes almost look comical with both sporting the purpling bruises, and if I weren't so determined to keep collected, I might laugh.

"She's always been a disappointment," he scoffs. "Just like you. You could never be like your brother."

"Ah, but Eli isn't at your beck and call anymore either, is he? Tell me, Alexander. Have you heard from him this week?"

The hand gripping the pen he's holding tightens, and I hear the plastic creaking under the pressure. "What did you say to him?"

"Me?" I shake my head. "I didn't say anything. I think he just finally realized the same thing the rest of your *family* did a long time ago. That you're a worthless piece of shit."

Alexander drops the pen, slamming his hands on his desk. "If you don't get the fuck out of my office right now, I'll—"

"You'll what?" I step closer to his desk, placing my hands on the wood and bracing myself against it so I can lean in. I notice with satisfaction that he flinches when I do, just a little. "You want a repeat of the other day, Alexander? I'd be happy to break more of your face."

"You're lucky I didn't call the fucking police," he growls. "You really think you could take me head-on in court? With my connections?"

"I'm hoping it doesn't come to that, since I imagine you'll

already have your hands full," I answer blithely, shrugging. "But that all depends on you."

"Is there a point you plan on making?"

"Right." My lips curl in another slow grin. "Do you know what your problem is, Alexander?"

He says nothing, just continues to glare at me.

"Your problem," I go on, "is that you've gone unpunished for so long that you think you're untouchable."

"Because I am," he answers smugly.

"I'm sure you really believe that," I laugh. "But that's the problem with men like you. If you go unchecked for too long . . . you stop anticipating danger. You let yourself get comfortable."

"This is pointless," Alexander scoffs. "Just get the fuck out of my—"

"Do you want me to remind you about Bianca Casiraghi's trust fund, Alexander? Or do you remember? You *were* the one who handled the overseas transfer of the funds, weren't you?"

The intense gratification I feel when he blanches is an allover sensation, my body practically humming. His eyes round and his mouth parts, and for the first time in my entire life, Alexander Hart looks . . . truly afraid.

"You don't know what you're talking about," he stammers.

"Oh, I know *exactly* what I'm talking about," I assure him. "And I have *several* documents to prove it."

"You can't—there's no way—it's not possible."

"Like I said, Alexander," I tell him calmly. "You've let yourself get too comfortable. You stopped anticipating the danger." The smile on my face feels feral, predatory even, but I enjoy watching Alexander quiver like prey. "But the danger found you just the same."

"You little shit," he seethes. "Whatever you think you know—"

"I know that you falsified legal documents," I tell him. "I know that you forged signatures. I know that you helped your buddy Lorenzo steal from his own wife for years to build his business and enjoyed a big, fat payoff for your trouble. That was the year you left the firm you worked for, wasn't it? You started your own that same year, if I remember correctly."

"You'll never prove it," he flounders. "You have no idea the people I know. I'll never allow it to see the light of day."

"Oh, it's much too late for that," I chuckle. "We've already handed everything over to Bianca. I thought she might feel overwhelmed having to dive into a criminal case so soon after winning that draining divorce case against her scumbag husband—sorry, I know you're buddies—but funnily enough, she seemed more than up for the challenge. We all have no doubt that she'll gain another win, with all the evidence she got from me and Eli."

I take a second to enjoy Alexander's shock, because it is absolutely delicious, but only a second.

"That's right," I say. "Your perfect son, the one whose mind you poisoned for years, finally had a moment of clarity. I guess you shouldn't have trusted him with a key to your office." I lean in a little closer. "Once again, you just got too comfortable."

Alexander moves to stand, vibrating with anger and acting like he might grab me, but I beat him to the punch. I wrap my hands around the collar of his shirt, pulling him over his desk so that his face is inches from mine.

"I would love to beat you half to death right now," I tell him, my voice a deadly calm. "But that would be too good for you. So instead, I'm just going to inform you of three things, and you're going to listen, understand?"

"I don't have to listen to a fucking—"

I tug at his collar so hard that he makes a choking sound.

"I said, *do you understand?*"

He looks livid but finally seems to realize that I have no qualms about hurting him if it comes to it. He nods stiffly, his eyes bulging and his mouth a hard line.

"One." I hold up one finger for effect. "You can expect to hear from Bianca's legal team within the week. Two." I add another finger. "You can expect to hear from *me* not long after, because if you think a court will continue to grant control over my mother while you're facing criminal charges, you're even dumber than I thought." He makes an indignant sound, but I barrel onward, not letting him speak. "And three." Another finger, his eyes flicking to my hand with a mixture of fear and loathing. "If you fight me on this business with Mom, if you even lift a single finger to try to block me from transferring her conservatorship from you to me, I will make sure that you rot in prison. We both know that you'll never see jail time because of this business with Bianca; I'm sure you'll throw money at it until you're sure that won't happen, but I think we both know that if I wanted to keep digging, I'd find more. A person like you doesn't just *stop* being a piece of shit. I can guarantee you've got a fuck ton of skeletons in your closet, and if you even try to fight me . . . I'll make it my mission in life to find every fucking one of them. I won't stop until you're rotting in prison. Do you understand?"

"You're making a big mista—"

I cinch the fabric of his collar until another strangled sound escapes him. "*Do you understand?*"

He looks like he'd like nothing more than to murder me, but I'm not bothered by it. The feeling is most certainly mutual. He glares at me for several long moments, finally giving me a stiff nod. I know that's as good as I can expect from him.

I release my hold on him more roughly than necessary, shoving him so that he tumbles back into his chair haphazardly. He's still looking at me with murder in his eyes, but I shoot him a smile as I straighten my jacket.

"I'm glad we could reach an understanding. You have a good life, Alexander."

He waits until I'm turning to leave to start shouting—an outraged burst of venom at my back about the mistakes I'm making, about how much he's going to make me pay—but I'm already out the door and slamming it shut, leaving all my thoughts about Alexander Hart behind it. I don't spare any glances to the house this time on the way out; I'm finally free of it. It means nothing to me now.

Dani is still leaning against the car outside when I step down the stairs leading from the porch, her arms crossed and her eyes full of concern, like she was poised to storm the castle at any moment if she thought I might need her.

"Did you hurt him?"

I shake my head. "Not really."

"Pity," she says blandly.

I fucking love this prickly woman.

I pull her against me, shoving my fingers into her hair and pressing my lips to hers briefly, staring into her gray eyes, which almost sparkle like silver in the sunlight. She really does make me feel . . . peaceful. I could get addicted to that feeling.

"Thank you for coming with me," I tell her.

"You should have let me come inside."

"Nah. You would have probably maimed him, and then I'd

have to study up on criminal law to defend you. Sounds like way too much work."

"Are you saying I'm not worth the effort?"

I grin. "I'm saying I'm not going to risk only seeing you once a month for conjugal visits."

"Wow, now who's greedy?"

I slant my lips against hers again, savoring it this time, keeping her close until she's humming into my mouth. "Always greedy for you, Dani," I mumble.

"Can we leave now? I kind of hate this place."

I peer over my shoulder, taking in the massive house one last time before nodding at her. "Yeah. Let's get the fuck out of here."

I don't look back as we drive away from the house.

I've got too much waiting for me ahead.

Thirty-Three

DANI

"WELL," MANUEL SAYS with a hint of amusement. "You've had quite an eventful couple of weeks."

"I'll say," I sigh.

"Big win, disclosing a relationship, aiding on a criminal case—I'd call that a full docket."

My lips tilt at the corner. "It's been interesting, to say the least."

"Well, kid," he says with a grin. "You held up your end of the bargain. So I'm going to hold up mine. I hope you're ready for more responsibility."

I ignore my racing heart. "You really think the other partners will go for it?"

"Are you kidding? Do you know how much money you just made this firm by pulling out a win like you did? I'll be surprised if they don't approach me about it first."

"I . . . Thank you. Really, Manny. I wouldn't be here without you."

"Oh, bullshit," he snorts. "You'd be here with or without me. You're good, kid."

"Still. I hope you know how much I appreciate you."

"Well, it never hurts to hear it." He nods at the door. "Now get out of here. You deserve a few days off."

I nod, beaming as I stand. "I'll see you at dinner this weekend?"

"I would never miss a night out celebrating with your parents," he chuckles. "They're always a good time."

"They're like children."

"But you love them."

"Yeah," I huff. "I really do."

"And will you be bringing your new man?" His smile is sly. "I have to admit, you really caught me off guard with Ezra Hart."

"No more than I did myself," I scoff. I can feel my expression softening. "But yeah, he's coming. His mother too."

"I can't wait. I'll try not to tell them all your embarrassing stories."

"You wouldn't dare."

"Wouldn't I?"

I roll my eyes. "Jackass."

"Love you too, kid."

I'm still grinning as I leave his office, immediately accosted by my two very overbearing best friends.

"So?" Nate is vibrating with excitement. "Is it happening?"

"Seems that way," I tell him.

"About time," Vera says. "Maybe you'll stop working so fucking hard now."

"Doubt it," Nate snorts. He waggles his eyebrows at me. "Going to see your boyfriend now, Duchess?"

"None of your business," I say sweetly.

"Oh, come on," he whines. "We give you all the details about *our* relationship."

"'Relationship' is a strong word," Vera grumbles.

Nate rolls his eyes. "Ignore her. She's still coming to terms with her feelings for me."

"Just know that I refuse to force her down an aisle chained to my wrist," I tease.

Nate wraps his arms around Vera's waist, laughing as she squirms away from the overexaggerated kiss he's trying to land on her cheek. He settles for pressing it into her palm, winking at me after.

"She'll come willingly."

"Shut up," she says, looking embarrassed for maybe the first time since I've known her. "Both of you."

"I'm happy for you guys," I say. "Seriously. At least I know all your bickering will have happy endings."

"Speaking of happy endings," Nate says. "Are you bringing Ezra to dinner this weekend?"

"I am."

"Are we allowed to grill him?"

"You are not."

He makes a face. "You're no fun."

"I know." I check the time on my watch. "I need to go. Ezra's making me and his mom dinner."

"So domestic," Nate sighs.

Vera slaps his arm. "Leave her alone." She smiles at me. "We're happy for you too, you know."

I nod. "I know."

"Call me later, yeah?"

"Sure thing."

I watch them go, already sniping at each other about something, and I have a feeling that will never change. Not that I can really judge, considering I'm going over to my idiot boyfriend's place and will no doubt be rolling my eyes at him at least a dozen times before he coaxes me into bed.

It's amazing how much the thought makes me smile.

EZRA'S MOTHER ANSWERS the door when I knock, ushering me inside.

"Ezra had to run to the store," she says. "Apparently he simply can't make curry without fresh garlic."

I chuckle as I step inside, following her to the counter. "Of course not."

"How was your day? Are they going to promote you?"

I've talked to Jackie many times in the last couple of weeks, and she's a far cry from the withdrawn, sad-eyed woman I first met in Alexander's house. Almost like being outside those walls has finally given her room to breathe, to find parts of herself she'd lost. She's hard not to love, I've quickly learned.

"Nothing official," I tell her. "But it looks that way."

"Wonderful," she says, looking genuinely proud. "You deserve it. Ezra told me all about how you helped Bianca. I've only met her a few times, but she always seemed very strong. I envied her."

"She is." I reach to place my hand over Jackie's. "But you are too. Look at all you've survived."

"I think you're giving me too much credit," she says gently. "But I'm trying to be."

"We'll be here for you every step of the way," I promise her.

"I know." She smiles at me. "Ezra is lucky to have you."

I shake my head. "Honestly, it's the other way around."

"He also told me that you're the reason we even have a case for transferring my conservatorship."

"I wish you didn't need one at all."

"Someday," she says with confidence. "But not yet. For now, I trust my son to take care of me."

"So do I."

"Anyway, I wanted to officially thank you. For everything you did for us."

"You don't have to thank me," I protest. "No one should be in the situation you were in."

"Still." She pats my cheek. "I'm grateful."

My chest tightens with emotion, and I manage a heavy nod. "I was happy to do it."

The door swings open behind us, Ezra stepping inside with a grocery bag in his hand. He grins when he spots us at the counter, and he shakes the bag. "Sorry. I tried to hurry."

"You're fine," his mother says. "We were just chatting."

"Jackie was telling me all your embarrassing stories," I tease.

"Did she tell you about the time I took my clothes off at the aquarium?"

I bark out a laugh. "Do I want to know how old you were?"

"Oh, this was just last year," he teases.

Jackie snorts. "He was three."

"Honestly," I scoff, "it wouldn't have taken much to make me believe he was a fully grown adult."

"He has always been a bit precocious," Jackie chuckles.

"Are my ladies hungry?" Ezra sweeps into the kitchen, pulling pans from under the cabinet. "One of these days, someone is going to have to cook for me for a change."

"But you're so good at it," I coo. "I'd hate to rob you of the joy of that."

He rolls his eyes. "So giving."

"I try."

"Did you talk to Bianca today?"

"I did," I answer. "They're moving forward with pressing charges."

"I'd love to be a fly on the wall for that trial."

"Oh, I fully intend to be sitting in the back row for it."

"Vindictive children," Jackie tuts, humor in her tone. "The both of you."

"Absolutely," Ezra laughs.

"Less talking, more cooking," I urge.

He shoots me a look over his shoulder, one I feel right down to my toes. He starts chopping things after, chatting with his mother about her day, and the ease of the moment, the absolute simplicity of sitting in this room with the pair of them and being surrounded by the love between them . . . it's mesmerizing. It gives me a sense of clarity.

"I'll be right back," I tell them both, excusing myself.

Ezra's brow furrows. "You okay?"

"Yeah. Just need to make a call."

They go back to chatting as I step out onto the balcony attached to Ezra's living room, sinking down into the patio chair and pulling my phone out to make a much-needed phone call. It only rings twice before she answers, and her voice is a balm. It always has been, I realize.

"Dani?"

"Hey, Mom."

"Hi, sweetheart. How was today? Good news?"

"It looks that way," I tell her.

"Wonderful!" Her voice is brimming with pride. "So we're still grabbing dinner this weekend? I expect to meet this man of yours. Can't believe you kept him a secret for so long."

"Technically, you met him."

"And you didn't say a thing! Can't say I blame you for snatching him up though, such a handsome man, that Ezra."

"Mom," I groan.

"Sorry, sorry," she laughs. "I'll be good, I promise."

"I highly doubt that."

The silence stretches, and as always, my mother seems to have a better sense of my emotions than even I do.

"Are you okay, Dani? You seem down."

"I . . . Mom, I . . . I wanted to tell you that I'm sorry."

"What do you mean?"

"I've been . . . angry. At you . . . at Dad . . . I blamed you, I let myself believe that you stole my childhood from me by lying to me for so long, but I . . . I've realized lately that you *gave* it to me. That you both sacrificed your own lives so that I could have one for myself. I've never thanked you for that."

"Honey," she says thickly. "You don't owe us a thing. We love you. We did what we did *because* we love you. It was never a hardship for us. We didn't sacrifice a thing."

"I just . . ." I have to choke down my emotions. "I've always felt like I stole part of your lives. That you could have found happiness so much sooner if it hadn't been for me."

"Oh, sweetheart." She doesn't bother hiding the teary quality of her voice. "You listen to me. You are the sweetest gift your father and I were ever given. Bringing you into this world is our greatest joy. You have never stolen a single minute from us. Do you hear me? You *gave* us life. You didn't take it away."

I can't stifle the sob in my throat now, sniffling into the phone. "Mom."

"I wish you'd told me this sooner, but I'm happy you're telling me now. I don't want you feeling like this for even one more day. You're a gift, Dani. Understand? I need you to know that."

I'm nodding knowing full well she can't see it, unable to form actual words.

"Dani?"

"Yeah," I say shakily. "I love you, Mom. Dad too."

"We love you too, Dani. So much. There's nothing we love more."

"I'll see you this weekend, all right?"

"We'll see you then, honey."

I hang up the phone as a tear tracks down my cheek, but despite the way I can't seem to keep them in, I feel . . . happy. For the first time in a long time, I feel like everything is ahead of me. Like there's nothing holding me back.

The patio door opens, Ezra peeking out at me, his face immediately filled with concern when he notices me crying. "Hey." He rushes over to crouch in front of me, wiping a tear away with his thumb. "You okay?"

I give him a watery smile, gently running my fingers through his golden hair, trailing them down his cheek and over his jaw after, wondering how I got so lucky.

"Yeah," I tell him, meaning it. "I really am."

HOURS LATER IN Ezra's bed, long after I've told him all about my day and the phone call with my mother, I'm still marveling at how content I feel just to lie here with him. Sure, sex with Ezra is intense, and mind-blowing, and an experience like no other—but this is just as good, I realize. Lying here with him, just like this.

His fingers trail up and down my spine, his lips resting against my temple as his breath ruffles my hair. It's . . . bliss, if I'm being honest.

"You know," he mumbles. "I never thought in a million years that you'd be here in my bed like this."

I hum into his chest. "I did."

"Bullshit," he laughs.

"No, I did," I sigh. "I think that's why I was so adamant not to let you bring me into it. I knew if I ever ended up here, I'd never leave."

"Wow, Dani. You are so obsessed with me."

He yelps when I pinch his side.

"Asshole."

He grins against my hair. "I know."

"So what now?"

He leans back, meeting my eyes. "What do you mean?"

"I mean . . . what happens now?"

"Whatever we want, Dani." He pushes my hair away from my face. "Sky's the limit."

"Do you know what you're going to do for work?"

"What," he snorts, "you don't want to be my sugar mama?"

I pinch him again, and this time, he laughs.

"I'll think of something," he says. "I'm not worried."

"Well, I was thinking," I start carefully. "I'll be getting a promotion soon . . . and they're going to be looking to fill my spot. Might even ask me to recommend someone. I could put in a good word for you with a certain junior partner, if you're interested."

"Mm. Nepotism at its finest."

"I'm going to pinch you again."

"Stop it, I'll bruise."

"Stop being an idiot."

"Hm. I rather like the idea of working under you."

"This is not a sex thing."

"Everything can be a sex thing if you just believe," he teases.

"I'm dangerously close to rescinding the offer."

"I'd love to work with you," he chuckles, kissing my forehead. "With you, under you . . . doesn't make any difference."

"I *do* like the idea of being your boss," I say thoughtfully.

"Mm. You just wait. It'll be a sex thing eventually. I love role-play."

"And . . . you'd really be okay with that? It could get awkward if you were to . . . change your mind about me one day."

"Dani."

I have to force myself to meet his gaze again, my chest fluttering with nerves. "Yeah?"

"You're being stupid again."

I narrow my eyes, but he just laughs, pulling me up for a hard kiss.

"I am never"—his lips press to my cheek—"*ever*"—they briefly touch between my eyes—"changing my mind about you. You're stuck with me, Sour Patch."

I hate how needy my voice sounds. "Forever?"

"Abso-fucking-lutely," he says firmly. His lips find mine again, holding them for so long he's practically breathing me in. "There's never going to be a 'last time,' Dani. Not for you and me."

I feel the last few bricks of the careful walls I've built around my heart crumbling away with his words, and even though I might never fully understand how we got here—I'm happy to just be grateful that we did.

There's never going to be a "last time," Dani. Not for you and me.

I smile against his mouth, and for maybe the first time since I met him . . . I don't feel an urge to argue.

Not even a little bit.

Epilogue

DANI

TEN MONTHS LATER

"THANK YOU SO much again, Ms. Pierce," Mrs. Lyndon says with tearful eyes. "I feel like I can finally relax."

"The hard part is over," I assure her, people filing out of the courtroom around us. "We'll talk next week and get everything finalized, okay? Go celebrate tonight with your daughters."

"I will," she says happily. "We'll talk soon."

I pat her shoulder, letting her go find her daughters in the crowd. Mrs. Lyndon's husband is an abusive piece of shit, and seeing him ordered to pay out a healthy alimony and child support while losing any rights to custody is a sweet victory that *I'll* definitely be celebrating. I make sure to give him a smug smile when I pass his still-fuming form spitting venom at his lawyer. Almost feel sorry for the guy.

The lawyer, not Mr. Lyndon, mind you.

I blow out a breath when I step out of the courtroom doors, happy to put this day behind me and go home to hopefully a very large glass of wine and Ezra's cooking. Six months after moving in, and I still rarely cook. Ezra jokes that it's my own personal stance against the patriarchy. I let Ezra joke about whatever the hell he wants as long as he keeps cooking.

Speaking of.

"Hey there, boss," a familiar voice calls.

He's still just as smug looking as the first day I met him—that stupid face and body are still lethal distractions, just welcome ones now. He is *my* idiot, after all.

"Aren't you supposed to be in court right now?"

He holds out his hand, tugging me into his side when I take it. "They asked for a continuance." He kisses my cheek. "So we got out early."

"And you just couldn't wait another second to see me, huh?"

"You know I'm greedy for you, Sour Patch," he chuckles.

"Well, I'm glad you're here. You can drive me home. I need a bath and a glass of wine."

"Long day?"

"It's definitely been a Monday."

He tucks a stray piece of hair that's escaped my ponytail behind my ear. "June is supposed to be the season of weddings, not divorces."

"You'd think," I huff. "Are you ready to go?"

"Do you mind if I drop off these documents on the fifth floor first?"

I notice the manila envelope in his hand. "Sure, that's fine. Is that for the Franklin case?"

"No, this is something new that came in."

He winds his fingers through mine as he leads me to the elevators, and I lean into him when we settle against the back wall.

It's almost funny, the drastic difference between this moment and my first memories of sharing elevators with Ezra, and I smile at the thought.

Ezra notices. "What?"

"I used to hate how pretty you were," I muse.

"Were? You don't think I'm still pretty?"

I roll my eyes. "I think you know you are."

"Don't scare me like that," he mock scoffs. "You know how fragile my ego is."

"About as fragile as it is small," I snort.

He laughs, turning to kiss my temple.

"Is your mom coming over this weekend?"

"Mm-hmm. I invited your parental unit too."

"Wow, the whole unit? What's the occasion?"

"Do I need one?"

"For a party?" I laugh through my nose. "No, not usually."

"I'd invite Vera and Nate, but I heard they're staying another week."

I make a face. "They've already been there for three weeks. Is it a honeymoon or a sabbatical?"

"God. Them eloping was not on my bingo card."

"If you recall, it *was* on mine."

"Yeah, yeah. You haven't let me forget it."

The elevator doors slide open to the fifth floor, and Ezra keeps his hand wrapped around mine as we move through the wide hall that leads to the county clerk's office. "What case was this for again?"

"I didn't say it was for a case," he answers cryptically.

I cock my head at him. "What's it for then?"

He doesn't answer right away, just flashes me that light-up-a-room grin, tugging me forward until we're outside the county clerk's door.

"Ezra, what's going on?"

"It's June," he says.

My nose wrinkles. "Yeah?"

"And tomorrow is a random Tuesday."

"Are you having a stroke right now?"

He holds out his envelope, gesturing at it with a tilt of his head until I take it from him. I slide it out of his fingers, still thinking he's hit his head or something until I crack it open.

Then all of the air leaves my lungs in a rush.

"Ezra, what . . . ?"

"Did you know in the state of Texas, the seventy-two-hour waiting period to file a marriage license can be waived by a judge?"

I swallow around the growing lump in my throat, running my fingers over the embossed letters of the thick cardstock reading *Marriage Certificate* across the front.

"Ezra, what is this?"

"I know a guy," he says with a grin.

Ezra reaches out to open the envelope, and there, sitting on top of a blank certificate waiting for two signatures, is a diamond ring. He picks it up with nimble fingers, gently taking my left hand and holding it while my right still clutches the envelope, trembling slightly.

"So?" He holds the ring inches from my fingers. "What are you doing tomorrow?"

"Ezra . . . are you sure?"

He grins. "As sure as I am that you're going to say yes."

"You are so fucking sure of yourself," I can't help but laugh, even if it is a little manic.

He slides the ring on my finger like it's a foregone conclusion, bringing it to his mouth and brushing his lips there. "You love that about me."

"No idea why," I answer wryly.

"You still haven't actually answered me."

"Sounds like I don't have much choice."

His lips curl. "Well, you can always object."

"Something tells me I'd be overruled."

He pulls me close, the folder flattening between us and his lips hovering over mine. "Absolutely, Ms. Pierce."

I can feel my own mouth curving, the smile forming there so big it almost hurts, my eyes watering as my chest swells.

"Well?" His lips brush against mine in a barely there kiss. "What do you say?"

I wrap one arm around his neck. "I'm sure I can pencil you in."

"I would expect nothing less, Sour Patch."

I slant my mouth against his, laughing. "That's going to be Mrs. Sour Patch to you."

"I'll call you whatever you want, Dani," he hums against my lips. "As long as I can call you mine."

And as it turns out, I'm absolutely fine with that agreement. No one is more surprised than me by that realization.

Fucking Ezra Hart.

I never even stood a chance.

ACKNOWLEDGMENTS

Gentlepersons. This is the book of my heart, but it wouldn't be here without several people continuing to hold my hand. (That joke will never get old, because it's not really a joke. I'm a mess and a half.)

To Cindy Hwang, for being the best editor I could have ever dreamed of meeting. I am so grateful that you continue to take chances on whatever silly idea pops into my head.

To my agency and my wonderful agent, Jessica Watterson. Your patience and understanding continue to be a balm to my spirit. I may be a neurotic mess, but knowing you're only a text away is a forever comfort. (For me, at least. To you, I am so sorry for all the messages.)

To my team at Berkley: my Bejeweled Babes™, Kristin Cipolla and Jessica Mangicaro, for always being the biggest of cheerleaders; Elizabeth Vinson, for always staying on top of all the things I would surely forget; Rita Frangie Batour, for always being fantastic at what she does (and a special shout-out to Monika Roe for another amazing cover); and all the other people working behind the scenes to make my dreams a reality.

To my therapist: Now that I've had two years in this industry, you are literally the glue holding me together.

To those I am lucky enough to call my friends, in no particular order:

My wife (listen, it might as well be legal at this point), Kate Golden, for being my voice of reason even on my most unreasonable days. I cherish the day our agents pushed us together like errant toddlers and said, *"Be friends!"*

To Keri, my heart sister, for always being the one person in the group chat brave enough to tell me to say "Fuck it" when that's the last thing I feel like I can do. I am grateful for you every day.

Daddy Kristen, for always being there to let me know that it *is* in fact going to be okay. You were this book's biggest champion before it ever saw the light of day, and I am so grateful for all the hours you toiled away holding my hand and helping me shape it into my favorite work to date.

To Elena Armas, whose voice notes are oftentimes the highlight of my day. Thank you for always being down to let me cry back to you in sometimes even *longer* voice notes. I am always glad to hear your voice.

To Amber, for always telling me my feelings are valid even when it feels like they aren't, and for always knowing the right thing to say even when I didn't know I needed to hear it.

To Vanessa, for always taking the time to be there for whatever silly question I've just asked, and there are many. It's a rare thing to meet someone so lovely so close to home in this wide world of bookstagram, but I am happy that you are only a short drive away.

To Ruby Dixon, for being one of the most supportive people in this crazy ride I'm on. I am so grateful to you for always checking in to make sure I haven't slipped into madness yet.

To Jessica Patrick, for always taking the images in my head

and turning them into the most wonderful pieces of promo art. Your talent astounds me.

To my friend Kevin, who, after many years as a prestigious and practiced lawyer, decided to sit down with me and go over my silly romance novel to make sure it wasn't complete ridiculousness. I am sorry I printed you a version without the sex scenes; they probably would have made it more fun, at least.

To all the bookstagrammers, bloggers, journalists, BookTokers, librarians, and reviewers who continue to make this possible. I see you and appreciate you always.

To the *readers*: I am so grateful for every single one of you, because without you, I wouldn't be here. You are what makes this a possibility. Thank you, from the bottom of my heart, for picking up this book.

And to my husband, who is happy to tell me when I am being ridiculous (which I often am). You are the only thing that keeps me sane some days, and I love you dearly.

Keep reading for a preview of

The Mating Game

The sequel to The Fake Mate
by Lana Ferguson!

One

TESS

"WELL, THE GOOD news is . . . you're not dying."

I gape at the pretty, smiling ER physician—Dr. Carter, she said her name was—who is regarding me carefully, having looked up at me from her clipboard, which I assume has the results of all the blood tests we did earlier.

"Do you know what's wrong with me?" I wring my hands together. "Is it some sort of weird twenty-four-hour bug?"

This seems unlikely to me, given the severity of the symptoms I've been experiencing since yesterday, but I suppose it's still a possibility.

Dr. Carter glances down at her clipboard again, flipping a page and reading something there. "I wanted to ask a few follow-up questions, if that's okay?"

"Sure," I answer tightly, wishing she would just give me some clue as to what's wrong with me. "That's fine."

"Your parents . . . You listed they're both betas?"

I nod. "That's right."

"And your siblings?"

"Also betas. We all are."

She presses her lips together briefly. "Do you have any family history of crossbreeding with shifters?"

"Excuse me?"

"Sorry." She gives me a polite smile. "It's relevant."

I think back, trying to mentally tick through my family tree for as far back as I can recall. "I think . . ." I frown, trying to remember. "I think my great-grandmother was a shifter, actually. I never met her though. She died before I was born."

"Hmm."

I watch as she scans through her notes again, every second that passes making my anxiety climb higher. Twenty-four hours ago, I was perfectly healthy and packing for my trip here to Denver, excited about a new job. Travel is nothing new to me; my contracting business, Rustic Renovations, takes me all over the country, but this is the first time I've had to get off a plane and take an Uber straight to the nearest emergency room.

It started with cramps—terrible, *terrible* cramps—followed by a fever and cold sweats and lots of nausea, and by the time the plane landed, it was clear all the other people on my flight were worried I was carrying some sort of plague, given my awful appearance. Even now, I can feel my chestnut bangs clinging to my forehead with sweat, and it's only the IV in my arm feeding me occasional doses of high-powered nausea meds that's keeping me from hurling all over the speckled white tile of the little room I'm in.

"Well," Dr. Carter starts carefully. "Your blood tests yielded an abnormal spike in your hormone levels. Your progesterone, estrogen, and cortisol levels are all three times the amount they should be. Your endocrine system is having a hard time processing the influx. That's what's causing all the unfortunate symptoms you're experiencing."

"I don't understand. Why would my hormones be out of whack all of a sudden? Is it like menopause? I'm only twenty-eight!"

"Nothing like that. It's . . . Well." She sighs, pulling the clipboard to her stomach and holding it against her white coat as she offers me a sympathetic look. "This might come as a shock, Ms. Covington, but . . ."

I lean in, my ass scooting to the edge of the hospital bed, which has me instinctively reach behind to make sure my panties aren't flashing anyone from the gap in the back of my paper gown. "What? What is it?"

"What you're experiencing isn't entirely out of the ordinary. In fact, it's something most shifters experience at the end of puberty."

I blink. "But . . . I'm a beta."

"Yes, well. It's not *entirely* unheard-of for a recessive gene to present itself later in life."

"That's . . ." I run my fingers through my hair, no doubt making my bangs stick straight up, but I can't focus on that right now. "That's impossible."

"Not impossible, I'm afraid," Dr. Carter says gently. "Just unlikely."

I try to process what she's saying, but it sounds faraway, like she's speaking to someone else. There's no way that I could suddenly be—

I force a swallow. "So, what? Am I going to suddenly sprout ears and a tail?"

"No, no," Dr. Carter assures me with a laugh as she reaches to tuck one honeyed tendril of her hair behind her ear. "Nothing so sudden as that. You will, however, feel the urge to shift in the near future. I have all sorts of pamphlets I can give you that are chock-full of information about what your body is going through. Although, I've never seen a case with such a late presentation as yours . . . so I can't guarantee your experiences will be exactly the same."

"I just . . . don't see how this could happen."

"It's just a little hiccup in your genes," she says with a shrug. "It will be an adjustment, but I can promise you your life won't be turned upside down entirely."

Easy for her to say.

"Any other surprises I have to look forward to?" I know I sound petulant, but I think it's allowed after the day I've had. "Am I going to start craving more red meat and sniffing strangers?"

Her smile is a little tighter, and I realize I'm being slightly offensive.

"Sorry," I amend quietly. "This is just a lot."

"I get it," she says. "It's funny, my mate eats his steaks practically rare. I'm always teasing him about it. I can tell you *I've* never had any special feelings about red meat, and as for sniffing strangers . . . You *will* start to experience an increased sense of smell. Every shifter has a particular scent, and unless they elect to use suppressants—which is usually only the case in certain professions or environments—you are going to experience those. It might cause headaches at first, but with time you will become more acclimated to the sensation."

"Great," I mumble dejectedly. "Just great."

"If I'm being candid," Dr. Carter goes on, "I have other suspicions about your lab results."

I stifle a groan. What else could possibly be going on with my body? "What?"

"It's just . . ." She holds out her chart, indicating a sloping graph that makes no sense to me. "Your particular levels of these hormones are indicative of a secondary designation."

"A secondary designation?"

"It's rare, incredibly rare, even . . . but then again, so is your situation as a whole. So it wouldn't be all that surprising at this point."

"I'm not following."

"I think you might be an omega, Ms. Covington."

I'm blinking dumbly again. "What?"

"Like I said, it's very rare, and in this day and age . . . it really isn't all that different from being a shifter."

"I know what an omega is," I say absently. "I have a friend who—" I swallow thickly. "How can you be so sure?"

"Well," she laughs. "I *am* one, for starters."

Fuck. Foot in mouth. Again. "Sorry. I'm sorry. I am not usually this much of an asshole."

"It's fine. Really. I can't imagine what it must be like to face this so suddenly."

"If you're an omega as well, can you tell me what I can expect? If that's the case?"

I could always ask my friend Ada, but I haven't even figured out how I'm going to tell her, or anyone else for that matter.

"Like I said, it really isn't all that different in most cases. If you start googling, you're likely to go down some undesirable Reddit threads that are mostly nonsense, so you can just ignore those. All it means is that your heats might be a little more frequent. Possibly more intense as well."

"My *heats*?"

Oh God. That absolutely hadn't crossed my mind yet.

"Yes," Dr. Carter explains calmly. "Usually, a shifter going through puberty will experience less intense heats—we call them 'juvenile heats,' to be exact—meaning that they won't last the full ovulation cycle and won't have the same level of, ah, need."

"Need?"

"Need to, um . . . copulate."

"Oh, fuck," I groan.

Dr. Carter gives me a small smile. "Precisely."

I might laugh if my entire world wasn't tilting on its axis.

"So . . . what do I do in the meantime?"

She considers this for a moment. "I'm going to prescribe you some hormone regulators, but the dose will be very mild. Just enough to alleviate some of your symptoms. We don't want to interrupt your body's cycle of change, after all. I can also get you something for the nausea and cramps. Other than that . . . I would strongly suggest that you spend the next few weeks or so at home, if at all possible. It's impossible for me to predict exactly what other symptoms you might experience while your body adjusts to the new hormone levels, and being around other shifters might make things more uncomfortable. Shifting isn't permitted inside city limits, but I can get you a doctor's note explaining your condition in case there are any unplanned incidents. Otherwise, there are several nice heat clinics on the edge of the city, where you would be able to shift comfortably. Normally, you would need to schedule weeks in advance, but again, I can get you a doctor's note explaining your special circumstances."

My mind whirls. Unplanned shifting? Heat clinics?

"I can't hole up for weeks," I argue. "I'm here for a job."

"Any chance you could work remotely?"

"I'm a contractor. I do renovation for cabins and lodges and such."

"Ah. That's a pickle."

"It is," I remark dryly.

"Well, I obviously can't force you either way," Dr. Carter says. "I can only suggest. But I would keep a close eye on your body. You don't want to overexert yourself."

"But the meds should help, right?"

"A little," she says. "As I said, we don't want to medicate you so much that your body can't process the change it's going through. This is a natural thing. For the most part, we just have to sort of let it run its course."

Perfect, I think. *Just perfect.*

"Okay," I say with a nod. "Okay. This is fine. Just . . . If you could get me those prescriptions you mentioned, I can deal with the rest."

"If you have any more trouble, don't hesitate to come back in, okay?"

"Sure," I answer, knowing that's unlikely. The jobsite is almost two hours away. I won't have time to pack up and head out every time I get a cramp. "Of course."

"Right. I'll get you those prescriptions before I release you." She starts to turn toward the door but pauses, giving me one last concerned look. "Oh. One more thing. It's very unlikely, but I should mention that you should steer clear of alphas."

"Alphas?"

"Another secondary designation," she tells me. "Their phero-mones, like yours and mine, are stronger than your average shifter. Being around one might wreak havoc on your system." She shrugs. "It's probably a nonissue. They are also incredibly rare." A small, strange smile touches her lips. "But then again . . . you never know."

I watch her go, still stuck on *pheromones*. Nothing about any of this feels like real life.

I check my phone when she leaves, seeing that my brothers have responded to the group text, asking if I landed okay. It takes all I have not to laugh at that. I am definitely not ready to have this discussion with my family. I don't even know what I'm going to say to my brothers when they fly in to join me on the job at the end of the week.

The job.

I groan. I'm still expected to show up at the small ski lodge this evening—a little place just up the mountain, near the neighboring town of Pleasant Hill. The woman I've been speaking to, Jeannie, seems nice enough, and I can only hope that she won't notice if I have to escape to the bathroom to deal with an influx of cramps or sweating or God knows what else during the next few weeks while I oversee the renovation.

I laugh dryly.

At least things can't get any worse.

"MADE IT TO Nowheresville yet?"

In hindsight, I probably should have let Ada's call go to voicemail. It's only been a couple of hours since the nice doctor at the ER informed me my entire life was changing, but since my best friend is like a shark smelling blood in the water when it comes to sussing out my moods, I doubt I can keep any of this from her for long.

"Almost," I tell her, slowing for a stop sign. "It's really off the beaten path."

"Never a good sign. That's how you get axe-murdered."

I roll my eyes. "I'm not going to get axe-murdered."

"That's what every person who gets axe-murdered thinks. No one wakes up thinking, 'Oh, today I'm going to get axe-murdered,' but then, before you know it—you're human firewood."

"I am officially putting you in time-out from those true crime podcasts."

"You'll change your tune when I keep you from becoming human firewood."

"How about we stop using the term 'human firewood' when I'm this close to a secluded ski lodge that I'll be staying at alone until my brothers fly in?"

Ada snorts on the other end of the line. "Thomas and Chase are in more danger than you are. They're pretty, but they don't have the same hardware upstairs as you. Kyle, maybe."

"Hey, now," I laugh. "That's not very nice."

"I'm kidding," she says. "You know I love those big lugs. But still, there's a reason you're the brains of the operation, and they're the muscle."

"And cameramen," I correct.

"And cameramen," she agrees.

"How cold is it there?"

"Somewhere between frozen toes and cracked lips."

I can practically hear her shudder. "No thanks."

"Definitely a far cry from Newport."

"I'll think of you while I'm on the beach later," she says with sympathy.

"That makes everything better."

"Obviously. Are you feeling better? Did you end up going to get checked out?"

I bite my lip, considering. Ada would understand. I've never asked for the ins and outs of what she is—but that doesn't mean I haven't picked up bits and pieces over the years that we've been friends. I'm not ready to tell anyone yet. Not when I haven't figured out my own feelings about it. I'm already half panicking enough as it is without her hysterics added to the mix.

"I feel better," I tell her. It's not a *complete* lie. I *do* feel better after the meds Dr. Carter gave me. "Not dying, at least."

"Just make sure you get checked out if you start feeling shitty again. It sounded like you were really suffering when I talked to you last."

"Maybe I ate something bad," I offer, knowing that's not the case. It *could* be a possibility though, in an easier turn of events.

"Have you heard anything back from HGTV?"

"Not yet," I sigh. "They said it could be a couple of weeks."

"Yeah, well, they'd be stupid not to green-light the show. You haven't had a TikTok fall under a million views in months."

"My brothers are optimistic, but . . ."

"You're the worrywart."

"That's me," I laugh. "It just comes down to the fine print. I don't want to jump into anything that is going to make our job not fun anymore, you know? I don't want to totally be beholden to *their* whims."

"I get that," she says. "What does your dad think?"

My hands tighten on the steering wheel, my jaw clenching. With everything happening today, my problems back home are the last thing I want to discuss.

"I don't know," I tell her honestly. "I haven't told him about it yet."

"You haven't told him?"

"No, and I told my brothers not to tell him either."

"But why?"

"Because . . ." I frown, thinking of the awful year he's had. That we've *all* had. "I don't want to get my mom and dad's hopes up if it doesn't come through. I'll tell them when I have good news."

"Babe, that's a lot of pressure to put on yourself."

"I know," I sigh. "But what choice do I have?"

I can practically see the sympathy in her eyes even from so far away, my chest constricting when I think about everything riding on this deal. Of the *good* it could do when it comes to dad's medical issues.

"This is all contingent on whether or not HGTV passes," I grumble.

"Shut up," she tuts. "If they do, then they're walnuts."

"Walnuts?"

"Felt appropriate," she tacks on. "If they *do* pass on it, they suck, and I will boycott their channel."

"You and I both know the day you give up *Property Brothers* is the day you're six feet under."

"They're hot twins with hammers. I won't be judged for this. Just a sec." I hear her shuffling on the other end for a moment before her voice returns. "Can I call you back? That's Perry's school on the other line."

"Absolutely. I'll talk to you later, okay?"

"Sure. Call you later."

She disconnects the call, and I'm suddenly even more glad that I decided not to tell her yet about everything happening with me. It's not that I don't trust Ada enough to tell her what's going on, it's just that I know how much she worries—it's the mom in her—and if I tell her about everything that's happening, there's a good chance she'll be packing up her and her son, Perry, and hopping on the first flight out. She has enough going on with the whole single mother thing; she definitely doesn't need any of my drama stressing her out even more. I'll give myself a few days to wrap my head around it first.

It doesn't take much longer after I hang up with Ada to see the end of the driveway. A faded wooden sign that reads THE BEAR ESSENTIALS WILDERNESS LODGE leans at a not-so-straight angle to signal that I'm at the right place. I can just make out the lodge nestled in the pristine white of the surrounding snow as I drive up, the log siding stark amid the wintry scenery. A deck wraps around the front to lead down into a set of stairs heading up to it, and on either side of the heavy wooden door there is a series of wide windows that go all the way up to the roof. The sky behind it is now a rich array of pinks and purples as the sun begins to sink below the horizon, giving the entire thing more of that *postcard* feel—save for the wear and tear.

It's still . . . pretty, mostly. But it's definitely seen some hard years. There are broken rails on the stairs that I notice as I get closer, a few missing shingles on the roof—even the sign above the door is faded and chipped, as if long overdue for a touch-up. I'm already making a mental note of all the people I'm going to have to call back in Denver to contract some work out to.

It's less picturesque than the one (literally, there was only *one*) photo that I saw on the very basic website, and I'm gathering now that it was most likely a dated photo. I doubt they've updated it at all since building it.

"Kind of a funny name for a lodge," I mutter to myself as I shift my rental car into park.

I sit in the car for a minute so I can shoot a text to my brothers, following that up with one to my dad to let him know I arrived at the jobsite. I stare down at my phone as I watch the little dots pop up with his impending response, a small smile touching my mouth when he replies, **You be careful out there, kiddo.**

It feels weird keeping all that's happened today from him, considering I tell him everything, but with what he's going through . . . I don't want to add to his stress. In fact, it's imperative that I don't, considering the state of his heart.

I step out of the car, letting the door shut behind me, to get a better look at the place. There's an old Bronco parked just outside, the forest-green paint still shiny despite the vehicle being at least thirty years old by my best guess, and it somehow looks like it's in better shape than the lodge itself. I've really got my work cut out for me with this one. I eye the broken railing that seems to have cracks and rotting wood as far as the eye can see; I *really* have my work cut out with this one.

I'm staring at the railing so intensely that I almost miss the front door opening and someone stepping outside, but I catch a large, dark shape out of the corner of my eye, stark against the light flakes of the gently falling snow—and it's hard to focus on much else when the person finally comes into view. He's heading right for me, and I can feel my mouth part at the hulking size of the man walking down the rickety stairs.

Tall is an understatement; this man looks more than a foot taller than I am, and I'm five foot four. But more than that, he is *wide.* Shoulders that seem to go on for miles in the thick red plaid of his coat, a broad chest that stretches the black-knit thermal shirt beneath—it's like he stepped right out of *Lumberjack Weekly*, with his trimmed beard and gray beanie with dark curls poking out of it that are just a shade or two darker than his eyes. I most likely spend a second too long studying the soft-looking mouth that peeks out from his scruff, but honestly, given that this stranger might be one of the most attractive people I have ever seen—and I have seen *a lot* of people—I think it's probably excusable. He comes to a stop right in front of me, and my gaze goes up and up and *up*, to the point that I'm forced to crane my neck at this giant of a man.

"You Esther?"

I blink, the abruptness of his question taking me off guard. "Tess."

"Jeannie said an Esther was coming."

"Yeah," I answer. "I go by Tess."

He shrugs. "Fair enough."

"Sorry." I stick out one gloved hand. "I'm the contractor Jeannie hired for the renovations. Do you work here?"

His eyes flick to my outstretched hand, but he doesn't take it. "Looks that way."

Jeez. Talk about frosty.

He's still frowning at my hand, and I draw it back slowly, my eyes lingering on the way his mouth turns down at the corners. The expression only makes him look more rugged, and I think to myself that he really does give off some sort of lumberjack vibe, albeit a really terse one. I'm pretty sure there's a Harlequin romance on my shelf at home that he modeled for at some point in his life. All that's missing is an axe, really.

I can't help but laugh at that, recalling Ada's and my conversation about being murdered out here. The guy arches a brow at the giggle that escapes me.

"Something funny?"

I wave my hand in front of my face. "Not unless you think murder is funny."

"Excuse me?"

"Not, like, *actual* murder," I correct, sort of. "I mean, well, okay, I guess *kind of* actual murder. My friend made this joke when I was on my way that I was going to get murdered out here, and I was thinking you totally give me lumberjack vibes, and that got me thinking about axes, which got me thinking about the murder again, and—"

I notice he's staring at me as if I've lost my mind.

"This is probably one of those things that should have stayed in my head."

He continues to frown at me for exactly four more seconds, then: "I'm not gonna argue with you there."

"Right. Um." I clear my throat. "Is Jeannie around? I would love to introduce myself in person after all the emails we've exchanged."

"Jeannie's down the mountain. Had something come up at her place."

"Oh. When will she be back?"

"Tomorrow, I figure."

"Oh."

I don't really know what else to say to that. This is all going very differently than I pictured, but I guess that's par for the course considering how this entire trip has been.

The bear of a man nods toward my car. "You got luggage?"

"Hmm? Oh. Yes. Sorry. I can—"

He sort of grunts in response but says nothing. It surprises me when he steps toward the car to open the door to the back seat and grab my bag—so much so that I reach out to try to stop him, earning me a puzzled look.

"You don't have to," I tell him, a little distracted by how dark his eyes look up close. "I can get my things."

There's a scent tickling my nose—one that reminds me of rain and sunshine—and I think to myself that it seems terribly out of place here in the snow. Maybe it's his cologne? It's really . . . nice, actually.

He looks from me to the bag and back again—finally shrugging before he releases it to turn and start to stomp up the steps to the main deck. He taps his boots against the last stair as I'm left to my own devices. I remember myself after only a few seconds, grabbing my bag and hurrying after him. He leaves the front door open when he slips inside, disappearing into the warm glow of the lights beyond.

"Sorry," I offer again as I step in after him. "I didn't catch your name."

"Didn't give it," he tosses over his shoulder as he shrugs out of his flannel coat.

"Totally something a murderer would say," I tease with a cluck of my tongue.

He turns to look at me strangely even as I try for what I hope is a friendly smile. "Hunter," he concedes. "Hunter Barrett."

Hunter.

I almost laugh at the utter appropriateness of his name. He definitely looks like a Hunter.

I close the door behind me and let my eyes sweep about the

room. There's a giant elk head mounted behind the front desk—its horns decked in dusty old Santa hats despite it being October. An old brass chandelier that has seen better days hangs above us in the wide entryway; the thick cobwebs dangling between the fixtures make me grimace as I stare up into them. The walls are a rich stained wood that feels warm even covered in dust, and I think to myself that with a little TLC, they could shine up nicely.

All that's missing is a bearskin rug.

Honestly, I'm not yet convinced I won't find one with further exploration.

I notice Hunter rounding the front counter built of treated cedar—reaching above his head to pull off the beanie he's wearing. The hair beneath is a thick heap of dark curls that frame his face and make him seem wilder, somehow—not to mention the way I'm filled with a sudden curiosity as to what it might feel like if I pushed my fingers through them. He climbs up to take a seat on a wooden stool behind the counter, settling there as he braces his hands on the counter in front of an open ledger.

"So, you do work here, right?"

"Sort of goes with owning the place, yeah," he tells me with a slight smirk.

I blink dumbly. "You're the owner?"

"Last time I checked."

My mouth parts in surprise, and it takes me all of three seconds to realize that I made murder jokes to my new would-be employer of sorts, most likely giving him the impression that I'm completely unhinged.

Perfect.

Two

HUNTER

WHEN JEANNIE TOLD me that she was hiring someone to renovate the lodge, I was wholly against it for a myriad of reasons. I still am, truthfully. I've fought my cantankerous aunt every step of the way from the conception of this half-baked plan right up to her informing me that someone was well on their way, but I have to admit, of all the people I might have pictured showing up at the lodge with a mind to "fix up the place," this tiny scrap of a woman is the furthest thing from anyone my imagination toyed with.

Her soft chestnut hair falls in her eyes, her bangs just long enough that she seems to make a habit of blowing them away from her face. Her big brown eyes give her a permanent quizzical expression that would almost be cute if I wasn't determined to dislike her. Plus, she really is positively tiny. How in the fuck does she expect to overhaul this entire place? I don't think they even make stepladders that would allow her to reach some of the higher bits.

Her owlish eyes are even wider as she comes to terms with the fact that it is actually *me* who she's working for rather than Jeannie, more or less, and her admittedly plush pink mouth makes a perfect O shape as she blinks her long lashes repeatedly.

"But I . . ." Her lips purse in a pout. "But I've been talking to Jeannie all this time."

And I can't help it; the irritation that she's here in the first place is still there, bubbling just beneath the surface, and her puzzled look and scrunched nose, which are one step away from being downright adorable, aren't enough to eradicate it.

"Probably because I didn't want to hire you."

Her mouth drops open. "Excuse me?"

"Nothing to excuse," I answer flippantly.

"You didn't want to hire me?"

"Wasn't as convinced as Jeannie is that we need all these renovations." I shrug, eyeing the way her arms cross over her chest, her shoulders hunching up around her ears, making her look like a cat that's three seconds from hissing. "You been doing this for very long? Kind of tiny for a contractor."

That gets the rise out of her that I'm looking for. "*Excuse* me?"

"Didn't mean anything by it," I say, keeping that same disinterested monotone in my voice. "Just an observation."

I watch her bristle, her fists clenching at her sides as she takes what I assume is meant to be a menacing step toward me moments before she thrusts out a finger in my direction. "I've been doing this for *ten years* now," she sputters. "My dad did it for eighteen years before that." She gestures wildly around the room. "I could rip this dingy little place down board by board and put it back together twice as nice if I wanted to."

I feel a pang of irritation at her assessment, a memory creeping forward of another time someone called it as much. "Dingy, huh?"

"Shit." Her expression turns sheepish as she reaches to unwind the scarf from around her neck, looking flushed suddenly. "I shouldn't have said that." She narrows her eyes, pointing a finger at me again. "But you shouldn't go around making snap observations. If you don't want me here doing this job, just say the word, and I'll turn straight around and go back to the airport."

I still don't really want her here—that hasn't changed—but honestly, now I'm almost intrigued to see what she has planned. I eye her cheeks, which are tinted pink with an ire that seems bigger than her petite stature, strangely curious about this woman who looks like she would have no qualms with, at the very least, *attempting* to kick my ass despite being half my size.

"By all means," I tell her drolly. "But then again, you're already here. I'm sure you'll do a bang-up job, Miss Fixit."

I'm rewarded with another gaping expression, her lips mouthing the moniker back at me in a daze. "Oh, sure," she huffs, throwing up her hands. "Since I'm already here."

"Exactly." I lift my arms above my head in a stretch, and my black Henley strains across my chest. "Well . . . there's no one staying here right now, so you can pretty much just take whatever room you want. All the suites are upstairs. They're all available except the one to the left of the landing. That's mine. There's an attached bath in every room. Living area is just through there." I nod my head toward the wide entry across the room. "Got a pool table, if you play. Jeannie cooks breakfast, lunch, and dinner— gotta be down by eight in the morning if you want to catch breakfast though. Lunch is at twelve, give or take a few, and dinner is at six. Got it?"

She nods at me with visible confusion, and I round the counter, sticking out my hand. She glances at it with a brief frown, flicking her gaze back up to my face warily before sliding her palm against mine.

"Okay," she says. "I think I've got it."

"Good." This close to her, I get a blast of something heavy and sweet, and my nostrils flare of their own accord as I try to breathe in more of it, but it's gone as quickly as it came. *The fuck was that?* "Well . . ." I say, clearing my throat and wrenching my hand from hers. "Welcome to the Bear Essentials Wilderness Lodge."

I move to leave her there, because I suddenly feel strange, but I barely make it to the stairs before she's calling out, "I just . . . pick my own room?"

"Seems the only way you'll get the one you want," I toss over my shoulder. And because I can't help myself, I turn to give her a smirk. "Probably don't want me to know where you're staying anyway," I say seriously. And when she gives me a puzzled look: "Since I might be an axe-wielding murderer."

She flushes again, and I feel a tinge of satisfaction at her discomfort.

"Don't you want to show me around and tell me some of your plans for the place?" she calls.

"Not really," I answer, already starting up the stairs. "Jeannie is the one insisting on this little redecorating project."

She makes an indignant sound. "I'm not a *decorator*."

"Of course not, Miss Fixit." I raise my hand above my head to offer her a little wave. "Breakfast is at eight," I remind her. "Have a good night."

She makes that same disgruntled squawk, and I hear her shoes slapping against the floor as if she's following me, and even from several paces away, I am hit with that strange scent, one that makes my steps heavier for the briefest of moments before it dissipates. I frown at my feet, turning again and narrowing my eyes at her as she skids to a halt. Jeannie definitely would have told me if— But it's hitting me again, causing goose bumps to break out across my skin, and without even realizing I'm doing it, I'm stomping back down the stairs to loom over her.

She shrinks only for a moment before rising to her full height to stare me down. It might be amusing if my heart wasn't beating so fast.

"Are you an omega?"

She visibly blanches. "W-what?"

I can feel my heart thudding behind my ribs, because there's no way Jeannie would have subjected me to this. Not after everything.

But I know this woman has no idea about my past, so I try my best to keep my tone from sounding as irritated as I feel.

"I'm only asking because," I try again, going for less aggressive but fearing that I might be failing, "I'm not on suppressants."

"Why would you even ask that in the first place?"

"Because . . ." I lean toward her, dragging in an inhale as if compelled. "You smell like an omega."

Her mouth falls open. "That's— That's a really rude question, isn't it?"

She asks as if she isn't entirely sure of the answer.

"Maybe," I say truthfully, "but if you're going to be staying here, it would probably be a good idea to take precautions. I wouldn't want you to have an incident."

"An *incident*?"

She acts like I'm being outrageous. Surely she can scent me? She has to know how bad of an idea it is for both of us to just co-habitate in this enclosed space for however long without any kind of barrier.

"I . . . Yes," I say, genuinely confused by her confusion, but what's more, I can't fathom having to endure shared space with another omega. Not after what happened. I can hear my own ag-gravation in my tone now. "Something like this would have been nice to know ahead of time. It's honestly a bit rude not to disclose this sort of thing knowing you'd be sharing a space."

She snorts. Actually *snorts*. "Wow. Day one, and already I'm dealing with this crap."

"What?"

"I'm fine," she says through gritted teeth. "I can do this job regardless of what I am, and I'm not going to let you sit there and discriminate just because I'm—because I'm a—"

"An omega?"

Her cheeks go bright pink. "Yes. That. You have another thing coming if you think you're going to insinuate I can't do my job because of some hormonal bullshit."

Huh.

I have to admit that her answer takes me by surprise; I've never met an omega who seemed almost offended by their own designation, but then again, I've only met one other (two, if you count Noah's mate), and *she* certainly wasn't embarrassed by what she was. On the contrary, she reveled in it. Which is exactly why the idea of being forced to live under the same roof as another one for so long makes my insides twist.

I suppose I could just grab some suppressants from the pharmacy in town if she insists on being stubborn—maybe she has some sort of condition that makes her incapable of taking them?—but then again, this is *my* place. Why should I?

Because she smells fucking mouthwatering.

There's something in an omega's scent that calls to someone like me; it's a tiny zing of unbridled want that creeps up my spine with just the simplest of inhales, one that I know all too well. It's bone-deep in our DNA to feel these things in each other's presence, and even if I'm currently the only one apparently feeling them, that doesn't mean it's not still a terrible idea, her being here.

I take a step back from her, sort of at a loss. She still looks offended. Worked up, even. And while I have no desire for her to be here, doing what she's planning on doing, I wasn't intending to be outright *rude*—regardless of how uneasy she makes me.

"Oh . . . kay," I say slowly. "Well . . . all right then. Just thought I'd mention it, considering."

"Considering," she scoffs.

I wonder if Mackenzie was this hostile to Noah when they met.

Miss Fixit is still glaring at me as I slowly turn back toward the stairs, and I hold my breath while I take them two at a time, needing to put distance between me and the sweet-smelling, tiny contractor who might actually want to murder me.

I don't slow down until my bedroom door is closed and locked behind me. I'd had a lot of expectations about meeting the contractor Jeannie finally wore me down to hire—but nearly being barreled over by her big brown eyes hadn't even remotely been in the realm of possibilities I'd dreamed up. I'd prepared myself to be cold to her, even downright unwelcoming if I had to be—

anything to give some sort of final protest against this entire debacle that Jeannie insists is necessary. And I tried. I really did.

But little Miss Fixit wasn't having any of it.

There's a ghost of a smile on my mouth as I remember the way she tore into me; she's such a tiny thing, and yet, when she let me know what's what, she reared up like a brown bear protecting her cubs on the mountainside. And I shouldn't find that cute. I also shouldn't have found myself at a loss for words even for a moment while studying her soft waves the color of tree bark and her full mouth the same blushed shade as the hellebores that grow up the mountain.

And her *scent*.

I can still practically taste the richness of it—like warm honey straight from the hive with a touch of something headier, something that could make me dizzy if I let myself have too much of it.

Tess. I test her name in my head, liking the sound of it. Soft, like her. Except she isn't. Not really. I can tell that Tess is nowhere near as soft as she looks. I can discern that after only a few minutes with her. Which means that it's going to be a hell of a lot harder than I anticipated to treat her like I originally planned. To make sure that she is all too aware of how I'm against all the changes she'll bring. I close my eyes, letting my head thunk against my bedroom door as I try to push the pursing of her mouth out of my mind. No, I can keep my distance, I think. I can make sure she knows exactly how I feel about her being here, sweet scent or no. Because I can't let someone like her rush into my life and turn it upside down. Not again.

The last time nearly broke me.

Illustration by Jessica Patrick

Lana Ferguson is a *USA Today* bestselling author and sex-positive nerd whose works never shy from spice or sass. A faded Fabio cover found its way into her hands at fifteen, and she's never been the same since. When she isn't writing, you can find her randomly singing show tunes, arguing over which Batman is superior, and subjecting her friends to the extended editions of *The Lord of the Rings*. Lana lives mostly in her own head but can sometimes be found chasing her corgi through the coppice of the great American outdoors.